The Pacific Rim and the Western World

About the Book and Editors

Analyzing the economic, strategic, and cultural elements that shape the attraction--and the friction--between the Pacific and Atlantic communities, this book integrates European perspectives into a discussion that has traditionally been dominated by Asian and U.S. voices. The authors take as their theme the uncertainty created by the Pacific Rim's new role in shifting the international balances of political and economic power.

Economic uncertainty has been fueled by Asia's trade surpluses with Western Europe and the United States, with the West viewing its system of free world trade as working to the greater advantage of the Asia Pacific. Strategic uncertainty pivots on the U.S.-USSR superpower rivalry and on the growing influence of Japan and the PRC on the strategic balance in the Pacific Basin. A more subtle and powerful constraint surfaces in the realm of culture--in differing perceptions among the people of the Asia Pacific and the West concerning liberal values and the liberal underpinnings of the present system of world trade.

Philip West is associate professor of history and East Asian languages and cultures as well as director of the East Asian Studies Center at Indiana University, Bloomington. *Frans A.M. Alting von Geusau* is professor of law and international relations at Tilburg University, the Netherlands, and director of the university's John F. Kennedy Institute.

The Pacific Rim and the Western World

Strategic, Economic, and Cultural Perspectives

edited by
Philip West and
Frans A.M. Alting von Geusau

Westview Press / Boulder and London

Westview Special Studies on East Asia

This Westview softcover edition is printed on acid-free paper and bound in softcovers that carry the highest rating of the National Association of State Textbook Administrators, in consultation with the Association of American Publishers and the Book Manufacturers' Institute.

Published in 1987 in the United States of America by Westview Press, Inc.; Frederick A. Praeger, Publisher; 5500 Central Avenue, Boulder, Colorado 80301

Library of Congress Cataloging-in-Publication Data
The Pacific Rim and the Western world.
(Westview special studies on East Asia)
Bibliography: p.
Includes index.
1. East Asia--Politics and government. 2. East Asia--Economic conditions. 3. Pacific Area--Politics and government. 4. Pacific Area--Economic conditions. I. West, Philip, 1938- . II. Alting von Geusau, Frans Alphons Maria, 1933- . III. Series.
DS518.1.P274 1987 330.99 86-24586
ISBN 0-8133-7338-7

Composition for this book was provided by the editors.
This book was produced without formal editing by the publisher.

Printed and bound in the United States of America

The paper used in this publication meets the requirements of the American National Standard for Permanence of Paper for Printed Library Materials Z39.48-1984.

6 5 4 3 2 1

Contents

Tables and Figures

TABLES

FIGURES

Preface

The papers in this volume were presented at a Colloquium held from May 29 to June 1, 1985, in Eindhoven, The Netherlands, on the theme, "The Growing Importance of the Far East in a Nervous World: Challenge to the West." Participants in the Colloquium represented high officials, business leaders and scholars from fifteen different countries.

The Colloquium was hosted by the John F. Kennedy Institute at Tilburg University, which is grateful to Professors Drs. H. W. J. Bosman, P. van Veen, L. Bartalits and J. van Lith, for their work in the preparatory commission for the Colloquium. The Institute is indebted to N. V. Philips Gloeilampenfabrieken, the Royal Netherlands' Academy of Sciences, and the Commission of the European Communities for their financial support towards the Colloquium.

Eleven of the chapters in the volume were presented at the Eindhoven Colloquium and revised and updated during the summer of 1986. Chapter 1, by Philip West, was written in 1986 to serve as an introduction to the volume. Chapter 6 by Professor Lawrence Klein was a lecture delivered on the Bloomington campus of Indiana University in January 1985. The concluding chapter by Frans Alting von Geusau, Director of the J. F. Kennedy Institute, reflects the discussions and the concluding session of the Colloquium.

The contribution of the volume, we believe, lies in its probing the range of Western anxieties about the Asia Pacific and its attempts to articulate Asian sensitivities about the "liberal" West. The Eindhoven Colloquium revealed that the differences in interpreting political, economic, and strategic issues within the Atlantic and Pacific communities are sometimes as large as the differences that separate them. The continual refinement of the questions and the examination of assumptions and cross-cultural perceptions--all part of an emerging "Pacific Rim consciousness"--were almost as important to discussions in the Colloquium as was the rigorous analysis of the data.

Our special thanks to Anna Leis Vugs, executive secretary, and Tineke Kleine, assistant secretary, of the John F. Kennedy Institute at Tilburg University for their invaluable help in organizing the conference; to Sue Weaver, Peng-chong Lee, and Margot Lenhart of the East Asian Studies Center at Indiana University for their help in pulling the manuscript together; and to Susan McEachern at Westview Press for her encouragement and patience with the manuscript.

Philip West
Frans A.M. Alting von Geusau

1

The Pacific Rim and the Western World: A Cultural and Historical Introduction

Philip West

The purpose of this introduction is to offer a larger framework for the papers of this volume. That framework is pieced together with the broad strokes of the cross-cultural historian, and it should place the tensions, the hopes, and the fears between the Asia Pacific and the liberal West [both are defined below and graphically presented in the map shown in Figure 1] into a broad perspective. Despite expanding world trade and greater communication, anxieties are keenly felt on both sides. Protectionist sentiment is strong in the West, while the countries of the Asia Pacific are both more dependent on trade with the West than before and also fearful of that protectionism. At stake may well be the system of world trade that since the days of World War II has brought unprecedented prosperity to the world.

Without belittling the importance of genuine cultural differences, I begin by assuming that neither the liberal West nor the Asia Pacific is a fixed entity. At any given time there is greater pluralism on either side than is often allowed by the other. Only in recent history has the West been identified as liberal per se, while only in the last two decades has the Asia Pacific been recognized as a dynamic economic force in the world. Another assumption in the introduction is that responsible discourse requires a critical examination of the vocabularies of culture and society.

The early Western adventures into the Asia Pacific, prior to the 20th century, were prompted by the "search for gold." Current encounters, at least those occurring in the last two decades, are produced by the search on both sides for expanding markets and new kinds of "gold"--advanced technologies and quality consumer products at bargain prices. In the earlier encounter the Asian role was

FIGURE 1

COUNTRIES OF THE WORLD DRAWN IN PROPORTION TO THEIR SHARE OF THE WORLD POPULATION

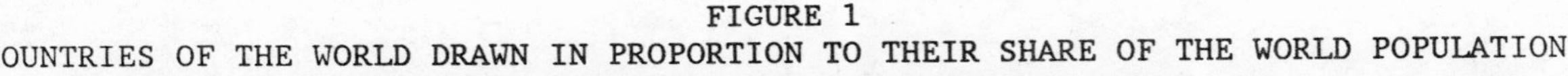

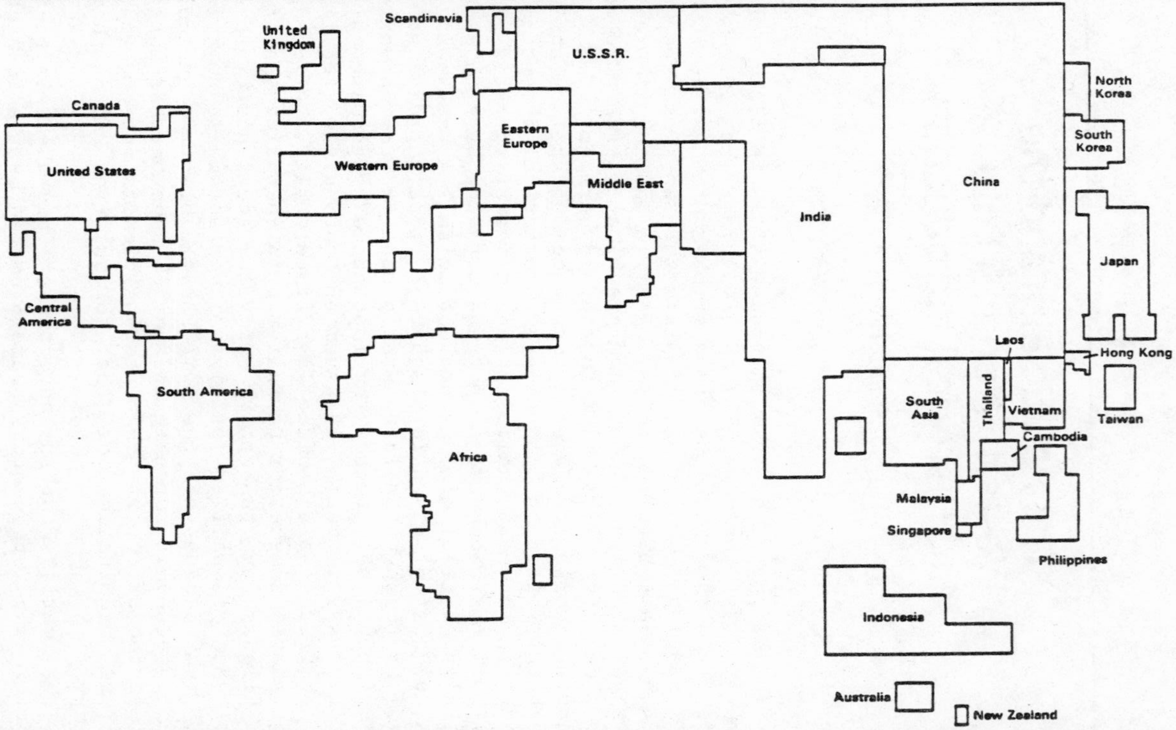

Source: World Development Report 1985 (New York: Oxford University Press) p. 39.

protective and reactive, while the Western role was expansive and assertive. Now, the peoples of the Asia Pacific in modern times have been forced to alter their views of time and of international relations, and in the process they have benefited greatly from the system of free trade. It is our perceptions of their activity appearing to be more vigorous than our own and resting on a set of values different from our own that feed Western anxieties.

SOME DEFINITIONS

The first broad strokes are reminders of some key geographic, demographic, and economic points of reference. Geographically, the Asia Pacific coincides roughly with the western rim of the Pacific Ocean. Because of their unique economic and demographic importance, Japan and China received most of the attention at the Eindhoven Conference, as they do in this essay. The Asia Pacific also includes the Asian Newly Industrialized Countries (NICs): that is South Korea, Taiwan, Hong Kong, and Singapore; as well as the Association for Southeast Asian Nations (ASEAN): Indonesia, the Philippines, Thailand, Malaysia, and Brunei. Singapore is also one of the ASEAN countries. Vietnam, North Korea, and Cambodia enter the discussion less as economic forces and more as extensions of Soviet influence. Australia and New Zealand lie on the Western Pacific, but they are not central to this discussion. The political and cultural orientations of Australia at least, are more Western than Asian, and while their proximity creates some bonding with the Asia Pacific, its role in this discussion is small.1/

The Soviet Union also lies on the Western Pacific, and the majority of the people living in the Western half of its landmass are Asians. But the Soviet-style economic system impedes participation in Pacific Rim activities, while its military policy is perceived by both Asians and the liberal West as a threat to political and military stability in the region. Still, geographic proximity encourages a greater economic role for the Soviet Union and a potentially less threatening one militarily, to the extent that its economic role can be enlarged. The liberal West, geographically, is made up of the industrialized countries of North America (with major attention given to the United States), the European Economic Community, and the European Free Trade Association. These countries are listed in Table 1.

TABLE 1
DEMOGRAPHIC AND ECONOMIC STATISTICS
FOR THE ASIA PACIFIC AND THE INDUSTRIAL WEST

Country	Population (millions) 1982	GNP (billions) U.S. 1982	GNP per cap. $US 1982	Exp/Imp Bil. $US 1982	Avg. Ann. GNP Growth 1970-82	Trade Growth 1970-82
ASIA PACIFIC						
China, PRC	1008.2	260.4	310.0	38.5	+7.1	+5.6
Indonesia	152.6	90.2	580.0	39.1	+8.4	+7.7
Japan	118.4	1,069.1	10,080.0	270.8	+7.0	+4.6
Vietnam	57.0	na	na	2.1	na	na
Phillippines	50.7	39.9	820.0	13.2	+5.0	+6.0
Thailand	48.5	36.8	790.0	15.4	+6.7	+7.1
South Korea	39.3	68.4	1,910.0	46.1	+15.0	+8.6
North Korea	18.7	18.1	923.0	1.7	na	na
Taiwan	19.2	49.9	2,457.0	45.4	+12.3	+8.4
Malaysia	14.5	25.9	1,860.0	23.2	+5.6	+7.7
Cambodia	6.1	na	na	na	na	na
Hong Kong	5.2	24.4	5,340.0	11.3	+10.7	+9.9
Singapore	2.5	14.7	5,910.0	48.8	+8.0	+8.5
	1,540.9	1,697.8		555.6		
OTHER W. PACIFIC						
Australia	15.2	164.2	11,140.0	46.2	+5.6	+3.1
New Zealand	3.2	23.9	7,920.0	11.3	+2.9	+1.8
UPPER NORTH AMERICA						
U.S.	231.5	3,009.6	13,160.0	467.1	+4.7	2.7
Canada	24.6	289.6	11,320.0	123.4	+4.2	+3.4
	256.1	3,299.2		590.5		
EUROPEAN ECON. COM.						
West Germany	61.6	662.9	12,459.0	332.2	+5.4	+2.4
Italy	56.3	344.6	6,840.0	159.6	+4.5	+2.8
Great Britain	55.8	473.2	9,660.0	196.7	+4.8	+1.5
France	54.4	537.3	11,680.0	208.2	+6.2	+3.2
Spain	37.9	181.6	5,430.0	52.1	+6.9	+3.1
Netherlands	14.3	136.5	10,930.0	128.7	+3.8	+2.4
Belgium	9.9	85.2	10,760.0	110.3	+4.6	+2.7
Greece	9.8	33.9	4,290.0	15.3	+4.1	+7.0
Denmark	5.1	57.0	12,470.0	32.6	+3.5	+2.1
Ireland	3.5	17.1	5,150.0	17.5	+3.8	+7.0
	308.6	2,529.3		1,253.2		
EUR. FREE TRADE ASSOC.						
Portugal	10.1	21.3	2,450.0	13.4	na	+4.5
Sweden	8.3	98.8	14,040.0	58.3	+2.8	+1.7
Austria	7.6	66.6	9,880.0	35.2	+3.3	+6.5
Switzerland	6.4	96.7	17,010.0	54.6	+4.1	+0.7
Finland	4.8	48.9	10,870.0	26.5	+3.6	+3.0
Norway	4.1	56.1	14,280.0	32.9	+5.5	+4.3
	41.3	388.4		220.9		

*Figures roughly comparable to those from the World Bank are taken from the Asia 1985 Yearbook, Hong Kong, Far Eastern Economic Review, pp. 6-9.
Sources: World Bank, World Development Report, New York, Oxford University Press, 1985, pp. 218-223, 234-235.

Within the geographic context, the interplay among demographic and economic factors creates the dynamism and the tension between the Asia Pacific and the liberal West. Of the total population under discussion here, 2.15 billion souls, almost three fourths are Asian, with China alone accounting for more than all the Western nations combined. Numbers of people alone do not add up to power and influence per se, but since the days of Marco Polo demographic size has dominated Western images. Population size is also very much on the minds of Asian leaders, as objects of pride and also as problems.

The economic power of the two realms is almost the reverse of population size, as Figures 2 and 3 show. North American and European economic power, as measured in GNP, overwhelms that of the Asia Pacific by a factor of three to one. When economic power is expressed as GNP per capita, the difference between the average in the Asia Pacific and the average in the liberal West is almost six to one.

Even in world trade, where the Asia Pacific role is rapidly expanding, the countries of the liberal West command an almost four to one advantage in merchandise exports and imports, compared to all of the Asia Pacific. European trade volume is well over that of North America or of the Asia Pacific, but it is mostly intra-European in nature. Powerful as Japan and the United States are in world trade, especially in the Pacific, their dependency on foreign trade and their value of foreign trade in per capita terms are far less than most of Europe. Contrary to the impression created by the deep penetration of Japanese goods in markets worldwide, Japan's dependency on foreign trade, calculated by dividing trade values by GNP in 1983, was little more than one half that of Italy and Great Britain and less than one half that of West Germany. Per capita trade figures for the Asian NICs, however, are comparable to those of Europe.2/

ECONOMIC CHALLENGES

If Asian demographic size suggests market opportunities for Western goods only in the uncertain future, and if Western dominance, in economic power and trade, compared to the Asia Pacific, is still large, why is there so much anxiety?

FIGURE 2A
POPULATION IN THE ASIA PACIFIC & INDUSTRIAL WEST

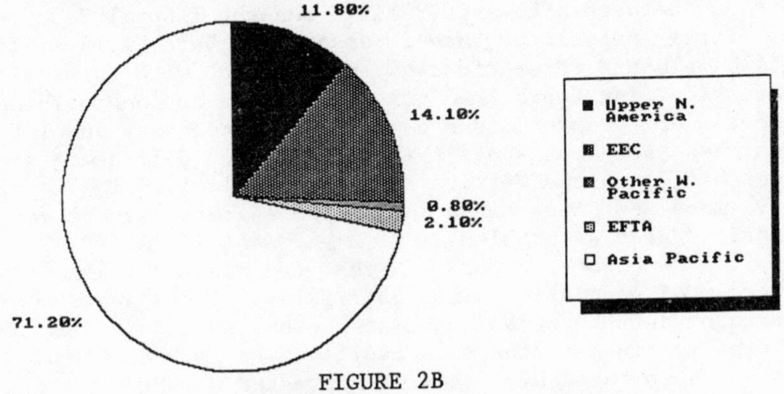

FIGURE 2B
POPULATION IN THE ASIA PACIFIC

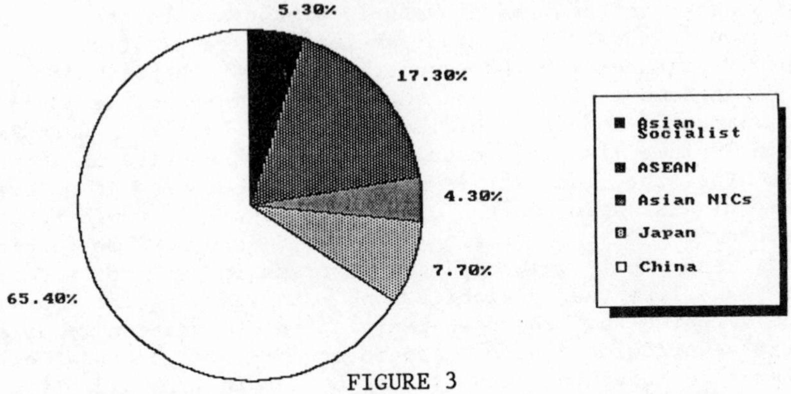

FIGURE 3
PERCENTAGE SHARES OF WORLD GNP AND TRADE VOLUME

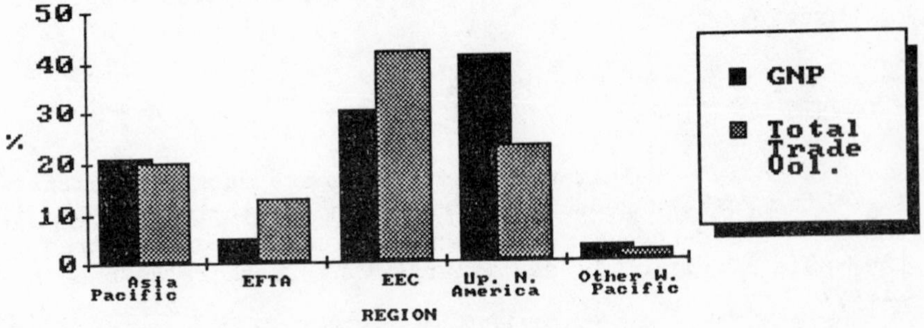

Sources for Figures 2 and 3 are derived from Table 1.

One clue to European anxiety is its declining contribution to the increases in world trade over the last twenty years. This decline is not to be confused with trade volume itself, wherein the European share remains very high. The declining role of European trade is disturbing in the context of a sevenfold increase in total world trade over the last fifteen years--$565 billion in 1970, $1,832 billion in 1976, $3,404 billion in 1982, and $3,975 in 1984. Between 1964 and 1973, as Figure 4 indicates, the European contribution to the increase was almost half of the total, 46.6% in exports and 47.5% in imports. For the same ten year period the American contribution was one third that of Europe, while Japan's was roughly half that of the United States and the Asian NICs was less than half that of Japan.

FIGURE 4
COMPARATIVE CONTRIBUTIONS TO INCREASES
IN WORLD TRADE FOR SELECTED YEAR PERIOD

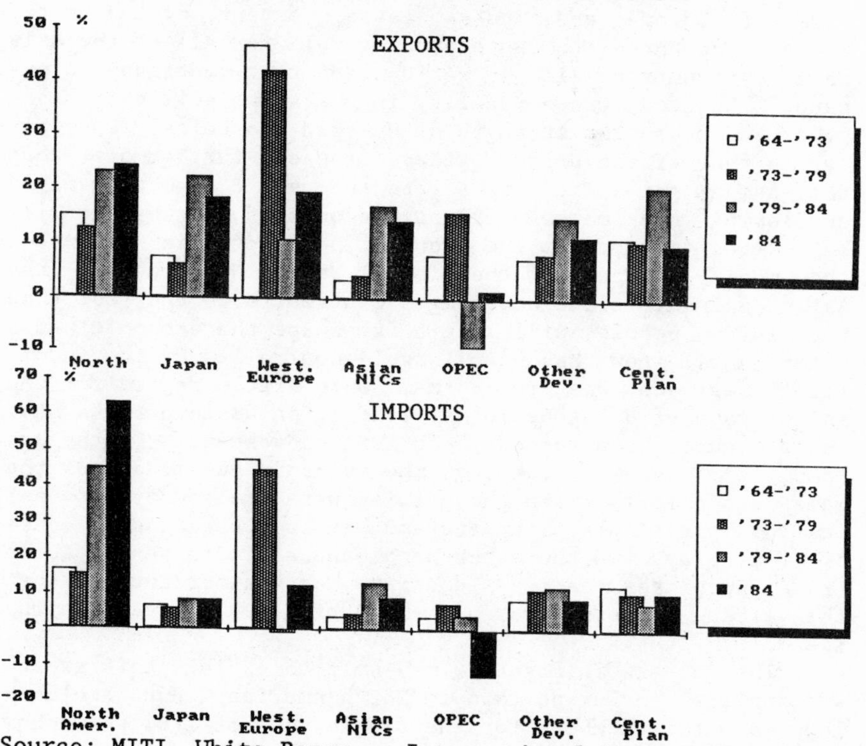

Source: MITI, White Paper on International Trade, 1985, p. 2.

Ten years later, however, we find dramatic reversals taking place. The West European contribution to the increase in world trade, between 1979 and 1984, had declined eightfold, showing a negative 1.1% contribution in imports. By contrast, the North American contribution to the increase in total world trade had more than doubled, while Japan's increase had also doubled and the contribution of the Asian NICs, as Figure 4 again shows, increased threefold. These figures reflect the importance of the American market in expanding Asian trade in the world, and they help to explain the world's "discovery" of the Asian NICs.3/ In recent years China has seen rates of economic growth greater, even, than the Asian NICs--9% in 1983 and 12% in 1984. Its increased trade activity is commensurate with this growth. And although China's trade volume is still less than half that of Taiwan's, this growth further contributes to Western perceptions of the Asia Pacific as a dynamic and expanding part of the world.

Thus, one clue to Western anxieties is the declining role of Europe and, to a lesser extent, of the United States, compared to an expanding role for all of the Asia Pacific countries--in a world trade that continues to expand. Granted, trade vitality in the Asia Pacific is highly dependent on the strength of Western economies, especially on that of the United States. Granted, furthermore, that the Asian gains in trade are the result of more rapidly developing and market oriented economies and that it will be a long time before the economic power of Asia will match the moving targets of the liberal West. Nevertheless, the Asian gains in trade advantages contribute to the fear that the Asian people will begin to shape the economic order which until now has been largely controlled by the industrial West on Western terms, with little regard for the Asian ways of doing business. Trading on Western terms has, to be sure, been turned to an Asian advantage. On the one hand, to suggest changing the rules in the middle of the game, especially when those rules were created by the West in the first place, understandably creates an Asian sense of foul play. On the other hand, annual increases in Asian trade surpluses easily leads to Western perceptions that the Asian traders are not competing on a level playing field.

The numbers in Figure 4 may help to explain this greater anxiety in Europe than in North America. But, a closer look at the numbers for the single year of 1984 shows how trade patterns continue to shift, in this case in favor of Europe. To be sure, the European contribution in 1984 is far from the 1964-73 period, but it is a rising one. Furthermore, the Japanese contribution, and even the Asian NIC contribution, show declines. The European increase and the Asian decline are the results of larger shifts within trade patterns that seem to have little to do with protectionism per se. The American role for 1984 remains dominant.

By virtue of its early and forceful impact on world trade, compared to other Asia Pacific countries, Japan is the most frequent target of Western cries for protectionism. To focus alone on Japanese trade surpluses, however, is to misrepresent the full nature of the challenge. Western trade deficits also exist with other Asia Pacific countries, who in turn have their own large deficits with Japan. Protectionism directed primarily against Japan, furthermore, will have profound effects on the whole of the Asia Pacific.

Japan's economic miracle still leaves the experts baffled. Westerners alternate between fear and admiration of this new power. When Herman Kahn pasted together one of the first books on Japan's economic miracle in 1970, the impact of Japan's performance was only dimly recognized and Japan's trade surpluses with the industrial West were too small to cause alarm. The response to Ezra Vogel's suggestion of Japan as number one, published nine years later, was more of a shock because the audacious title of his book had a ring of truth. The world's focus of attention on Europe and the United States over the previous century has ill-prepared Westerners to be second to anyone.

The immediate challenge is the reduction of Western trade deficits, which have become a powerful political issue in both Europe and the United States. As bad as the American deficit is to Japan in per capita terms, that is $400 for every individual Japanese in 1984, it is worse for the Asian NICs, $800 for every Taiwanese and $1000 for every citizen of Hong Kong.4/ Smaller deficits might soften the cries for protectionism, but even with a weaker dollar relative to other currencies, lower American interest rates, and a smaller national debt, Western trade deficits are likely to remain for some time to come.

Behind the problems of unbalanced trade are differences in economic performance in the world economy. The Asia Pacific countries have sustained economic rates of growth in the last quarter century more remarkable than for any other part of the world. These growth rates may extend into the next decade and possibly the next century. Impressive as this projected growth may be, the economies of the industrial West, even with lower rates of growth, will still dominate world trade, while great disparities within the Asia Pacific will also be maintained. Though Japan's growth rate was among the highest in the world in the 1960s and 1970s, it is projected to hold stable at 4% until the turn of the century. At that rate, its share of world GNP would remain between its current 20 and 21 percent. The other Asia Pacific countries, including China, the Asian NICs, and the ASEAN countries, are also projected to have high growth rates, and yet their combined share of world GNP by the turn of the century may be only a little more than that of Japan and still less than half of the United States.5/

Projections are a risky business, because the variables affecting economic growth and trade are difficult to select. There are both bright and dark prospects on the horizon. On the bright side, inflation in the developed countries has tapered off, while technological innovation and capital investments have increased. On the dark side are: the massive budget and balance of payments deficits, notably in the United States; the sluggishness of the Western economies; the large external debts of developing countries; and the growing strength of protectionist sentiment in the industrial West.

Current projections on world trade are made even more difficult because the reports and discussions of trade are focused on the trade in goods and ignore, for the most part, the rapid growth of trade in services. Incomplete as the reporting is, some evidence suggests that the trade in services may be as high as one-fourth the value of trade in merchandise and that it is growing more rapidly. These trends reflect the growth of the service sector in the economies of developed countries in general. In the industrial West, the service sector accounts for as much as 60% of the total labor force, or almost twice that of the manufacturing sector.6/

The anxiety that feeds protectionist sentiment in the West issues from the pinch of trade imbalances with the Asia Pacific and from the expectation that Asian economic dynamism may increase the trade indebtedness in the future. It also springs from the uncertainty about the ability of the industrial West to compete successfully, and Western expectations that Asian economic dynamism may continue to increase Western trade deficits indefinitely. In this context, it is easy to see the appeal of focusing on the short-term benefits of protectionism, the protection of jobs and of righting the trade imbalances. Protectionism, in the long run, however, is a different matter. According to the World Bank, there is "abundant evidence to show that import restrictions do not save jobs, do not improve the balance of trade, and add upward pressure on the real exchange rate." The bank stresses the "perversity" of protectionism, because "not only do its roots lie in a failure to adjust, but its adoption simply compounds that failure."7/

The well known industrial policies of the Asia Pacific are the bone of contention. Government protection of infant industries and those targeted for their export potential was one key to Japan's industrial policy until the mid-1960s. Protection then covered government programs for gaining access to foreign technologies and for research and development. Incentives were created for firms to move into particular areas of research and production through special loans and tax credits. Although Japanese government protection was diminished and even disappeared in some industries such as automobiles, electronics, and steel, it has continued in other key areas such as telecommunications, semiconductors, and computers, where the global competition and added value are high and the trade potential is excellent.8/

Japanese writers concede the government's deliberate use of industrial policy to create trade advantages. They also concede the problems Westerners face in negotiating with Japan, bureaucratic barriers, complex distribution channels, and complicated inspection procedures--all of which impede the entry of foreign products and investments into Japanese markets. These and other complications are related to what Karl von Wolferen has in mind in his discussion of the "Central Democratic State" (CDS).9/ In his view, and that of Chalmers Johnson who coined the phrase, the CDS is both a clue to Japan's rapid industrial development and to the difficulties faced by Westerners in working with Japanese bureaucracies. Similar industrial policies, that encourage closer cooperation between business and government, also characterize the Asian NICs and the countries of ASEAN, not to mention China. The "erasing of the dividing lines between private and public sectors," to use von Wolferen's words, gives the Asia Pacific countries an unfair advantage.10/

There is no gainsaying charges that the Asia Pacific is taking advantage of the world trade system. Only the city states of Hong Kong and Singapore are truly open markets. Formal and informal barriers to entry of Western products and investments remain great for the other Asian NICs and the ASEAN countries in general, while those of China are so difficult to manage that foreign investments and market access are problematic at best.

Because Japan is the primary focus of attention in the liberal West, a closer look at the charge of unfairness is in order. To begin with, many Western firms, such as BMW, IBM, Procter and Gamble, etc., successfully operate in and export to Japan and other Asian countries. Moreover, Western trade disadvantages are related to a demand among Asian consumers for product design, quality levels, and customer services not often found in Western imports. More important in the assessments of Japan today, is its responsiveness to Western pressures in recent years. Japanese tariff reductions begun, however selectively, since World War II, gained momentum in 1968 with the Kennedy Round. Out of the new agreements in the 1982 and 1984 Tokyo Round, Japanese tariffs, according to the World Bank, were "lowered to levels not seen before in this century."11/ Prompted by fears of retaliation from the United States, Korea and Taiwan are now also reducing tariff barriers, although they are still far behind Japanese reductions.

Prior to Japan's acceptance of the General Agreement on Tariffs and Trade in 1963, Japanese restrictions in customs tariffs and import quotas were much higher than in the United States and Western Europe. Since then, however, reductions have occurred to the point where it could be argued that the Japanese market today may be no less open than Western markets. According to the Keizai Koho Center, the average Japanese tariff on all industrial imports in 1984 was 2.8%, compared to 4.4% for the United States and 4.7% for the European Economic Community. Furthermore, in 1984, Keizai Koho figures show Japanese tariffs on computer and software imports to be 4.9% compared to 4.5% for the United States and 17% for the EEC.12/ William R. Cline, of the Institute for International Economics, argues that Japan's visible non-tariff barriers may be even less than those of other industrially advanced countries. That is, 22.1% of Japan's manufactured imports in 1984 were subject to such barriers, according to Cline, compared to 45.1% for the United States and 36.5% for France.13/ These figures are not offered here to conclude the debate. They do, however, force a critical examination of charges of unfairness by one side against the other.14/

Other Asian countries are as troubled by trade deficits with Japan as is the liberal West, but because their market-oriented economies are highly dependent on an open world market, they are as fearful of Western, especially American, retaliation against Japan as they are of Japan's dominance. Lee Kuan Yew, Prime Minister of Singapore, regards American threats to close its markets in an attempt to solve "temporary difficulties," as "preposterous," and he asks, "Is America willing to write off the peaceful and constructive development of the last 40 years that she has made possible?" Mahathir, Prime Minister of Malaysia, is more exercised by the "economic Cold War between Japan and the United States" than by the Soviet threat. Either as trade enemies or as favored bilateral partners, Japan and the United States, in Mahathir's words, are feared like two elephants fighting or making love. In either case, the grass, or the rest of the Asia Pacific, will be trampled or squashed. Mahathir decries the "political illiteracy" of protectionism on either side of the Pacific.15/

The enormous trade deficits with Japan, dependence on world markets, and fierce competition among themselves are the anxieties of the Asian NICs, the ASEAN countries, and China.16/ Their export-driven sucesses of recent years are by no means guaranteed to continue. As global markets change, the competitive edge of one decade may be lost in the next. The shifts from heavy to light industry and from manufacturing to services may be a mark of economic progress generally, but successful adjustments are difficult to make. Whether or not the cultural resilience and economic dynamism of the Asia Pacific will continue into the coming years, or be able to withstand Western protective measures, should they occur, is not at all clear.17/

POLITICAL CHALLENGES

Unsettling as economic trends may be, strategic and political uncertainties may be even more unsettling. Few would deny the close relationship between economic and political development. But just what that relationship is, remains unclear. At the heart of political anxieties is the role of the Soviet Union in the Pacific Ocean. A different kind of anxiety is tied to the question of political succession of the present older generation of Asian leaders.

Socialist Countries and the Asia Pacific

The anxiety over the military role of the Soviet Union is greater for some Western leaders than concerns over growing trade imbalances with the Asia Pacific. China, too, provokes unease because of its Soviet-style political organization and ideological orientation. In the rivalry between the superpowers in the Pacific, China's role was regarded largely as an extension of Soviet power until the Sino-Soviet split in the 1960s. Since then, China's more independent role in the Pacific region, has softened Western anxieties. And yet the legacies of the Cultural Revolution, a disaster of China's own making, continue to create suspicion. This suspicion is heightened in the minds of non-Chinese, especially by memories of China's past dominance and expansion and by the ties between China and the Overseas Chinese who control much of the economic power in Southeast Asia.

The concerns at the Eindhoven Conference with strategic questions, especially the influence of the Soviet Union, were by no means uniform. In charting the historical development of superpower rivalry in the Pacific Basin, Laszlo Bartalits is as critical as anyone of Soviet behavior, but the United States does not escape his criticism altogether. In his analysis of American policy, James Armstrong gave high marks to the Reagan administration, despite the preceding half century of American blunders. The result is a stronger position, politically, in the Pacific region for the United States than for the Soviet Union. The importance of historical patterns in assessing China's strategic role in the Pacific region is discussed by this author in another paper. Finally, Janamitra Devan's paper reminded the conference of ASEAN fears of China's motivations and behavior.18/

An active Russian interest in China goes back to the Treaty of Nerchinsk in 1698, but it was not until the 19th century with attempts to break the isolation of Tokugawa Japan and the creation of the city of Vladivostok, that Russian influence spread to the shores of the Pacific. Japan's victory over Russia, in 1905, blunted the Russian advances in Korea and China's northeast, but Russian influence continued to spread through literature and later ideology. It would be hard to overstate the influence of Marxist-Leninist ideology on the twentieth century developments of China, Korea and Vietnam. The rift with China in the 1960s has again altered the Soviet presence on the Pacific Rim, but the defeat of American forces in South Vietnam in the spring of 1975 created in effect a power vacuum that quickly has been filled by the Soviet Union.

Compared to the size of its military power on the Pacific, Soviet economic influence and volume of trade are small, although some increases are recorded. For example, Soviet trade with China has increased fourfold in five years to $2 billion in 1985. This figure, however, is not much more than China's covert trade with Taiwan. Soviet trade with Japan, furthermore, stood at $4.3 billion in 1985, which was less than the figure in 1980. Soviet trade with Vietnam and North Korea is apparently larger--no figures are available--but it is closely linked to military aid and occurs largely outside the framework of Pacific Rim trade in general. To be sure, the Soviet Union, Vietnam, and North Korea stand to benefit from expanding global trade, and various "liberalization" measures have been discussed to capture that advantage. North Korea is said to be watching closely South Korea's impressive economic and trade performance, while Vietnam over the past half decade has engaged in a number of "reforms" in its attempt to emulate some aspects of China's new "open door" policy.19/

By virtue of their demographic and economic size, the influence of the socialist powers in the Western Pacific must be reckoned with. But short of major reforms, the socialist economic model has little, if anything, to offer this late into the 20th century. Although its political and economic structures are still shaped by the Soviet model, China's impressive economic performance in the last ten years is explained largely by the degree to which it has departed from that model.

The differences in performance between the Asian NICs and the Asian socialist states, as revealed by a glance at Table 1, have almost laid to rest the debate over the comparative advantages of market-oriented and centrally planned economies on the Pacific Rim. Continuing debates about the advantages of socialism spill over into critiques of American policies the world around, but the debate is staged largely by intellectuals and political minorities groups. Even in such sensitive areas as income distribution, where centrally planned economies with their emphasis on planned distribution were thought to have an edge, the debate favors the advanced and newly industrialized countries with a market orientation.20/ Short of a decisive turning away from its own economic model, similar to that of Hungary or China, current reforms in the Soviet Union cannot be expected to bear much fruit. As the creator of its own model, its ideological orthodoxy, and its own "world order," the Soviet Union can make similar moves only with great difficulty, while North Korea and Vietnam, with their deep-rooted suspicions of China, cannot be expected to weaken their ties with the Soviet Union for some time to come.21/

One clue to the behavior of the Soviets in the Pacific, in addition to superpower rivalry, is the traditional fear of inaccessibility to the sea. Its presence there and hostile stance projected against the market-oriented economies of the Asia Pacific may be an attempt to compensate for the harsh judgment history has made on the Soviet experience. Asian perceptions of superpower rivalry have changed dramatically in the last decade, since Vietnam's economic and political disasters over the last decade and since China's radical departure from the Soviet model. Asian hostility to the Soviet model is so deep that it can only be contained by police force and government-generated xenophobia in North Korea and the Indochina peninsula. The greater threat to the interests of the liberal West in the Pacific may not be the differences between itself and the Asia Pacific, but rather the expansion of Soviet power. My intent in offering this observation is not to strengthen anti-Soviet prejudice. If the United States fares better in Asian judgments about the Cold War, it is because its economic and political orientation is better suited to the economic dynamism and political directions in the Asia Pacific.

Asian Political Traditions

Surprising as it may seem to those whose images of Asia are shaped largely by news reports, one distinctive asset of Asian political traditions, is the relative stability and continuity in leadership of the last quarter century.22/ To be sure, Mao Zedong's last years of rule during the Cultural Revolution, and the opposition of students and rival political leaders outside the normal political process in South Korea, Thailand, and the Philippines, provoke images of chaos and instability. Nevertheless, remarkably long periods of political leadership have characterized the Asia Pacific in recent years: Mao and Deng in China; the Chiang generations in Taiwan; Park and Chun in South Korea; Lee in Singapore; Suharto in Indonesia; Kim in North Korea; and yes, even Marcos, prior to his ouster, in the Philippines. The correlation between this political stability and the economic dynamism of the Asia Pacific appears to be a positive one, especially when compared to the general political instability elsewhere as in Africa, the Middle East, and Latin America.

The relative stability of Asia may erode, however, if the problems of political succession are not resolved. Asian political preference for age, experience, and personal charisma produces one kind of stability not seen in the liberal West. But, in Asian contexts, these patterns of patriarchal authority also produce tendencies toward cults of personality, senility, bureaucratism and personal favoritism.23/ Just how the balance between the strengths and weaknesses of age works out may vary from one individual to the next within the same political tradition. Mao Zedong's senility and personality cult may have been the worst example of this weakness, and his legacy provokes recurring doubts about China's political stability. On the one hand, in the context of Taiwan's spectacular modernization, the question of Chiang Kai-shek's misuse of personal power is moot. Deng Xiaoping, on the other hand, appears to understand how the concentration of power in the hands of an aging leader can undermine political effectiveness, and in order to prepare for his retirement, he has skillfully brought younger leaders with similar persuasions into high positions.

Complicating the abuses of personal power is the general lack of political institutions to protect the rights of citizens, to tap the energies of opposition forces and the talents of younger people, and to carry out the smooth transfer of power when an older leader dies. Indeed, one clue, to fundamental differences with the liberal West is the lack of a political culture in the Asia Pacific that legitimizes and produces a loyal opposition. These political uncertainties cast a certain pall over the economic successes in some of the ASEAN countries and, to a lesser extent, among the Asian NICs.

KEYWORDS IN WESTERN LIBERALISM

The questions raised in this section of the essay are the subject of vigorous discussion, on both Asian and Western sides. My purpose in this section is to reflect on the use of a few keywords that shape the current discussion. By showing how meanings of the same word change over time and differ across cultures, these broad strokes are intended to soften anxieties. An overly present-minded and unreflective use of keywords such as "liberal" and "individualism" often divide Asia from the West more than is warranted.

A possible starting point is one of Webster's definitions of liberalism as "a philosophy based on belief in progress, the essential goodness of man and the autonomy of the individual, and standing for tolerance and freedom for the individual from arbitrary authority in all spheres of life." Raymond Williams takes the discussion a step further, in his various studies of "keywords," beginning with the reminder that liberalism has not had a long tradition in the West, nor has it always carried positive connotations. According to Williams, the word "liberal" did not come into English usage until the 14th century, and as it became a doctrine of "certain necessary kinds of freedom," it also essentially became a "doctrine of possessive individualism."

Williams' probes into the etymologies of words reinforces this varied, at times contradictory, understanding of other keywords. The earliest uses of the word "equality," for example, were in relation to physical quantity, while specific social meanings for equality were not given until the American and French Revolutions. The word "democracy," which is often traced back to Greek origins, until the 19th century, frequently carried a strongly unfavorable connotation. The word "individual" originally meant indivisible. In this paradox the modern use of the word emphasizes one's separation or distinction from others, while the word indivisible implies a necessary connection. This "record in language of an extraordinary social and political history" indicates just how far word usage can stray from original meanings.24/

To underscore the pluralism of the liberal West and contradictions among groups which would all plausibly claim to be anchored in a liberal tradition, we find that interest groups diverge when it comes to perceptions of trade with the Asia Pacific and of the free trade system itself. It is surprising that these contradictions have not surfaced more often in public discussion. When, for example, the question of free trade is raised, three very different interest groups, according to Kenichi Ohmae, may be identified: consumers, corporations, and politicians. Fundamental misperceptions about the attitudes of these three groups obscure the true nature of protectionism and the liberal values and institutions it is designed to protect. According to Ohmae, consumers share many tastes and habits in common. They simply wish to buy the best products and services at the lowest cost, regardless of country origin. Of course, when the job security of consumers, as workers, is threatened by foreign competition, they quickly and understandably become protectionist. If they are secure, however, their interests as consumers can rapidly undermine previous opposition to foreign products: witness the spread of Asian produced consumer goods among working class people in the whole of the industrial West today.

The role of corporations in world trade is different. Their purpose is to make money. With little regard for trade balances one way or the other, they frequently move capital or plants overseas in order to make more money. Indeed, if the total activity of corporations were recognized, and not just export trade, 1984 would reveal, it is argued by Ohmae, that the American corporate experience in Japan is still largely a positive one. The value of the goods that an American corporation either exports to Japan or produces in Japan to sell to Japanese consumers, Ohmae continues, is roughly equal to the value of Japanese goods, either exported to or produced by Japanese companies in the United States, or $69 billion in 1984. According to Ohmae, direct operations by American corporations in Japan in 1984 were three times the size of Japanese direct operations in the United States.25/

The primary government interest is in the balance of payments. The purpose of governments, Ohmae argues, is a political one, that is, their interest is to comply with perceived demands from pressure groups who can influence their positions or divert public criticism away from potentially negative political actions. Given the trade imbalance with Japan, protectionism by political leaders in the West may be seen, Ohmae suggests, as a convenient way to divert criticism away from the larger mismanagement or neglect. When Western political leaders put pressure on Japan to open its markets, they mean to increase direct exports, and they largely ignore the desire of consumers and advantages that direct operations abroad can bring to the economy.

An excellent example of this diversionary role is the American government's vexation with Japan over beef and citrus. These two issues have become political footballs, as it were, and bear little resemblance to actual trade practice or significance. The statistics on American exports to Japan of beef and citrus suggest that however protected these two agricultural products may be there, it is unrealistic to expect the Japanese to do much more. In fact, in 1983, Japan's imports accounted for 68% of total U.S. beef exports, 73% of pork exports, 22% of orange exports, 51% of grapefruit exports, and 78% of lemons and limes exports.26/ Given the small volume of American beef and citrus exports to Japan relative to other agricultural products such as soybeans and other grains, a complete opening up of the Japanese market in these two product areas would likely have only negligible effects on the trade imbalance, while the present demand to "open up" Japanese markets in these two areas distorts the larger role Japan already plays.

Each of these groups may represent a certain part of Western liberalism: consumers with their interest in more and better quality for less, regardless of a product's national origin; corporations with their interest in making money; and governments whose focus on trade deficits may be little more than attempts to cover its own mismanagement. The first two groups, over time, do not necessarily perceive the challenge of the Asia Pacific as a threat to their interests. Of course, major corporations in industrial sectors that have lost out in international competition can easily become protectionist, that is, until or unless it becomes possible for them to regain competitiveness or to locate offshore, as indeed many Western firms have done. But even government, which has raised the cry for protectionism louder than other groups have, is not united on the issue, as the sharp division between the Congress and the President of the United States shows. Such is the problem facing anyone trying to generalize about attitudes and perceptions in the liberal West today.

Another keyword in the liberal lexicon, individualism, is also illuminating in our attempt to understand Western anxieties about the Asia Pacific today. Unlike the liberal framework of world trade that has benefited the Asia Pacific and has increasingly earned its support, the question of individualism touches upon a more profound difference and a more sensitive issue. In reading Donald Munro's recently edited study of individualism and holism in China, one is struck by how often Western Sinologists cite individualism as the key difference between Chinese cultures--and all of East Asia for that matter--and the modern West. Munro's book also echoes Williams' reminder that the currency of individualism in the West is a recent development, only since the Enlightenment.27/ The identification of individualism with major cultural themes in the liberal West is buttressed by Webster's reference twice to the individual in defining liberalism.

To be sure, as a core theme, individualism may be more uniquely an American and less a European orientation, and some might even argue that it represents an aberration of the best of the liberal tradition in the West. Whatever the proper context, individualism is not an altogether negative quality in the Asia Pacific, as our later discussion of conscious attempts by the Japanese to make education more "individualistic" will show. Indeed, the rugged American individualism expressed in music, entertainment, and even business practices, continues to fascinate, if not frustrate, Asians and Europeans alike. Though generally critical of the liberal West, Luigi Barzini finds words of admiration for this peculiarly American "spiritual wind...a sacreligious Promethean element...an impious challenge to God's will." Extreme though it may be, American sensibilities informed by individualism "dominate the world in large and small matters," while American hopes, Barzini claims, have become "universal man's hopes too."28/

Prized as this individualism may be, its effect on Western culture is increasingly called into question, not only among skeptical outsiders but within American society itself. Whether it is the malaise of workers in the factories, or teachers in schools, or the trauma of children and parents of broken homes, or the violence in the streets, or the nihilism of acid rock, or the blurring of right and wrong, this individualistic side of American culture is undergoing serious scrutiny. Already a century and a half ago, Alexis de Tocqueville noticed the American "restlessness in the midst of prosperity" and that above the "freest and best educated of men" a "cloud habitually hung on their brow." Americans then seemed to de Tocqueville to be "serious and almost sad even in their pleasures." How could such a restless and competitive people sustain enduring relationships when "they clutch everything and hold nothing fast?"

Among the many current books concerned with the problems of individualism, there is one written by a team of sociologists headed by Robert Bellah, who with his colleagues describes an "ontological individualism," a belief in which only the individual is a firm reality. Carried to an extreme, these "habits of the heart," a phrase in the book's title taken from de Tocqueville, have produced the "widespread feeling that the promise of the modern era is slipping away from us." In this liberal world, "so incoherent that it seems to be losing the significance of its own ideals," the generosity and goodwill of individuals is fragmented and small-scale, and their attempts to relate to the "large-scale forces and institutions" become impossible. It is this frustration that creates the "pathos underlying many of the conversations about work, family, community, and politics."29/

Bellah's pessimism is by no means universal in liberal America, but it is pervasive enough to force a serious reconsideration that is confined not only to thinkers and writers. It is also occurring, if only covertly, among American and European workers employed in firms and factories owned and managed by Japanese. Until recently, there were voices, including experts on American management and on Japanese culture, who claimed that, however admirable Japanese management practices might be, there was little point in discussing its adoption in the West because of unbridgeable cultural differences. Judging by the experience of many American workers in Japanese firms, however, the opposite seems to be the case. From auto-assembly plants to consumer electronics, American managers and workers in Japanese owned and managed firms are surprisingly satisfied, while unions in these manufacturing sectors are increasingly frustrated. Rugged individualism and its extension into the familiar pattern of adversarial relations between unions and management, for so long the symbol of the American work place, are yielding to the appeals for greater job security, greater cooperation between labor and management and the common concern with greater productivity for the firm as a whole. The hardhat is worn not only by rugged individualists, seeming not to care for others, but it is also worn by workers who believe in harmony, teamwork, and commitments that go beyond the next paycheck.30/ To be sure, Japanese managers, setting up firms in the West, are careful to insist on harmony as the principle of organization and to protect the firm from union activity that is anti-management. The adjustment by Western workers to Japanese communication styles has taken place nonetheless. It has been made easier by the flexiblity of Japanese management, which yields at times to the American-style "top down" decision-making pattern, instead of the "bottom up" pattern more familiar to Japanese firms. At times it has even yielded to union activity in an attempt to coopt it.31/

LIBERALISM IN ASIA

If the peoples of the Asia Pacific appear less than enthusiastic in their commitments to the liberal world order today, they may have good reason. Until recently, liberalism, defined loosely as a political philosophy, was perceived by most Asians as a threat to the very fabric of their cultures. Liberalism's stress on equality in human and international relationships appeared to conflict with the prevailing hierarchical pattern in Asian social and political organization and in foreign relations. Recently in the West, liberal and libertarian voices have placed the rights of the individual far above the claims of the group, while for centuries personal freedom and individualism in the Asia Pacific have been criticized as forces for confusion and disorder.

Just why Asian peoples have resisted the inroads of liberal thinking may be related to their recent encounters with the West when economic, political, and even cultural liberalism was introduced into Asian cultures by military force. Captain Elliott's disregard for the pleas of the Dao Guang Emperor to stop the British trade in opium, and his contempt for the efforts in 1839 of Commissioner Lin Zexu to control the trade in Canton, were justified in the name of "free trade." The British and French pillage of the beautiful Yuan Ming Yuan palaces in Peking in 1860 (palaces ironically designed by Jesuit architects employed by the imperial court a century earlier) was associated with the demand for "equality" in diplomatic relations. Thereafter, Western ambassadors permanently established their embassies in the same city as the Chinese Emperors and, in one move, undermined the ritual hierarchy that had defined China's orthodox view of the world. The Open Door policy of Secretary of State John Hay, of 1898, may have protected China's territorial integrity, but it did nothing to change extraterritoriality, whereby Western traders operated according to their own laws in disregard of Chinese laws. The 1912 partial return to China of the Boxer indemnity by the government of the United States in order to establish one of its prestigious "liberal arts" colleges, Qinghua University, has been portrayed as a generous move in the heyday of imperialism. But one is also reminded that the indemnity of the Boxer Protocol of 1901 was the harshest of the many indemnities forced upon China as its most recent reward for losing every war with Western powers in the 19th century.

Abhorrent as this violent introduction of liberal ideas and institutions into the Asia Pacific may be, Asian leaders have become surprisingly liberal in their outlook and in their response. These examples of violence are by no means the whole story of violence in modern Asia. Indeed, the greater violence may be that of Asians against Asians, whether it is Japan against the rest of the Asia Pacific during the Pacific War, or Mao Zedong or Pol Pot against millions of "intellectuals" who were insufficiently "red." Furthermore, despite Western violence, Asian leaders in the last century have been attracted to the ways of the "liberal" West, because of the promise of "wealth and power," sufficient to rid Asia of the Western military presence.32/ Few educated Asians today would suggest a return to their premodern patterns of social and political hierarchy, not to mention their 19th century systems of foreign relations and closed trade. Even the leaders of Asian socialist countries today would not deny the benefits of "free trade." Indeed, the advantage of economic and political interdependence between the Asia Pacific and the liberal West has been accepted to the point that if any one country were to threaten that tie, it would challenge one of the most powerful--and welcome--developments in the last half of this century.

Reconsiderations of their traditions will not likely lead Asians to the point of an individualism that threatens the distinctive coherence or the dominance of the group in human relationships. Nevertheless, the attractions of liberalism to the peoples of Asia are more than economic. Since the turn of the century their leaders have become more liberal in political thought. Even as patriarchal family patterns prevail, the value of equal opportunity for all, regardless of age or sex, is gaining in popularity. Even as the interests of the group continue to dominate human relations, the concepts of individual choice, personal freedom, and human rights have taken root in Asian cultures. And even as political institutions remain authoritarian in comparison to those of the liberal West, Asian leaders place great premium on democracy and are moving, with some glaring exceptions to be sure, toward greater political freedoms and accountability through open political processes.

Compared to the strength of liberal institutions in the West, liberalism in Asia may appear relatively undeveloped, but its presence is unmistakable. Despite the vigilance of Asian peoples towards Western cultural influence generally, the Asian absorption of Western ideas continues. Even the music, eating habits, and fashions, which carry with them the overtones of individualism, are being absorbed, as far away as rural Shaanxi in China. In Japan, furthermore, in contrast to Western attempts to learn from Japanese management which is heavily group oriented, we find a vigorous questioning among Japanese managers and workers about the very system that seems to have propelled them into the center of our attention. There, young people do not wish to work as hard as their parents did; women, generally as highly educated as in the West, are no longer willing to be treated as inferior either in the home or in the workplace; and even managers are questioning the so-called lifetime employment system. A recently formed Ad Hoc Council on Education, appointed by Prime Minister Nakasone has called for a "transformation of uniformist education to individualistic education," while strengthening traditional values. Former Vice Minister of Education, Hiroshi Kida, has recommended that "more individual activity" must be introduced into the schools in order to promote creativity.33/

Indeed, even in China, where economic levels would seem to work against middle class values and where socialism has reinforced traditional collectivist attitudes, there appears to be a growing pluralism. These liberal tendencies, furthermore, are taking root not just as transplants from the West but as extensions, if only as minor themes, of particular Chinese traditions. Not recognizing the possibilities of the pluralism in their past may be the result of ignorance, both Western and Chinese, as well as a kind of nationalistic stereotyping, generated by Chinese leaders themselves. That stereotyping, painted onto public opinion with a broad brush, was put to political use in order to mobilize the masses in the cause of national salvation. Now that China is politically "saved," and that it is turning to the West for its economic improvement, this pluralism is once again emphasized. Using traditional motifs in Chinese law to bolster the legal modernization of today would have been inconceivable during the Cultural Revolution. Its widespread use today, including the notion of rule by law if not rule of law, increases the possibility of a greater pluralism in their minds and also in Western interpretations of Chinese thought.34/

In pre-modern Chinese thought, even liberal themes appear to have existed. Unlike modern Western individualism, traditional Chinese liberalism rests on the belief in the importance of the individual's responsibility and independent action. This peculiar Chinese emphasis on individual action is closer to the word "individuality," which Williams reminds us, has a "longer history" than individualism, and stresses "both a unique person and his (indivisible) membership of a group."35/

The possibility of a "liberal tradition" in China has been argued forcefully by William T. deBary, the doyen of American specialists in Chinese thought. DeBary's argument has a bearing on the way the links or the conflicts between the Asia Pacific and the liberal West are perceived. He reminds us that there is a term for individualism in Chinese (geren zhuyi) which was borrowed from a Japanese term invented in the late 19th century. Its connotation has been predominantly negative. Its use and misuse by the state during the quarter century of the Communist Revolution until Mao's death was so pervasive that the charge of individualism by the Party was sufficient to humiliate millions of Chinese people and drive hundreds of thousands of intellectuals from public life and office and many to their death.

This unrelenting attack by the state has encouraged scholars to explain Chinese hostility to individualism as the combined result of Stalin-like statism and authoritarian Chinese tradition. To argue, however, that unrelenting hostility against individual action is the necessary consequence of China's political culture is misleading, according to deBary. Similarly, China's more liberal frame of mind today is not merely the result of Western influence. Chinese tradition is not so monolithic, nor can present behavior be reduced to such simple explanations. The themes within the many schools of Chinese philosopy are complex and may conflict. In seeking roughly equivalent meanings for the term individualism and also for liberalism (ziyou zhuyi), deBary argues, Chinese translators were not at a loss for words to express these new concepts, nor were they forced to fall back on transliteration as the only way to represent Western ideas that were new to them.36/ Indeed, deBary offers a "vocabulary of Neo-Confucian individualism," which is scattered throughout the Confucian classics and which exhorts the individual to rely upon himself to discover the meaning of the Tao and to assert himself against arbitrary political authority. To be sure, self-cultivation and freedom as freedom from selfishness, passion and ignorance are quite different from dominant themes in American individualism today. For that matter, however, thoughtful defenders of the liberal tradition in the West are equally concerned that the pursuit of freedom not become mere license.

The implications of these considerations for Sino-Western relations today is summarized by deBary as follows:

> For Westerners to adopt too narrow or culture-bound a definition of "liberalism," will be as self-defeating as was the attempt in China to limit Neo-Confucian orthodoxy to one particular school of thought. To see liberalism as having roots only in a Western past means confining and condemning it to an increasingly attenuated future. For Chinese, on the other hand, to see it as a foreign body, unassimilable to their own lives and culture, may likewise inhibit a natural growth from their own roots or [from] the process of cultural hybridization which today is the natural outgrowth of living together in the modern world.37/

Although not all scholars of Chinese thought would agree with deBary's emphasis, the possibility of a greater historical pluralism in China lies at the heart of this essay.

MANAGEMENT AND INNOVATION

Growing doubts within the West about the efficacy of liberal values coincide with the growing impact of Asian sensibilities on the West. As world trade has begun to shift from the Atlantic to the Pacific, ideas have followed. The discovery of new and better competitors can spill over into new ways of making things and of ordering realities. The net effect of travel, furthermore, triggers new considerations, while the net effect of migrations in recent years, notably the dramatic increase of Asian immigrants into the United States and Europe, can also weaken ethnic and cultural barriers.38/ Over the last century, the experiences of Asians with the West and in the West have raised doubts about traditional identities. Indeed, these doubts are a record of struggle mixed with hope, and they are an enduring theme in modern Asian literature. Continuing travel to, study in, and competition with the West, will sustain those doubts, even as traditional identities are affirmed. For the first time in modern history, these doubts are now occurring with comparable intensities on both sides of the world. For the first time in almost two centuries, the liberal West may be as much on the receiving side as the giving side of cross-cultural history.

One expression of this introspection, of these self-doubts, is the current admiration for Japanese management among Western economists and businessmen. To be sure, many of the principles of Japanese management were adopted from the West in the 1950s, as Michael Yoshino demonstrates.39/ "Just-in-time production," for example, now closely identified with Japanese organization, was originally Henry Ford's idea. But there are dimensions of their management philosophy that appear to be distinctively Japanese. The extent to which these qualities are cultural or simply organizational, or are Japanese or Western, is moot.40/ What is instructive here is that these ideas are perceived in the West to be Japanese and worthy of emulation.

Given the extent of public discussion about Japanese management, it is appropriate to begin with Peter Drucker, one of the first defenders of this cross-cultural exercise and one of the most highly sought-after consultants in American business today. In his first article on Japan in 1971, Drucker warned against the "folly" of "imitating" Japanese management because it is "deeply rooted in Japanese traditions and culture." Still, he believed it desirable to try to "emulate" Japanese management because it addresses successfully the most important concerns of top management in the West, namely: making effective decisions; harmonizing employment security with productivity; and developing young professional managers. One lesson to be considered, in Drucker's view, is spending more time on "defining the question" before proceeding to the "answer." Another lesson is the implementation of a more "bottoms-up" decision-making process, which sounds surprisingly democratic for "hierarchically" oriented Japan, and relies less on the "top-down" process more typical of Western, or at least American, management. A third lesson is the Japanese emphasis on "lifetime training," as one alternative for overcoming the "extreme specialization and departmentalization plaguing American businesses." "Continuous" training extends the learning curve into the adult years and in part accounts for the high rates of productivity growth in Japan.41/

Drucker's suggestions have been implemented in surprising ways by the mid 1980s. To offer one example, the president of the Chrysler Corporation, Lee Iacocca, was sufficiently impressed with Japanese management and communication techniques that when Chrysler signed the joint venture with Mitsubishi in March 1985, he proudly announced that Mitsubishi would not only contribute capital and technology, but would also take responsibility for "dealing with state and local governments in site selection, in the building of the plant, in dealing directly with unions, and in day-to-day operations."42

In addition to the debates over the value of Japanese and other Asian forms of management, there is a more subtle dispute over the relative strengths of inventiveness and technological creativity. At the summary session of the Eindhoven conference, two commentators tried to soften Western anxieties by affirming that the Japanese edge, economically, is only a function of their superiority in applied technology. Applied technology, however, builds on the basic and advanced technology produced largely in and purchased from the West. Similar arguments may be heard in public and private conversations about Japanese abilities to "imitate" and "borrow" from other cultures, a theme that is echoed again and again in even the most elementary discussion of Japanese history and culture.

With its greater emphasis on spontaneity and individual creativity, the argument goes, the West will continue to maintain an edge in developing breakthroughs in the more significant areas of basic research and inventions. It is an edge that by their very nature Asian cultures are unable to develop. They may be well suited to innovation, that is, to developments within the parameters set by Western inventions. But, when it comes to breaking through those parameters or creating new ones, they are at a disadvantage. Invention and basic research, compared to innovation and applied research, are considered to be the more creative and, in time, should redress economic imbalances. As proof of its cultural superiority, the argument maintains, the West will continue to draw Japan and other Asian nations toward Western ways of thinking and organization. Even as technology transfers are now a two-way street between Asia and the West, the more significant transfer, the argument proposes, will continue to be from the West to Asia.

A cursory glance at some statistics offers support for this Western assertion. For example, among the hundreds of Nobel prize winners in science, only four have been native Japanese.43/ To cite another set of figures, in 1983 the value of technology exports for the United States was U.S. $7.6 billion, while, for the same year, that of France was U.S. $1 billion and that of Japan was only U.S. $.5 billion.44/

Lest these claims appear to be merely the result of a Western bias, Japanese voices can be found to support the claim. Hideki Yukawa, the first Japanese Nobel prize winner, for example, confessed that his best work occurred while thinking in English, while another Japanese Nobelist, Leo Esaki, has claimed that "Japanese culture...is overly sentimental, too aesthetic, too intuitive and irrational." Esaki, who for twenty years has worked for IBM, thought his fellow Japanese were "too obsessed with form and peripheral behavior without being able to get to the heart of the matter."45/ Japanese teachers of today vigorously debate the limitations of their education system which they perceive as stifling creativity and ill-preparing the young people for the rapidly advancing technologies that will keep Japan competitive on the world markets.46/ Even the report of the Long Term Credit Bank in Tokyo that analyzed Japan's high technology industries in 1983, argued without qualification that Western countries still maintain a clear edge in advanced technology. To anchor its point, the bank cited a German study, completed in 1976, that divides technological change into three categories: revolutionary ones, remarkable ones, and improvements on existing technologies. According to that study, Japanese inventions accounted for only 6.6% of the 380 chief revolutionary inventions identified, while the United States accounted for 67.4% and Great Britain for 8.9%.47/ Lack of Japanese protest to this argument may not surprise those who have a keen appreciation for just how adaptive Japanese can be, even to the point of accepting almost wholesale the Western critique.

Countering the claim that invention is more significant than innovation, or that the distinction between the two is significant, or that the West is more inventive than Japan, are other figures and arguments. Japanese patent applications between 1975 and 1980, for example, increased at a rate of 20% per year, while the increase in the United States over the same years remained static. Indeed, the total number of patent applications by country, in 1981, were 215,000 for Japan, 85,000 for the United States, and 28,000 for the United Kingdom.48/ The simple counting of patent applications, without weighing their relative value, may not be a valid measure of inventiveness, innovation, or creativity. When correlations are carefully made, the figures do, however, mean something.49/

Japanese technological creativity, whether as invention or innovation, is further expressed in a field defined as "mechatronics," that is, the ability to combine mechanics and electronics and to fuse existing technologies in creative and concentrated ways. Their excellence in mechatronics may be one expression of the theme of miniaturization in Japanese culture. Customers the world around admire the fruits of mechatronics in calculators the size of credit cards, and digital watches no larger than two quarters put together and capable of doing seemingly innumerable things, which are all available for the price of a few dollars. Video cassette recorders and tastefully designed small cars are other examples of their unique talents in mechatronics. Indeed the penetration and domination of Japanese VCRs in European markets are associated with one particular strain of European protectionism. Perhaps the largest advantage that mechatronics brings to the Japanese is in the design and production of micro-chips and robots. In 1984, according to the Japan Industrial Robot Association, the total population of robots in Japan was 67,300, as compared with 15,200 in the United States and 19,700 in Western Europe. Impressive as these figures are, robotics measured as units per industrial worker was more highly developed in Sweden than in Japan.50/

John Jewkes, in his study of the sources of invention in the West, concludes that there is no support for the view that inventions can be predicted, which is contrary to claims by either the liberal West or the Asia Pacific that they may have an edge in the areas of technological creativity. Nor is there any way to assign a preference between the "two worlds of authority and questioning, of tradition and novelty, of conservatism and radicalism, of stability and progress, and of continuity and change."51/ According to Jewkes and his colleagues, the "spectacular view of modern invention," that is, an image of a "typical lone inventor of the 18th and 19th centuries," working by himself in a "garret or garage," has all but disappeared. In the 20th century at least, the inventive profile is less spectacular and individualistic and more group-oriented and systematic. It is a cooperative process between research institutions and large firms and between science and technology.52/

As precise correlations between cultural factors and inventiveness remain to be established, it is interesting to see how another Japanese scientist addresses these questions. Unlike his Nobel compatriots, the Vice President of Sharp Corporation, Tadashi Sasaki, sees many competitive edges, not just one. Sasaki divides the question of technological creativity or innovation into five different categories, beginning with the "revolutionary principle invention" in which Europe has been superior, followed by the United States, and trailed by Japan. The other categories are "future technology," "high technology," "applied technology," and "improved technology." In the last two categories, Japan surpasses both Europe and the United States, and in the very last category, Sasaki gives a rating of "surpass" to Japan and "inferior" to both Europe and the United States.53/

As a fillip to Sasaki's argument, Gene Gregory, a professor of international business at Sophia University in Tokyo, has argued that Japan is uniquely suited to continuing innovation precisely because of, not in spite of, its "cooperative mode of management." According to Gregory, the very structure of Japanese firms encourages innovation and creativity because engineers as well as skilled workers participate in a "value-added accounting system." This is a system that is able to assign values added at various levels to the relative inputs into the innovation process. The effect of such an accounting system is to reinforce the sense of "team performance." A comparable system, Gregory claims, does not exist in Western firms.54/ To the extent that Sasaki and Gregory are right, the liberal West may not have an edge over the Asia Pacific in the critical areas of technological creativity and inventiveness.

Other countries are contributing to the sharpening of the competitive edge of the Asia Pacific. Korean inventiveness and mechatronics are well known, as is the applied technology of Taiwanese firms. If the scientific and technological genius of China, which until the 16th century was in many ways superior to the West, can be revived, creativity and innovation in the Asia Pacific will be greatly enhanced. There are some signs that this is taking place. The debates over the nature of innovation, over the relative valuation of invention and innovation, and over which side of the world may have the edge in either, will likely continue for years to come.

CONCLUSION

The anxiety that feeds protectionist sentiment in the liberal West has many roots. Trade imbalances are the most obvious. While trade protectionism, in the short run, may make sense for some infant industries and for the preservation of jobs, the causes of protectionism, the World Bank reminds us, lie in the "failure to adjust," and its adoption "simply compounds that failure." Moreover, charges that the Asia Pacific is more unfair than the liberal West in its trade practices are softened by significant changes in recent years. Asian trade surpluses with the West are due increasingly to their competitive edge, a fact more readily appreciated by consumers and corporations than by many politicians.

Political concern that shades into anger over the growing influence of the Soviet Union in the Pacific Basin is another source of Western anxiety, as papers in this volume show. Protection against that threat has little to do with economic protectionism. There is a hope, however distant, that the dynamic interaction between the Asia Pacific and the liberal West will reduce that threat not by destroying it head on, but rather through a diversion of attention that broadens the horizon of possibilities and softens the mindsets of the Cold War. Such a broadening can include the Soviet Union and offers new ways of defining national security and national interest.

Cultural and historical factors compound economic and political anxieties. They are mutual, and they run deep. For Asians, it is the memories of Western violence that ushered in liberal ideas and institutions into the Asia Pacific beginning in the 18th and 19th centuries. Asian leaders also fear that the extremes of liberalism, expressed as excessive individualism, may undermine cherished ways of defining and ordering Asian realities. The 20th century for Asian peoples has been a process of painful and profitable absorption of Western science and technology. But it is "erroneous and at times fatally dangerous," in Jun-ichi Kyogoku's view, to conclude hastily that Japan and the Asia Pacific in general, share with the West the "same institution of society, the same institution of knowledge, and particularly the same cosmos of meaning." Kyogoku recognizes that a certain "progress belongs to science and technology," but in "morality, art, and politics," there is "no progress" on either side.55/

Westerners perceive that Asian cultural orientations give them a competitive edge that is either unfair or undesirable. The stronger group orientation in Asia clashes with the sanctity of individual autonomy in the liberal West. Asian cultures are also more comfortable with close ties between business and government, while Western critics, in the name of "free trade," regard Asian "industrial policies" as unfair. Westerners also argue that Asians take advantage of trading opportunities that are made possible by a system that rests on liberal values but they do too little to maintain that system. To what extent suspicions on both sides are comparable in degree is moot, and the perceptions of fairness and unfairness will no doubt remain in the eye of the beholder for a long time.

Western anxieties about Asian economic vitality spring largely from huge trade deficits. To place these anxieties in perspective, it is important to remember that in economic size, as measured either in GNP or sheer trade volume, the Asia Pacific is still quite small when compared to the liberal West. Furthermore, there is no guarantee that the trade surplus edge of the Asia Pacific will be maintained. Asian countries confront problems of their own, among them political succession, shifting and temporary economic advantages, trade vulnerability on world markets and, of course, fierce rivalry among themselves. Even if the Asian "edge" does maintain itself, the most optimistic forecasts would still leave the Asian economic size far behind that of the liberal West. Indeed, the roots of Western protectionism seem to be buried in the recession of the early 1980s, while the economic story of the liberal West in the mid 1980s looks more hopeful. Because perceptions are deeply imbedded and often lag behind changing realities, it is hard to predict the depth and length of protectionist feeling against the Asia Pacific. The lag may be too long to avoid severe consequences.

"Knowing is difficult, doing is easy," Sun Yat Sen once said. Knowing, for Westerners as they face the Asia Pacific, means looking within, identifying the "enemy within" as clearly as the "enemy without." In his conclusion, twenty years ago, to a volume on the Pacific Rim, Wilcomb E. Washburn stated that progress toward the creation of an early European "world view" emerged as the result of "self-doubts" introduced out of contact with the Asia Pacific. Grotius' writings on international law in the 17th century, for example, were prompted by European contact with Asia. The Asia Pacific also provided an "unexcelled classroom and laboratory for the children of the Age of Enlightenment." The "greatest returns," in Washburn's eyes, were not the "wealth of the Orient," but the "education of the European mind."56/ If the mutual anxieties between the Asia Pacific and the liberal West are fairly addressed, the future holds a promise of "great returns" in education, culture, *and* possibly wealth for both sides.

NOTES

1. For a recent list of Australian publications on the Pacific Rim, see *Pacific Studies 1985 Catalog* (International Specialized Book Services Inc., 1985) pp. 21-24. For another opinion on Australia's interest in the Asia Pacific see Derek Davies, "Traveler's Tales," *Far Eastern Economic Review* (December 1985):39. Following a recent visit to Australia Davies recounts his disappointment over Australia's journalistic coverage of Asia: "All that talk about Australia being part of the region...has not had much impact on editorial priorities. East Asia seems largely thought of as a threatening, unstable region." Davies noted that in 1975 there were 14 Australian staff correspondents in the whole Asia Pacific region. Ten years later there were only 16, with none from the commercial TV or radio networks.

2. *Japan 1985, An International Comparison* (Tokyo, Keizai Koho Center, 1985) p. 31.

3. GATT (General Agreement on Trade and Tariffs) press release, March 14, 1985, as reported in the *White Paper on International Trade, 1985* (Tokyo: Ministry of International Trade and Industry, 1985) p. 2.

4. *Far Eastern Economic Review* (5 September 1985):52.

5. "Outlook for the Growth Rates and Share of GDP in the Pacific Region," Prospects for the Pacific Age: Economic Development and Policy Issues of the Pacific Region to the Year 2000, prepared by the Planning Bureau, Council for Economic Research on the Pacific Region for the 21st Century (Tokyo: Economic Planning Agency, July 1985) p. 10.

6. Jetro White Paper on World Trade, 1985, The World and Japanese Trade (Tokyo: Japan External Trade Organization, 1985) p. 10. Also see Wall Street Journal, 7 January 1986.

7. "The Roots of Protectionism," in the World Development Report, 1985 (New York: Oxford University Press, 1985) p. 39.

8. Thomas Pepper, Merit E. Janow, and Jimmy Wheeler, The Competition: Dealing with Japan, (New York: Praeger, 1985) pp. 187-288.

9. Chalmers, Johnson, MITI and the Japanese Miracle: The Growth of Industrial Policy, 1925-1975 (Stanford, California: Stanford University Press, 1982.)

10. An excellent summary of the close tie between government and business in East Asia can be found in Roy Hofheinz, Jr., and Kent Calder, The Eastasia Edge (New York: Basic Books, 1982.)

11. World Development Report, 1985, p. 40. Also see Park Un-Suh, "US-Korea Bilateral Trade Opportunities and Problems," in Korea's Economy (Washington D. C.: Korea Economic Institute, January 1986) pp. 10-14.

12. KKC Brief (Keizai Koho Center) 29 (July 1985):1-2.

13. New York Times 4 April 1985.

14. "Manufactured Import Markets: Open or Closed?" KKC Brief, (July 1985). See also Gary Saxonhouse, "The Micro- and Macroeconomics of Foreign Sales to Japan," in Trade Policy in the 1980s, ed. William R. Cline (Cambridge, MIT Press, 1983). Saxonhouse shows that in a sampling of 109 products, only 17 in the Japanese case were shown to be dependent on statistically signficant noneconomic factors. The share of these 17 products in total Japanese foreign trade was 4.9%, or the lowest rate among the advanced industrialized countries.

15. As quoted in Asia 1986 Yearbook (Hong Kong: Far Eastern Economic Review, 1986) pp. 12-14.

16. Japan 1985, An International Comparison (Tokyo: Keizai Koho Center, 1985) p. 33. According to the '85 Jetro White Paper on World Trade, both the United States and the EEC deficits with Japan were larger than their exports to Japan, while the deficit for Southeast Asia, which includes the Asian NICs, was $5 billion or one sixth of

their exports to Japan. As reported in Focus Japan 12.12 (Tokyo: Jetro International Communication) (December 1985) insert, "Japan Scene."

17. See The Competition: Dealing with Japan, Chapter 6 on "Japan's Declining Industries," pp. 247-287.

18. Richard Solomon, "American Defense Planning and Asian Security: Policy Choices for a Time of Transition," in Asian Security in the 1980s: Problems and Policies for a Time of Transition, ed. Solomon, (Santa Monica: Rand Corp., 1979) p. 5. For an excellent account of ASEAN perspectives including anxieties over Soviet influence, largely in Vietnam, and Chinese influence in Southeast Asia, see Linda Lim, ed., Southeast Asia Business, (Ann Arbor: Center for South and Southeast Asian Studies, University of Michigan, Summer 1985). See also Lim's "Rising Trade Tensions: Asian Perspectives," in Asian Issues, 1985 (New York: Asia Society, 1986) pp. 55-73.

19. Asia 1984 Yearbook (Hong Kong: Far Eastern Economic Review, 1984) pp. 195-198 and 281-287.

20. See for example the Table on "Income Distribution" in the World Development Report, 1985, pp. 228-229. Even in China prior to Mao's death, where egalitarian goals and policies were carried to an extreme, creating a more equitable system of income distribution was a problem. See, for example, William L. Parish and Martin K. Whyte, Village and Family in Contemporary China, (Chicago: University of Chicago Press, 1978).

21. Elizabeth Pond, "Shades of Communism, Soviet Model Stumbles into Computer Age," special report in the Christian Science Monitor, 7 January 1986, pp. 17-19.

22. See The Eastasia Edge, chapter 4.

23. See "Focus on Korea," Far Eastern Economic Review, (18 July 1985):47-74.

24. Raymond Williams, Keywords: A Vocabulary of Culture and Society (New York: Oxford University Press, 1983) (revised edition) pp. 117-119, 161-165, 179-181.

25. See Kenichi Ohmae, Triad Power: The Coming Shape of Global Competition (Free Press, 1985). Also see Focus Japan, 12.8 (August 1985):1-2.

26. Japan, 1984, An International Comparison (Tokyo: Keizei Koho Center, 1985) p. 18.

27. Luigi Barzini, The Europeans (New York: Simon and Schuster, 1983) pp. 233-35.

28. As quoted in Robert N. Bellah, et. al., Habits of the Heart: Individualism and Commitment in American Life (Berkeley: University of California Press) 1985, p. 117. For fuller accounts of de Tocqueville's comments on

individualism and its effects on American culture, see Richard D. Heffner's edited and abridged Alexis de Tocqueville, Democracy in America (New York: The New American Library, 1956) pp. 192-198, 254-256.

29. Habits of the Heart..., pp. 199, 277.

30. See James C. Abegglen and George Stalk, Kaisha, The Japanese Corporation: The New Competitors in World Business (New York: Basic Books, 1985).

31. See Sigmund Nosow, "A Lesson for American Managers: Learning from Japanese Experience in the U.S." National Productivity Review (Autumn, 1984):407-416.

32. Benjamin Schwartz, In Search of Wealth and Power: Yen Fu and the West, Western Thought in Chinese Perspective (Cambridge, Mass.: Harvard University Press, 1964).

33. See the special section, "Japan at Work," Far Eastern Economic Review (16 December 1985):69-85.

34. See Zhang Pufan, Zhungguo fazhi shi (A History of Chinese Law)(Beijing: Qunzhong Press, 1982)(in Chinese). This textbook for law students in China traces the development of law from the earliest times through each of the twenty-four dynasties. Interest in the past is sufficiently keen to allow the writers to include a lengthy discussion of law in the Guomindang period. When law in each historic period was relied upon, the writers argue, it buttressed the political order.

35. Keywords: A Vocabulary of Culture..., pp. 164-165.

36. William T. deBary, The Liberal Tradition in China (New York: Columbia University Press, 1983) p. 43.

37. Ibid., p. 106.

38. Christian Science Monitor 10 October 1985, pp. 3-4. Since 1980 one-half of all immigrants to the United States have been Asian, easily outstripping those from Latin America, 35%, and Europe, 12%. Their positive reception into American communities scattered throughout the country is accounted for by the outstanding economic and educational performance of the Asian immigrants, within the first generation. In recent years Asian-American students have outscored white students in college-entrace examinations by 32 points. This "tidal wave" moving across the Pacific is made possible by the relaxation of immigration regulations initiated by Attorney General Robert F. Kennedy in the early 1960s.

39. Michael Y. Yoshino, Japan's Managerial System: Tradition and Innovation (Cambridge, Mass.: MIT Press, 1968).

40. Thomas J. Peters and Robert H. Waterman, Jr., In Search of Excellence, Lessons from America's Best-Run Companies (New York: Warner Books, 1982).

41. Peter F. Drucker, "What We Can Learn from Japanese Management," Harvard Business Review (March-April 1971): 111-122. In discussing productivity, it is important to distinguish between actual productivity levels, which overall are still considerably higher in the West than in Japan, and productivity growth, where Japan, South Korea and Taiwan excel. It is the impressive growth rates, not the mere size of GNP or of trade volume, or even of productivity levels, that create Western anxiety. See Japan 1985, An International Comparison, pp. 74-75, for a summary of these comparisons.

42. Lee Iacocca, "Fairness First: A Level Playing Field for U.S. Japan Trade," in Speaking of Japan (Tokyo: Keizai Koho Center, July 1985) pp. 1-8. In concluding The Emerging Japanese Superstate (1970), Herman Kahn cautioned that Japan's "rising sun" had not reached its zenith, but rather had "just begun its climb." He hoped this study of his and the Hudson Institute would give some "guidance to the West on how to live with this incredibly apt student of... Western industrialization," p. 183. Though not as explicit then as Drucker in "learning" from Japan, and more cautious in predicting the future of Japan's relations with the West, Kahn's message is essentially the same. The recent study on Japan by Janow, Pepper, and Wheeler was also produced by the Hudson Institute and it was dedicated to Herman Kahn.

43. Gene Gregory, "Japanese Creativity," Far Eastern Economic Review (28 March 1985).

44. Japan 1985, An International Comparison, p. 26.

45. As quoted in The Competition: Dealing with Japan, p. 241.

46. See for example the special issue of Japan Echo, 11 (3 November 1984), that addresses the "New Formulas for Education."

47. Japan's High Technology Industries, p. 4.

48. Japan 1983, An International Comparison, p. 17.

49. Jacob Schmookler, Invention and Economic Growth (Cambridge: Harvard University Press, 1966) p. 18.

50. "Mechanical Men Steal a March on the West," in Far Eastern Economic Review (19 December 1985) p. 51. For a finer breakdown of figures on robotics, see Japan 1985, An International Comparison, p. 28. See also Makoto Kikuchi, Japanese Electronics: A Worm's Eye View of Its Evolution, (Tokyo: The Simul Press, 1985).

51. John Jewkes, David Sawers, et. al., The Sources of Invention (London: Macmillan, 1960) pp. 9 and 225.

52. Ibid., p. 32.

53. Tadashi Sasaki, "Towards the Asia Pacific Age, Seeking Beyond Science," in Asia-Pacific Culture: Its History and Prospects, (conference proceedings) (Tenri, Japan: the Tenri Yamato Culture Bureau, 1984) p. 14.

54. Gene Gregory, "The Dynamics of Japanese Innovation," in Journal of Japanese Trade and Industry, (January/February 1985):59-61. See also Masanori Montani, Japanese Technology: Getting the Best for the Least (Tokyo: Simul Press, 1982).

55. Kyogoku is a professor of political science at the University of Chiba, Japan, and his discussion appeared in "'Modernization' and Japan," in Experiencing the Twentieth Century, eds., Nobutoshi Hagihara, et. al. (Tokyo: University of Tokyo Press, 1985) p. 271.

56. Wilcomb E. Washburn, "The Intellectual Assumptions and Consequences of Geographical Exploration in the Pacific," in The Pacific Basin: A History of Its Geographical Exploration, ed. Herman R. Friis, (New York: American Geographical Society, 1967) pp. 326-334.

PART ONE

The Pacific Rim and World Politics

2

Soviet Strategy and the Pacific Basin

Laszlo Lajos S. Bartalits and Johannes Wilhelmus H.C.M. Schneider

When compared to its position at the close of World War II, the Pacific Basin, by the mid-1980s, has been transformed beyond recognition. Soviet policy, based upon the concept of interdiction on the Western shores of the Pacific, had acquired a definite naval dimension while American strategy, after wild gyrations, seemed more settled on an active policy of holding onto those Western shores. Policies of imperialism or hegemony being what they are, the Pacific is, for the time being, the foremost region in the world where these mutually exclusive policies may clash to secure future positions. What exactly, then, are superpower strategies in this area?

After an examination of the pertinent American policy, the situation of the ASEAN states, whose predominant security problem is Vietnam, will be discussed. This country, in turn, leads one to look at the possible development of its relations with China against the background of its relations with the Soviet Union. The Soviet military build-up is another matter, and the foreign policy position of Japan, the dominant industrial giant in the West Pacific region, also needs scrutiny. The Soviet threat may be differently perceived by the various states and therefore prompts the question as to strategy: is it once again the spectre of falling dominoes, or is it something else? In the conclusion, the findings to the above queries should fit into the wider picture of East-West relations.

AMERICAN POLICY

The overriding reality with which American foreign policy in the West Pacific has to contend is the present entanglement of the three other great powers: the Soviet Union, China and Japan.1/ America's past history in the area still heavily weighs in the balance: the Vietnam war, which followed the Korean one; the single-minded devotion to Taiwan as a stopgap for mainland China, a devotion skillfully entertained by a most powerful lobby; and the difficulties of adjusting the rapprochement with China to the changing realities. All require a rare combination of political skills to draft a new foreign policy. Yet, as has often been remarked, American foreign policy is usually rather reactive in nature except when there is a strong foreign policy team or an incidental powerful backing of public opinion. Present American policy does not seem to proceed from a well entrenched political concept and, in addition, suffers, as is certainly the case with Asian countries, from the confusing signals that proceed from the various organs within the Administration.

Nevertheless, that policy does begin with a number of assumptions that appear to be more or less a common ground among those concerned with the West Pacific area.2/ Japan remains the security centerpiece of America's strategic _dispositif_. A close second is South Korea, retained at so much cost. The Philipppines remain both a historic and a strategic asset because of the huge American bases located there. Taiwan, as already mentioned, will not easily be written off. Once the spectacular reversal of America's China policy was obtained, Taiwan became a further anchor-point. It is now out of the question that China will again become ostracized, if only for its own (huge) sake. Whatever time it will take before China becomes a truly great power, its firmly admitted potential can on no account be gambled away by the United States.

The real gap on the West Pacific rim is Vietnam, which still confronts America's memory with its most sensitive and emotional experience and which remains of great strategic importance. Though a true reversal of alliances by Vietnam does not look probable for the moment, the question over Vietnam's position is serious enough to make it a prime concern in American policymaking. Vietnam appears to be the true unfinished business in the Sino-American rapprochement. On the one hand, the problem of its relations either with the Soviet Union or with China is of decisive significance for the entire strategic set-up in East Asia, and, on the other hand, the extent of its Indochinese hegemony determines the policy of the ASEAN states.

For the United States, the China policy is probably the one which remains most subject to further definition.

Though China may no longer be looked upon as a clear bar against Soviet hegemonistic tendencies, as the common cry had it in the early days of the Sino-American rapprochement, and although it certainly can not be taken entirely for granted, it has nevertheless developed into a kind of informal ally of the West. China's clear economic reversal makes it highly unlikely that the party-to-party relations with the Soviet Union--a necessary condition for a true Sino-Soviet allegiance--will soon warm up. Neither are the state-to-state relations on the brink of turning into a firm alliance because of the by now conventional problems of the Northern frontier, of Afghanistan and of Kampuchea. Since Vietnam appears to hold the actual key that could break up this logjam, and since its alliance with the Soviet Union holds the key to the future division of spheres of influence in East Asia, American foreign policy in this region will partly be a policy of wait and see and partly one of holding onto its actual positions, so that it does not become shunted aside if there is a reversal.

America's China policy has already shown some changes of emphasis which, though perhaps more a matter of form than of real substance, may have had a tendency to throw the actual policy somewhat off balance; even more so since outsiders usually have difficulty in accurately assessing what exactly goes on in the American mind. There are few, if any, places in the world where matters of foreign policy tend to get mixed up, in public debate, with personal preferences. As an example, Alexander Haig's view tended to emphasize the more military side of the China card, while George P. Shultz appeared to revert to a more ideologically conscious diplomacy which did not neglect faithful allies such as Japan, South Korea and the Philippines.3/

The policies of both Secretaries of State have to be viewed against the background of President Ronald Reagan's accession to the White House. It meant the vocal return of the Taiwan lobby (the old China lobby). Reagan's electoral rhetoric was, by itself, enough to set back relations with China. Only, in 1983, was there a prudent change, no doubt initiated by the President himself. This laborious revision brought him to Beijing in 1984, much to the chagrin of his most loyal devotees who had not let themselves be educated by the demands of *Realpolitik*.

Yet, China is not exactly a country that allows the United States to determine its own policy. China, itself, has probably gone through most of the changes. In the rather short run, it has lost its ideological fervor to regain control over Taiwan, while China's determined drive toward economic modernization has made it far more open to Western markets, and hence to the United States. Its defense reappraisal and memories of the traumatic Soviet reversal of the early sixties, have combined to make China look to America for the procurement of defensive weapons. The future of Hong Kong now settled--at least on paper--and its active foreign policy which makes Beijing a center for diplomatic pilgrimage and which forces the Chinese to take up the pilgrim's staff themselves, has made it less uniquely dependent upon the United States. As a result, a number of factors likely to upset Sino-American relations have vanished, and associations between both countries are therefore likely to remain on a more even keel.

American policy in the central region of East Asia can hardly be looked upon in a vacuum. Toward the South, the ANZUS Pact is undergoing a drastic reappraisal, partly occasioned by anti-nuclear sentiments that may also irritate American strategic initiatives elsewhere in the world. Essential for the American policy towards Vietnam is the success of ASEAN's till now remarkably steadfast policy of containment towards Vietnam. There is just the possibility that the second crop of newly industrialized nations may count a few of these states among them. If so, then their ideological situation will starkly contrast with the terrible economic performance of Vietnam--a situation that ought to be rather comfortable for the United States.

Still farther afield are India and Pakistan, the latter of which is uncomfortably poised on the brink of developments in Afghanistan, a country that brings one back to the Sino-Soviet stalemate so central to the future of the West Pacific area. Tedious as negotiations with the Soviet Union usually are in so sensitive an area, one surely cannot discount the possibility of a settlement that might, by the same token, lead to a reassessment of the entire picture.

The reason Japan is not mentioned at this point is that America's policy toward this country is likely to remain stable in the foreseeable future. Nor has this policy been affected much by the vital change that Sino-American relations have undergone. This subject will be discussed further under Japan.

ASEAN OR THE CONTAINMENT OF VIETNAM

The ASEAN policy has been based on the precipitate withdrawal of the United States from Vietnam and the subsequent utter collapse of its political presence there. On the one hand, these countries moved directly into the line of fire and, on the other hand, the United States withdrew fully behind safely entrenched positions to sulk over its first big international defeat. The experience left the ASEAN states with bitter feelings of exposure and abandonment. In an area where memories of Vietnam's Indochinese hegemony are long and have been sharply revived by the invasion of Kampuchea and the insignificance of Laos under Vietnamese suzerainty, fear for their political future is understandable. Yet, alternative developments looked equally ominous.

Soon after America's withdrawal in 1978 and apart from the invasion of Kampuchea, there were two further developments of decisive importance: Vietnam's membership in the Council for Mutual Economic Assistance (CMEA) and the conclusion of a treaty with the Soviet Union, followed by weapon deliveries. Soviet influence was brought uncomfortably close, the more so since the American one was on the wane. Paradoxically, the historic threat of China, fully revived by the protracted Chinese support of communist subversion in Thailand and Malaysia, now seemed to fade.

This reversal has not taken place overnight, and it hinges on the wider Sino-Soviet relationship in the region. For one thing, the relationship between China and Vietnam did not survive the Vietnam war for an obvious reason: China's traditional fear of having a strong and Vietnam-dominated Indochina at its southern frontier. Even a superficial look at that extremely long frontier and at the countries bordering it and the pattern of their relationships makes it clear that China has obvious reasons to be nervous about any prospect of encirclement. Vietnam itself, thoroughly exhausted after decades of a fierce war, had only the Soviet Union to turn to, and from the latter's point of view, filling up the vacuum left by the American withdrawal was a chance too good to be missed. The final result of the reversal was that China, already in 1979, as a result of the invasion into Kampuchea and Vietnam, had taken over the position of enemy number one of the United States and thus was thrown back upon the sole and utter dependence of the Soviet Union.

The Soviet-backed invasion of Kampuchea was enough to make the ASEAN countries determined to hold out against Vietnam and withstand any of its overtures. Another reason may have been the attitude of Indonesia, the real giant among them, whose animosity toward the Soviet Union and China, through sheer political weight, made it less adamant towards Vietnam. However, the latter's harsh and exacting attitude prevented any real wavering in the support of Indonesia for ASEAN. The slowly renewed presence of the United States and the invasion of Afghanistan, which was rather surprisingly condemned in the third world at large, given its traditional and somewhat benign attitude towards Soviet dealings, could only strengthen the new rearrangement in Southeast Asia.4/

An obvious result of the Vietnam-Soviet relationship has been the lease of the ports of Danang and Cam Ranh, which reminds one of the historic surge of the Soviet Union towards the South in Europe with all of the attending Balkan upheavals.5/ The price which Vietnam can exact as a result of this lease--about a quarter of all foreign Soviet assistance goes to Vietnam--and its CMEA membership do not, however, permit it to attain a real economic growth or even to stem a steady deterioration. The sorry exodus of boat people on which international attention was rivetted by a United Nations conference, the growing political isolation over Kampuchea and the apparently high costs of this operation, all combine to make its plight a matter of utmost concern. Until recently, the dour revolutionary attitude, which even tried to curb Soviet influence in Indochina, showed little sign of abating. The prospect that Vietnam recently held out, to withdraw the bulk of its troops by the early nineties, heralded a change in policy which still has to prove itself.

Vietnam has not yet consented to an unrestricted use of its naval bases by the Soviet Union. The country has to measure the chances of its future in light of the price that an exclusive dependence on the Soviet Union would entail. Its economy in shambles and a number of its erstwhile leaders either dead or gone, it may choose a more pragmatic diplomacy. A first sign is the cooperation with the United States in tracing the bodies of Americans missing in action; another one is its more businesslike tone in dealing with the ASEAN countries. The real point of first importance is, however, the development of Sino-Soviet relations. Though the prospects seemed to improve at an early stage, the three obstacles so adamantly put forward by China--Afghanistan, the Soviet troops on its northern border, and Kampuchea--have effectively dampened the prospects of progress at an early stage. But, the prospect that the Soviet Union may negotiate away Kampuchea remains a sensitive issue overhanging Soviet-Vietnamese relations.

The ASEAN countries have reacted to these developments in a variety of ways: Moscow has been denied permission to have its ships call upon their ports, espionage has been dealt with ruthlessly, and Soviet efforts to establish closer relations have been turned down. The threat uttered by the Soviet Vice-minister for Foreign Affairs, Kapitsa, in Singapore, in April of 1983, had no effect and neither did the attempt by the Soviet Union to offer itself as the guarantee against Vietnam's expansion.6/ The ASEAN countries appear able to measure Soviet threats. Their strategy focusses on limiting that influence by restraining Vietnam. The idea that an agreement with Vietnam might force the Soviets out has found no takers. The countries seem to be well aware that, in the long run, China remains the main threat, though for the moment, Vietnam fits that role.7/

CHINA AND VIETNAM

The improvement in relations between Bangkok and Beijing in 1983 may have alarmed Hanoi and forced it to look for a way to ease the tension between the two countries. Real improvements in the relations between China and Vietnam have been limited. The tone has become more restrained. Vietnam, at one time, even released nine "infiltrators" and offered to stop the traditional exchanges of fire along the border. Yet, Beijing stuck to its opinion that Vietnam is doing its utmost to worsen relations and should demonstrate its good will by withdrawing its troops from Kampuchea.8/ Behind this Chinese posture of intransigence probably lies the galling experience that China received the worst end of the military incursions it undertook to teach Vietnam a lesson. In any event, the grand sweep with which Vietnam destroyed the ring of bases along the Thai border, and even inside Thailand in 1985, did not provoke China into giving it another lesson, although the tension at the common border remains high.

The real explanation for this somewhat subdued Chinese reaction probably has to be sought elsewhere. It is the change which has come about in China as a result of the advent of Deng's leadership. Defense matters are no longer given a clear priority as the four modernizations have evolved. China has resolutely given preference to economic priorities, and the results have been immediate and spectacular. Compared to the picture of a China that is looking with great determination towards the future, Vietnam cuts a poor figure as a revolutionary diehard sliding into stark economic failure. Here lies the real issue and challenge for East Asia. Deng has accurately assessed the chances of a giant that like China is poor, backward and with military muscle that is in no way commensurate to the mass it has to maneuver. Even the most determined and successful drive towards economic improvement will leave China a not yet fully developed country well into the next century.

If one only compares the imposing procession of dignitaries, diplomats and businessmen converging upon Beijing from all over the world with the silent ruin that Vietnam has slid back into, now that leftist propaganda has different targets to lash out at, there can be little doubt as to which country has to start mending fences. Considering what Vietnam has been, it will take all the possible pragmatism of a new generation of leaders to catch up with a world that has already long passed them by.9/

The economic prosperity that is so visible in quite a few countries in East Asia confronts Vietnam with the stark choice of either pursuing political domination, together with complete political isolation in the region, or reinserting itself by recognizing that it has irretrievably lost its lofty place at the center of the international stage during the war with the United States.

Whatever improvement there is going to be will have to pass through the settlement of the Kampuchean problem. The Soviet Union is involved since its aid and its political promise not to take this matter in its own hands are vital;10/ the ASEAN countries are involved since they link up every real improvement in their relations with Vietnam with a settlement that probably has to include Prince Shihanuk; the Chinese are involved since they have made Kampuchea one of the three main conditions to any real improvement in the Sino-Soviet relations. Vietnam has one quite solid argument: that it is not prepared to countenance the readmission of the Khmer Rouge, however much they still command the strongest guerilla forces.11/ Any political settlement that so vitally involves so many states remains difficult. It will have to wait for a profound rearrangement in the region. Any real settlement will have to pass through a political change within North Vietnam, that is, to what extent it will admit that its full dominance over Indochina is untenable.

Most countries in the region, if not all, think that time is on their side. Militarily speaking, Vietnam has called China's military bluff by going ahead with its 1985 destruction of all major rebel camps, including those in Thailand. That country now faces a rather tough refugee problem. For this reason, the Vietnamese carrot dangled in front of ASEAN nations, that it will withdraw the bulk of its troops by the early nineties, may have more substance than it is often credited with: Vietnam can afford to be so magnanimous because of its military strength and its confidence that it can hold onto its revolutionary gains in its own country. If so, from an American point of view, a more relaxed Vietnam might be willing to contemplate a certain phasing out of Soviet military (naval) presence, while the United States itself might win favor with ASEAN by seriously taking up Vietnam's apparent diplomatic willingness.12/

AMERICA AND CHINA

The advent of the Reagan administration clouded Sino-American relations. The utterances of the presidential nominee concerning China and the strong favor shown toward Taiwan were enough to make China nervous about the future of America's policy. The worst part was that the initial weapon deliveries to Taiwan showed a rather drastic disagreement between the partners on the subject of phasing them out. There are several reasons why relations returned to a more even keel afterwards. The United States learned to assess its relationship less on the strength of newly found emotions and more on enduring political realities.

One of them, of course, is Taiwan, which is slowly coming into the grip of a succession problem that could call into question the conception of the one China that has always inspired China's and America's policy. But China, in turn, appears to have relegated the Taiwan problem to a more distant future. One can only guess the reasons, but it seems safe to say that the prospect of the settlement of the Hong Kong issue has changed the outlook and may suggest the solution for the problem of Taiwan as well.13/ Once Taiwan is readmitted, as China may correctly guess, there will be little more than diplomatic protests. The interests of the Soviet Union paradoxically may come to coincide with the Kuomintang Government, if the latter were to become convinced of its complete isolation. Such a possibility cannot be easily dismissed.14/

Apart from Taiwan, the strategic position of the United States in East Asia, its naval presence in the area and its military involvement in South Korea, have been reassuring to China.15/ The Americans themselves are convinced of the necessity of a credible presence which also underlines their security relations with Japan.16/ But, relations with China also form a prominent part in the entire strategic set-up of the United States and its policy of containment in Asia.17/ The long American neglect of China was always an anomaly for which the United States paid an extremely heavy price in Korea and Vietnam. Apart from the impossibility of the United States to once again draw upon its military allies for such expeditions, any sensible policy of containment in East Asia has to be founded on local cooperation. Nor can it be expected of Japan in the future to accept a relationship with the United States that would upset entirely its relations with China. As long as the logjam in the Soviet-Japanese and the Sino-Soviet relations remains, the present strategic situation is likely to last because it fundamentally suits the participants.18/

There are two further issues which, in a wider context, are linked up with American policy in the Pacific. One is New Zealand, which, under ANZUS,19/ has called into question its relationship with the United States. ANZUS was a more or less understandable creation in the wake of the Second World War and the American withdrawal from mainland China. During the war, Japan's military conquests and its co-prosperity sphere, spanning the Western Pacific and all of Southeast Asia, had forced security problems on New Zealand. When mainland China turned communist and appeared to advance the Soviet sphere of influence, compounded with the Korean War, the frightening spectre of a communist onslaught conjured up the worst suspicions in the United States. In American strategic conceptions, the entire region had always been looked upon as an integrated area and, for the reasons mentioned above, the other ANZUS countries readily fell in with that conception. Australia's and New Zealand's long antagonism against nuclear experiments in the Pacific and nuclear weapons in general has led the latter country, under its socialist prime minister, to refuse to countenance any dealings with American nuclear propelled ships or those carrying nuclear weapons. The pretense that their presence is not disclosed, and so can be conveniently ignored, is no longer accepted.20/

One of New Zealand's arguments, apart from the specious one--that it would invite Soviet retaliation--is that the country is outside the sphere of direct Soviet influence. The proposition may be doubted. Though New Zealand (and Australia) are by no means in the direct firing line, there is some reason to believe that Soviet strategic conceptions--and these are ultimately the ones that count--have a wider reach than New Zealand confidently pretends to believe.

Though ANZUS has not formally been called into question, it may be doubted whether much has been left for the moment. The United State's obvious fear is, of course, the spreading of an anti-nuclear campaign in the East, similar to the one it faces in the West, where about a third of its allies refuse to contemplate the stationing of nuclear weapons in times of peace.21/ Nevertheless, the conception that New Zealand is really outside the sphere of Soviet strategy sounds convincing enough for the sake of (propaganda) argument.

The second issue is that America's concern with the Pacific Basin may well grow in importance, both in its own right, as well as for European concerns of not having any strategic links outside of a narrowly defined NATO area. There can be little doubt that an eventual confrontation between the Soviet Union and the United States will focus on East Asia22/ and change the hitherto "familiar" features of the East-West conflict.23/

SOVIET MILITARY BUILD-UP

The United States, China and Japan could hardly fail to note the truly gigantic military build-up of the Soviet Union in this area. Its strategic importance vitally affects an area that stretches all the way from Siberia in the North to Okinawa in the South, as well as from Alaska in the East to Mongolia in the West. All of the important bases of the two chief protagonists can be found here. This concern has been clearly reflected in the hearings before the American Congress, and the rapid build-up of the Soviet fleet in this area has not gone unnoticed.24/

Four reasons can be found for this startling display of power. The first one can be found in the deep running Sino-Soviet rift. It concerns the most vital issues between the two countries: the sharp disagreement on communist strategy; the ideological break after the de-Stalinization now superseded by the almost reverse positions of the antagonists; the determined third world option, originally taken by China, and conveniently coupled with a stinging rebuke of the unequal treaties imposed on China by a Czarist Russia and adamantly upheld by the Soviet Union; and the complete withdrawal of economic aid and drastic decline in trade, which is only now being slowly resumed. The heat behind the Chinese demands and the border clashes have led the Soviet Union to drastically reinforce its frontiers. The second reason is the Soviet fear that its almost empty Siberian spaces face the by far most populous state in the world. Only a concentration of superior fire power can provide a credible defense. Besides, such forces might be used to threaten China with a preemptive strike.25/ The third reason is the Soviet presence in the Indian Ocean, where its bases should be seen in the context of the overall Soviet effort to stand up against American naval forces all over the world. The fourth, and last, reason is Japan, which, as a potential military power, could quite possibly turn against the Soviet Union. Japan is, above all, worried about its extensive maritime communications upon which much of its economic vitality depends. The Soviet naval forces seem best suited to disrupt the traffic in sea lanes.

The Soviets have also reinforced their air force and navy by stationing them in great numbers on the Kurile Islands. The occupation of these islands by the Soviet Union remains a principal bone of contention between it and Japan.26/ This threat was enough to induce Prime Minister Nakasone to warn that he would turn his country into an unsinkable aircraft carrier--a statement none of his predecessors would have dared to utter.

Figures about the Soviet strength in the Far East indicate that there are some 40 divisions (370,000 men) and some 820 ships, totalling well over 1.5 million tons, "the largest of the Soviet fleets in numbers of ships and which has been growing consistently since the mid-1960s."27/ The number of aircraft, including naval aircraft, amounts to about 2,100, while about 30% of the Soviet strategic missiles are deployed along the Trans-Siberian Railway and in submarines of the Pacific fleet. It remains to be seen what the final impact of this concentration of power may be. Until now, Soviet naval deployment has been based more on a certain presence than on bringing to bear strategic pressures if need be, as is the case with the American fleet. The Soviet Union is, and remains for the time being, a continental power whose strategic doctrine is not dominated by maritime matters.

The Soviet position has its disadvantages. Its bases are far away from the European heartland. Vladivostok lies close to the People's Republic of China and can only be reached by the extremely vulnerable Trans-Siberian Railway or by air. The Soviet fleet is bottled up since it has to pass through the narrow straits under the control of Korea and Japan before getting out into the open sea. Such straits can be mined easily.

JAPAN

Although still only militarily important through its specific ties with the United States, but economically a colossus in its own right, Japan remains a key element in the Pacific Basin. It has already been mentioned that the relations between Japan and the Soviet Union have steadfastly remained bad and certainly the potential openings of previous decades are not to be found since the ties between Japan and China have improved. If the Soviet military build-up has been partly inspired by its geographical disadvantage, then Japan, by hemming in the entire Siberian Pacific coastline, will almost automatically have to bear the brunt if the Soviet Union wanted to break out in force.28/ If Japan were to block the straits of Tsushima, Soya and Sugaru, in addition to the passages between the Kurile Islands, it would have taken over an important strategic task from the United States.

Japan's own defense forces are slowly pushing through their constitutional ceiling, but any nuclear development by Japan itself remains out of the question. Japan has, however, remained extremely reticent about the strategic tasks it could clearly and openly admit to taking up. Japanese policymakers entertain, of course, grave doubts about the feelings of other East Asian nations if their country were to emerge again as the predominant military power in the region after having attained an economic status that already inspires occasional bad feelings.29/ Resistance in Japan itself to any outright military policy that is in keeping with the country's resources will most probably remain high for the foreseeable future. In strictly financial terms, Japan's outlays on matters connected with defense are bigger than the sums ostensibly devoted to it. Officially, in American eyes, Japan's increased defense spending should not remain behind the NATO countries.

The weight of Japan in the military equation depends a great deal upon the strategic designs of the United States. To what extent does it want Japan to shoulder a part of the burden, to take over an autonomous part of the Pacific defense set-up, or simply to underwrite whatever the United States wishes at any particular moment? Though the fundamental lines of American strategic thinking may be more or less obvious, the actual emphasis and the continuous reappraisal, which the American democratic vocal process imposes and forces out into the open, often distorts the issues in the eyes of outsiders and leaves them with a confused and often wrong impression. One further disadvantage of the strategy of the United States in the Pacific is that it is not tied up with anything approaching the military organization of NATO. Security matters are only too often a bilateral affair between it and Japan, where the Japanese are asked to accept the American way of thinking. Together with the by-now permanent American frustration with Japan's economic performance, the stage is set for military understandings whose main purpose is to paper over disagreement. It always remains a matter for speculation as to what really would happen if things were to come to a head.

Even if Japan considers the Soviet Union as its potentially most dangerous neighbor, it does not really want to join in an anti-Soviet alliance with China and the United States if it can help it. Its geopolitical situation forces it to seek a _modus vivendi_ with that neighbor. Economic relations between the two countries, though often described as ideally complementary, have really never flourished. Japan has been more concerned about its economic prosperity, the security of its supply lines for the import of raw materials and energy, and has thus been happy to leave military matters to others.30/ The bitter experience with the Soviet Union dating from the Second World War and the less than forthcoming attitude from that country, seems to preclude a reversal of alliance in the near future.

One of the strategic concepts, contemplated by the United States, would involve deterring the Soviets from military adventures in other parts of the world by threatening the security of the Soviet bases in Kamchatka and perhaps in Sachalin. Such a strategy could be called "horizontal escalation." Defined as a strategic principle, it holds that an attack by the Soviet Union on a weak point of the West should be met with an attack on a weak point of the Soviet Union. Though not formally adopted as official doctrine, the present administration appears to act on this principle.31/

CHINESE PERCEPTIONS

How do the Chinese assess the threat of the Soviet strategy? It may be useful to refer here to ideas set out by Professor Hua Di, of the Institute of American Studies in Beijing, at a symposium in Honolulu in February, 1985. He presented a frightening picture of Soviet ambitions that was much more disquieting than the often soothing Western analyses would suggest. The Soviets, Hua Di observed, strive for world domination, and to attain that goal it is necessary that the United States be forced out of Europe, Asia and Africa. The means to be used for this grand design are conventional forces and nuclear blackmail. In case of a big conventional war, so Hua Di suggested, the Soviets would have to rely on their ground troops because the Soviet Navy, notwithstanding its expansion, could only play a relatively minor supporting role.

Moscow would not be able to break through every line of European defense, since that would bring war too close to the industrial heartland of the Soviet Union. A conventional confrontation could be fought in Baluchistan, where it would be followed up by naval and aerial attacks on American reinforcements and logistics in the Pacific, the Indian and the Atlantic Oceans, as well as in the Mediterranean.32/ This conception explains the Chinese worries about the fighting in Afghanistan.

Hua Di went further into the widespread misconception concerning the 52 divisions (his figure) of Soviet forces in the Far East: they are all located only a two- or three-day distance from the Central Asian theater. Ten other divisions, encamped in the Trans-Baikal region, are intended for use in the East or in the South, where they could be backed up by eight divisions of the Central Strategic Reserve kept in Moscow. The Soviet Union is presently trying to cope with Afghanistan, while waiting for Khomeni to disappear so that they can grab Iran, as well as inciting the separatist movements in Pakistan, such as the Pathans. The Soviets continue to beef up their forces so that they can defeat the Americans rapidly in a conventional encounter.

Hua Di's scenario could be taken by Japan and other countries as a cue to acquire nuclear weapons as quickly as possible.33/ He also pointed out how ill-starred American assistance to Taiwan had been since it prevented full cooperation between China and the United States. Whatever the merits of this analysis, dangling such a price before the eyes of Americans remains a piece of skillful diplomacy. It suggests an almost self-evident conception of the necessity that China and the United States join forces in order to maintain peace in the Pacific and the world at large.34/

The weak point of this exercise remains the fact that the increasing Soviet military strength has not spurred

China to actually join forces with the United States. It may be obvious that China is not very inclined to join any anti-Soviet bloc and definitely embroil itself with the Soviet Union. For one thing, it would deprive China of a powerful card in its dealings with the Soviet Union. China is more inclined to keep its distance from both of the greater powers and to set store upon its position as a potential great power that is revered and sought out for that very reason.35/

This pragmatic approach has permitted China to behave in a positive way towards non-communist states in the region. China knows full well that its security depends on its relations with the two great powers and that it has to react prudently to their presence in the region. This pragmatic approach has become more pronounced under the Deng regime. One only has to compare the almost daily strident utterances in the heyday of the Cultural Revolution with the mostly economic and businesslike proclamations since Mao's death. The effort to play down grand strategy has, in any event, permitted China to look intelligently after its own interests and to keep future options more open.

For the moment, Chinese foreign policy is inspired by the overriding goal of containing the spread of Soviet influence towards the Pacific. This effort does not necessarily imply that China feels itself compelled to tighten its ties with Washington. The slogan--stressed by China since the Bandung days--that Asia ought to be reserved for Asians is interpreted by the present Chinese leadership to mean that it looks for convenient relations with other Asian powers such as Japan, the ASEAN states, and even the Pacific countries, Australia and New Zealand. The militarization of the Pacific in the wake of a Soviet-American confrontation runs directly counter to the most fundamental Chinese conceptions concerning the area.

The Soviet military threat since World War II, which welded the NATO states together, has not provided a sufficient basis for a common defense system in the West Pacific, and most probably will not do so. Geopolitical factors, as well as political and socio-economic differences, make it a most complex region. The two most important indigenous powers, China and Japan, each impress a character completely of its own. It has been impossible to weld together a coherent defense system, as the failure of the far more modest security alliances of the Dulles' era clearly have shown. The only opportunity, from America's point of view, remains a flexible approach that takes into account the complex nature of security aspects in this region.36/

SOVIET STRATEGY: A DOMINO POLICY?

The concept of a domino policy looks like a misnomer. If a country cannot get everything at once, it will have to proceed step by step. The Chinese conception has long been, and still may be, that the fundamental issue at stake is Soviet hegemony in Asia and its relentless press to establish first its influence, and second, to obtain a Soviet political hold in the minds of the rest of the world. Ironically enough, it was Mao Zedong who pressed the Soviets to crush the Hungarian uprising and corroborated with its former ally in a policy that China is, itself, now vigorously denouncing. The Chinese may be forgiven the thought that henceforth the Soviet Union will need no further encouragement in this direction. The question is then, whether this intention is really at the bottom of Soviet strategy in Asia.

The downing of the Korean airliner in 1984 sent very disagreeable shockwaves over the area. The high-handed way in which the Soviet Union threatened military reprisals in case of interference with its maneuvers, starting just when the search for the wreckage began, seemed to underline its tough attitude.37/ The Soviet Union, like China, has realized that the communist ideology and the virtues of the Soviet economy hold little attraction for Asia. As a result, the Soviet Union presses ahead, mainly with military means. According to a Rand Corporation study, the thrust of the already noted beefing up of the Soviet forces in Asia reflects, besides the customary targets, China, Japan and the American forces in the area, a widening circle of geopolitical interests. Its military capabilities in Northeast Asia are steadily and systematically linked up with those in South and Southwest Asia.

The Soviet forces in the north already have been briefly discussed. Their concentration along China's northern borders is a constantly felt threat that hangs over the discussion between the Soviet Union and China. The Soviet Union does not appear amenable to a withdrawal of some of its troops which might satisfy China and yet leave the strategic balance largely the same.38/

In Southwest Asia, Afghanistan represents only a very small portion of the entire Chinese border, but the destabilizing effect of the Soviet invasion is obvious. The first country to feel the heat is Pakistan, and through the customary play of alliances and counter-alliances, a large part of China's southern border might swing towards a camp friendly to the Soviets, if Pakistan were to disintegrate under the pressure. No wonder the three main Chinese objections against the Soviet Union are Afghanistan, the North Vietnam and Kampuchea. Together these areas constitute by far the larger part of China's endless frontiers.

This land circle is complemented by a Soviet naval presence which has its main base in Cam Ranh Bay. This huge base, once the pivot of the American war effort in Vietnam, offers the Soviet Union the possibility of defying the American military forces in this sensitive part of the western Pacific. Admiral James Butts testified to this effect in a hearing before the U.S. Senate.39/ The ASEAN states regard this presence as a potential threat to their vital shipping lanes. Professor Lee Yong Leng, Director of the Politicological Center of Singapore University, is of the same opinion when he states that the Soviet Union now has at its disposal the possibility of blocking the sea lanes along which oil is transported to Japan and South Korea. The expansion of this base's facilities has been going on for quite some time, but since November 1984 the pace has quickened with the arrival of fighter planes and bombers, which, according to Admiral Crowe, Commander of the U.S. Seventh Fleet, completes the aerial defenses of Cam Ranh Bay. The Admiral expressed full confidence in regard to the total balance of forces in the Pacific, but he was worried about the developments in the Philippines and within ASEAN. The Soviets now have, the Admiral observed, a warm water base more than 3,000 miles south of Vladivostok that can be used as a staging post for possible action in the Indian Ocean.40/

The question that remains is the degree of political control the Soviet Union has over it. Vietnam alleges that it is rented to the Soviet Union, but it is not clear to what extent Vietnam's political control may hamper Soviet maneuvers. According to Washington, the "facilities," as Vietnam pretends to call them, may be offered in compensation for Soviet aid there and in Kampuchea. If the Soviets have much freedom in using these facilities, their presence may be a great threat to the Strait of Malacca-- one of the obvious missing links in the chain of Soviet bases.41/ The Cam Ranh Bay base would, in any case, permit the Soviets to intervene as quickly as the U.S. naval forces. As Professor Lee points out, the security of the waters surrounding the ASEAN states is of critical importance for the control of the Malaccan Strait.43/

According to the Red Flag, the Chinese are of the opinion that the Soviet Union proposes to create an archlike shipping route connecting the Mediterranean with the Red

Sea to the Indian Ocean and to the Southwest Pacific and Japan. In such an admittedly grand design, there would be a link-up between the Pacific and the Black Sea fleet and hence a possible threat to the sea lanes of the entire area under discussion and beyond. Whether or not these ideas are flights of fancy, they are in tune with the Chinese ideas expressed above.

The most worrisome point is that even if one considers such grand designs premature for the moment, as they probably are, there is nothing in Soviet statements or in actual preparations and military deployment to contradict these ultimate goals. It is also part of the Soviet strategy to encourage potential adversaries to entertain such ideas. In that sense it is almost, by definition, a domino strategy.

A separate question is whether Vietnam, faced with a stern and continuing refusal by others to accept its political designs, may be tempted to stir up guerilla movements in the ASEAN countries. Western sources believe that there is little scope for renewed insurrection in Thailand. The previous guerilla movement has disintegrated and, moveover, no longer believes in the Maoist strategies of conquering the countryside. A part of it, however, may turn to urban guerilla tactics. Given the ASEAN's disinclination for communism, the Soviet Union would have to install Marxist regimes--a course they are not contemplating at the moment. Rather, the pressure they bring to bear appears as an effort to drive the ASEAN countries apart by inducing some of them to accept the Kampuchean situation as being irretrievably lost to them and not worth the risk of clashing with the Soviet Union over it.44/ Americans and their allies will have to muster sufficient military and political forces to counter the threat implied by this Soviet strategy.

CONCLUSION

Kremlin leaders have been much obsessed by the prospect of being a superpower on an equal footing with the United States. Their attainment of this status has been, at least in their own eyes, of comparatively recent date, since they mostly measure it in terms of (brute) military power. It remains for them to have this status effectively acknowledged both formally and politically. Their interest is, in particular, more directed towards the acceptance of their inherent right to interfere with the system of international relations in regions bordering their territory.

In practice, this policy is mainly directed towards Asia and the Pacific, where relations have not yet been entirely aligned. In that perspective, the influence of their most direct competitors, the United States and China, has to be limited and reduced as far as possible. Soviet leaders strive for their patronage to be accepted in a region under the guise of a security system, in and through which they exert effective control.

Yet, they often have to subordinate these efforts to their actual relations with China and the United States. It is the correlation of power within the triangle, Soviet Union-China-United States, which fully dominates policy-making in the Kremlin. Changes in policies directed towards other countries often result from changes within these triangular relations. Whenever the Soviet leaders detect a chance to increase their power at the cost of China and/or the United States, they will certainly make use of it, provided the risks remain acceptable. This political principle may be taken as a permanent feature of Soviet foreign policy. There are no indications which would lead one to suppose that this fundamental priority has been abandoned, or receives less emphasis, under the regime of Gorbachev.

The Soviet Union's geopolitical situation makes it a continental power that spans the greater northern part of the Eurasian continent and forces it to shift its defense perimeter as far outward as possible. China's geographic position implies that the Soviet Union will have to neutralize this influence--and that of Japan--especially by trying to reduce the American influence. The Pacific, then, is an area where the United States is determined to hold on to its influence. The Soviet Union sees its duty as spreading its influence and keeping open options for the time when China really may someday grow into an equal partner of the United States and the Soviet Union.

Unless a way can be found to conduct relations in such a sensitive area by means other than sheer power, the prospects are somber indeed.

NOTES

1. Raju G.C. Thomas (ed), The Great Power Triangle and Asian Security (Lexington, 1983) p. 1017. Jonathan D. Pollack, The Sino-Soviet Rivalry and the Chinese Security Debate (The Rand Corporation, 1982). Norman D. Levin, The Strategic Environment in East Asia and the U.S.-Korean Security Relations in the 1980s (The Rand Corporation, March,

1983). Joachim Schultz-Neuman, "Aktuelle Sicherheitspolitik im asiatisch-pazifischen Raum," Europaische Wehrkunde 33 (1984):146-150. See also Michael Yahuda, Towards the End of Isolationism: China's Foreign Policy after Mao (London, 1983) pp. 1-43. Harry Harding, "Change and Continuity in Chinese Foreign Policy," Problems of Communism 32, (March-April 1983):1-19.

2. On the American position in the Far East, see William Watt, The United States and Asia: Changing Attitudes and Policies (Lexington, 1982), and Raymond H. Myers (ed), A U.S. Foreign Policy for Asia: The 1980s and Beyond (Stanford, 1982). On March 5, 1983, Secretary of State Shultz addressed the World Affairs Council in Chicago. He revealed a number of new insights which were to govern U.S. policy towards Asia such as a lower priority attached to the role of China as a barrier against the Soviet expansionism and a higher priority in regard to Japan's role to contain the threat.

3. See also Takashi Oka, "Stability in Asia," Foreign Affairs 63 (1985):655.

4. Chinese leaders were not adverse, in those days, to confront Hanoi and Moscow, in veiled terms, with the possibility of a common Sino-American action. Cf., also Dennis Duncanson, "Die strategischen Hintergrunde des chinesischen Vietnam-Krieges" (Background of the Chinese war effort in Vietnam), Europa Archiv 34, (1969):336-343. John Franklin Cooper, "China and South Asia, Current History 83, No. 497, pp. 405-408 and 434-436. On Cambodia in general, see Oskar Weggel, "Entwicklungen der Indochina Frage seit dem Ende des Vietnam-Krieges, Gescheiterte Perspecktiven, denkbare Losungsansatze," (Developments in Indochina. Failed Perspectives and possible Solutions), Europa Archiv 40 (1985): 49-56.

5. H.J. Dietrich, "Perspektiven und Probleme in Ostasien-Westpazifik," (Problems and Future in East Asia-West Pacific), Europa Archiv 32 (1981):276-277. For an account of the American relations with Southeast Asian countries, see Gareth Porter, "The United States and South Asia," Current History 83 (December 1984):401-404, 436-438.

6. P. Schier, "Die Beziehungen der Sowjetunion zu Vietnam, Laos und Kambodscha," (Relations between the Soviet Union and Vietnam, Laos and Cambodia), Osteuropoa 34 (September 1984):675-676. Lau Teik Soon, "The Soviet-Vietnamese Treaty--A Giant Step Forward," South Asian Affairs (1980): 54-64.

7. Frankfurter Allgemeine Zeitung, 27 September 1983, p. 8. Neither was the Soviet Union interested in the ASEAN

conception of a zone of peace and security. H.J. Dietrich, op. cit., p. 280.

8. R. Petkovic, "China und seine Asiatische Nachbarn," (China and its Asian neighbours), Internationale Politik 36 (January 1985):12-13.

9. The most noteworthy leader, Le Duan, who succeeded the legendary Ho Chi Minh, finally died in July 1986.

10. On the possible re-establishment of friendlier relations after Gorbachev's access to power, see Far Eastern Economic Review 127 (March 1986):10-11. Cf., Le Monde , 22 March 1985, p. 1.

11. Newsweek, 8 April 1985, p. 22.

12. The International Herald Tribune, 26 March 1986.

13. The New York Times, 28 February 1983, as cited by Allen S. Whiting, "Sino-Soviet Relations: What Next?" Annals of the American Academy of Political and Social Science, No. 476 (1984), p. 149. See also Parris H. Chang, "U.S.-China Relations: From Hostility to Euphoria to Realism, ibid., p. 159-163.

14. J. D. Pollack, "China's Role in the Pacific Basin," Survival, Vol. 26, p. 171. "Standfestigkeit in der Chinafrage," (Standing Firm on China) Neue Zurcher Zeitung, 6 July 1984, p. 5. A sign that the heat has been allowed to drop may be found in the Chinese reaction to the Dutch relations with Taiwan. When the Dutch government gave permission for the delivery of two submarines to Taiwan, China reacted violently by cutting down the level of diplomatic representation and by refusing any commercial deals. See Ko Wan Sik, "The Dutch-Taiwan Submarine Deal: legal aspects," Neth. Yb. I. L., Vol. 13 (1982), pp. 125-141. Relations having been restored to normal, Beijing did not voice any objection to later deals which were admittedly much smaller and did not involve armaments.

15. United States-China Relations: Today's Realities and Prospects for the Future, Hearing on Foreign Relations, Senate, May 17, 1984.

16. H. J. Dietrich, op. cit., pp. 280-281. Global Political Assessment, No. 17 (1983-1984), p. 41. R. Petkovic, "China und die U.S.A.," Internationale Politik 39 (1985): pp. 16-17.

17. N. Z. Zeitung, 17 June 1984. The Economist, 30 June 1984, pp. 34-37.

18. International Herald Tribune, 12 June 1986.

19. The ANZUS cannot be compared to NATO. The former prolongs the war-time alliance directed against Japan. It has no integrated command-structure, no fixed headquarters, permanent staff or even secretariat. The 1951 agreement,

instituting the ANZUS, is a vague document, only 11 articles long, and lacking in precise details and legal terms. Its purpose, according to the preamble, is "to strengthen the fabric of peace in the Pacific Area." The three governments promise to consult one another in case any of them feels threatened.

20. See N. Z. Zeitung, 24/25 March 1985, p. 5. Michael Pugh, "Australien und Neuseeland: neue Wege in der Sicherheitspolitik," (Australia and New Zealand, New Avenues in Security Policy), Europa Archiv 40 (25 March 1985):175-184.

21. A former NATO Secretary-General once observed that during a NATO exercise, a country refusing the stationing of nuclear weapons was the first and only one to call for their use. The commanders were happy to refuse them their request.

22. W. Kraus and W. Lutkenhorst, "Atlantische Gegenwart--Pazifische Zukunft," (From Present to Future--from the Atlantic to the Pacific), Asien 10 (January 1984): 20-21.

23. P. Polomka, "The Security of the Western Pacific: The Price of Burden Sharing," Survival 26 (Jan/Feb 1984): 4-5.

24. See Dieter Heinzig, "Sowjetische Asienpolitik in den siebziger und achtziger Jahren," (Soviet Policy in Asia in the 1970s and 1980s), Osteuropa, Vol. 34, No. 9, p. 641-642.

25. W. Hyland, "Soviet Security in the 1980s," Adelphi Papers, No. 125, pp. 20-21. See also Harry Gelman, The Soviet Far East Build-up and Soviet Risk Taking Against China (The Rand Corporation, 1982), and Gerald Segal (ed.), The Soviet Union in East Asia, Predicaments of Power (London, 1983).

26. C. J. Blankenburgh, "De positie van Japan in Oost-Aziee (Japan's Position in East Asia), Int. Spectator, Vol. 38, (The Hague, 1984), p. 229. Tetsuya Kataoka, "Japan's Northern Threat," Problems of Communism 133, (March/April 1984):4-7.

27. "Asian Security 1984," Research Institute for Peace and Security (Tokyo) p. 70. for a more detailed description see ibid., p. 63ff. See also B. M. Blechman and Edward N. Luttwak (eds), International Security Yearbook 1983-84 (London, 1984), pp. 174ff.

28. See William T. Tow, "Sino-Japanese Security Cooperation: Evolution and Prospects," Pacific Affairs 56 (Spring 1983):57-58. Joseph Y. S. Cheng, "China's Japan Policy in the 1980s," International Affairs 61 (Winter 1984/85):91-107. For a survey of Soviet-Japanese relations, see Joachim

Glaubitz, "Zur Aussen-und Sicherheitspolitik Japans," (Japan's Foreign Policy and Security), Aussenpolitik 35 (1984):184-186.

29. P. Polomka, op. cit., p. 10. J. Glaubitz, op. cit., pp. 177-189, and Fr. A. Zeitung, 16 May 1984, p. 3.

30. J. Glaubitz, "Ein Jahrzehnt der Spannungen und Bewegungslosigkeit. Die Politik der Sowjetunion gegenuber Japan seit 1973," (A decade of tension and stagnation: the Soviet Union's foreign policy towards Japan since 1973), Osteuropa, Vol. 134, pp. 647-657.

31. M. Klare, M. Barang and F. Barnaby, "Asia: Theater of Nuclear War," South, No. 37 (November 1983), pp. 9-14.

32. Strategically speaking, Baluchistan is of interest to the Soviet Union. It is an area where leftwing guerillas operate. If the region were to secede from Pakistan and turn to the Soviet Union, the road to the Indian Ocean would be cleared. It is unlikely that, in such an event, the U.S. would not react.

33. This piece of advice seems to underlie the entire presentation: the suggestion would relieve China from the awkward responsibility of deciding alone whether or not to use nuclear weapons in defense of other Asian countries. If so, this suggestion would mean a strong invitation to the countries so advised to throw in their fate with that of China. However, such suggestions remain far too embryonic to suggest definite long-term Chinese strategic conceptions.

34. The Daily Telegraph (3 March 1985), p. 16.

35. P. Polomka, op. cit., p. 7.

36. Mike M. Mochiuzuki, "Japan's Search for Strategy," International Security 8 (Winter 1983-84): 152-179, and Masaski Nishihare, "Expanding Japan's Credible Defense Role, ibid., pp. 180-205.

37. T. Ch. Rhee, "The Military-Strategic Factors in United States-Korea Policy in the Changing Political Environment in East Asia," Korea and World Affairs 7 (Winter 1983):600-601.

38. Le Monde, (22 March 1985), p. 1, and The Economist 294 (30 March 1985):18.

39. The Daily Telegraph (26 March 1985).

40. The base was built by the U.S. during the Vietnam war as a supply facility. It was left behind in 1975 with its infrastructure intact when they left. In 1978, the Soviet Union and Vietnam concluded a Treaty of Friendship and, a year later, after the border clashes between China and Vietnam, The Soviet Union received full use of the base.

41. On the Soviet efforts to acquire control over the Malyan Strait, see Robin Edmonds, _Soviet Foreign Policy: The Brezhnev Years_ (Oxford, 1985), pp. 170-171.

42. _The Wall Street Journal_, 17 October 1983, p. 6, and Leszek Buszynsiki, "Vietnam's ASEAN Diplomacy: Incentives for Change," _World Today_, Vol. 40, No. 1, p. 29-36.

43. See Note 39, ibid.

44. See also David P. Chandler, Kampuchea: End Game or Stalemate?" _Current History_ 83 (December 1984):413-417 and 433-434. Pao-Min Chang, "Kampuchea in Chinese and Vietnamese Policies: The Root of Conflict," _Studies in Comparative Communism_ 16 (Autumn 1983):203-221.

3

U.S. Military and Political Interests in East Asia

James David Armstrong

ENDS AND MEANS IN U.S. POLICY

The most striking feature of American policy towards East Asia in this century has been its lack of consistency. Not only has the level of American involvement fluctuated wildly in line with changes in the perceived importance of the region, but actual U.S. interests have been defined in radically different ways even in times when the United States has accepted a major commitment to East Asian security. Moreover, quite dramatic shifts in the relative emphasis given by Washington to one part of the region over another have occurred during fairly short time periods. A wide gap has at times developed between declared interests and the resources devoted to their attainment while at other times, the resources that Washington has been prepared to allocate to achieve specific objectives have seemed wholly disproportionate to the goal in view.

A brief review of the history of American involvement in the Far East will serve to illustrate these points. U.S. interest in the Pacific developed concurrently with the opening up of the American West, but it remained primarily economic until the acquisition of Hawaii and the Philippines in 1898 transformed the United States into an Asian power of the first rank. The region's new importance to Washington was evidenced by the Open Door notes of 1899 and by its major role in bringing about a peace treaty between Russia and Japan following their war of 1904-1905. Such actions, in effect, amounted to an assertion that the United States was now a force to be reckoned with in the region, with important interests that needed to be respected by other powers. But although the United States initially seemed to favor Japan over the European powers, this preference was soon reversed as the Japanese immigration issue began to sour relations. Moreover, during the five years before the First World War, the United States embarked upon an aggressive period of "dollar diplomacy" with the evident aim of translating its financial strength into political power. Particularly worrying for the Japanese were American demands for the commercial neutralization of Manchuria. But, not for the last time in its involvement in East Asia, American aspirations were backed neither by a sufficiently strong military presence to demonstrate clearly America's capacity and will to support its interests by force if necessary, nor by any apparent readiness to engage in diplomatic bargaining that might have attracted Japan by holding out the possibility of a quid pro quo in return for concessions in Manchuria. Instead, the high moral tone affected by the United States merely irritated Japan and, more seriously for American interests, pushed it towards a rapprochement with Russia.

After the First World War, American power and prestige were at a peak and the United States was able to use its preeminence to persuade the other East Asian powers to accept, at the Washington Conference, naval limitation and other agreements that might have formed the basis of a durable international order in the region. However, the fifteen years following the Washington Conference witnessed a drift in the United States away from this high point of American involvement in East Asia, and numerous indications appeared, suggesting an apparent American disinterest in the problems of the region, or at least a disinclination to play any major role in resolving them. Then, with no action taken to check Japan's increasing assertiveness, the United States began to reverse its policies, making a number of decisions during 1938-41 that inexorably led to confrontation.

As the war in the Pacific entered its final year, the outlines of a new American design for order in East Asia emerged. Japan was to be an exclusive sphere of influence of the United States, under whose tutelage it was to progress towards a peaceful, democratic future. China was to be built up as a strong, democratic pro-American power, capable of playing a major role in a new equilibrium in the region. In pursuit of this objective, Washington was to try to bring about an end to the conflict between nationalists and communists in China. As for the Soviet Union, its acquiescence in, and even cooperation in building, the new order was to be purchased by American acceptance of an expansion of the Soviet sphere of influence in East Asia.

Finally, Korea was to come under some form of international trusteeship, although Washington was somewhat vague as to the precise details of this arrangement.1/

The substance of this new order was agreed upon at the Yalta Conference but, although the Soviet Union fulfilled its part of the bargain by signing a friendship treaty with China--receiving in return its promised strategic domination of the Sea of Okhotsk as well as various privileges in Manchuria--the other elements of America's grand design for the region never materialized. There are many reasons for this failure, including the emergence of the Cold War in Europe, but in at least three respects the failure was a result of American policy. First, American aspirations for China were always based on illusory perceptions of the country's potential strength, Chiang Kai-Shek's commitment to democracy and the prospects for a nationalist-communist coalition. Second, although Washington was prepared to devote substantial resources to its objectives for Japan--its greatest success in the region--uncertainty abounded as to how extensive its economic and military commitment to China and Korea should be. Last, American Far Eastern policy was inevitably affected by the death of President Roosevelt when his relatively conciliatory approach towards the Soviet Union was suddenly and significantly shifted to Truman's more uncompromising stance.

The post-war period was to witness a continuing unpredictability and oscillation in American policy in East Asia. In Korea, apparent American signals to the effect that there were strict limits to the extent of its willingness to underwrite South Korean security were a contributing factor in the North Korean decision to invade. Anxious about the possible impact on its credibility , the United States decided to interven and pushed the North Koreans back into their own territory. The U.S. decision started a process of escalation which eventually provoked a Chinese counter-intervention and a far longer and more costly war than Washington had originally anticipated.2/ China itself became the target of an over-emotional, unforgiving hostility that locked the United States into a rigid and often absurd posture. The effect was to hinder the United States in its ability later to respond with flexibility to the opportunities presented by the Sino-Soviet rift, and it contributed to the exaggerated importance later attached to Vietnam.

The Vietnam War itself may be seen as the tragic culmination of twenty years of American misperceptions, miscalculations and uncertainty in East Asia. Nor did its end bring about a new era of consistency or the steady pursuit of attainable objectives clearly linked to a carefully worked out assessment of U.S. interests. China was courted by Nixon and Carter, but the much less enthusiastic approach to Sino-American relations of the Reagan Administration produced a distinctly chilly atmosphere for a time that encouraged the Soviets into a renewed bid for a Sino-Soviet rapprochement. South Korea went through a profoundly destabilizing experience when President Carter made Seoul's human rights record a major yardstick for American policy and threatened to withdraw American forces until wiser counsel prevailed. The strains in American-Japanese relations during the 1970s and 1980s may generally be seen as the normal frictions that inevitably arise in any relationship between states, however close. Even here American policy is not above criticism, particularly for its occasional tendency to disregard the sensibilities of the Japanese.

One of the chief underlying problems of the policy of the United States in East Asia is that it has not always derived from a clear and enduring view of American interests. This is partly because U.S. opinion has long been divided as to the relative importance of the region as against Western Europe or Latin America. Even when massive resources have been devoted to achieving American objectives in East Asia, as in the Korean and Vietnamese Wars, this has often stemmed less from a perception of the intrinsic importance of the specific goals in question than from some confused notion of their symbolic significance or their role in demonstrating the credibility of the United States as a world power. It is not possible to define such purposes precisely. The impression served in fact to justify open-ended commitments that were out of all proportion to any reasonable assessment of American national interest. This was especially true in Vietnam.

Unsurprisingly, when attempts have been made to define American interests in terms of some broad concept or doctrine, these have either been too vague or have contained too many inner contradictions. They have offered little guidance on the crucial question of what resources are to be devoted to their attainment, or have foundered on the rock of American domestic politics. Moreover, one "doctrine" has often borne little apparent relation to another one. For example, the idea has sometimes been advanced--most famously by Dean Acheson on 12 January 1950--that East Asia is important for the purpose of providing the United States with "strategic depth": that the region gave it an outer "defensive perimeter" against Soviet aggression.3/

As is well known, however, the United States was to find itself defending countries (South Korea, South Vietnam and Taiwan) which lay outside Acheson's "defensive perimeter." These commitments helped to give rise to a wholly different concept of "containment" which, in turn, led to a search for a more realistic set of policies, enshrined in Richard Nixon's "Guam Doctrine," the main thrust of which was that Asian states should undertake more of the burden of their own defense. Associated with the Guam Doctrine was the vaguer notion that American policy should seek to construct an overall balance of power in East Asia.

However, these two conceptions still left open the fundamental questions of just how significant the Far East was in American policy, what was the relative importance of one part of it as against another, and what resources should the United States devote to attain its objectives there? The Nixon presidency was unable to resolve these issues after its China initiative and its withdrawal from Vietnam due to domestic and Middle Eastern crises that befell it.4/ The Carter presidency complicated matters by injecting human rights considerations into America's Far Eastern policy and also elevating the Sino-American relationship to the level of a major strategic partnership, with formal recognition occurring in January of 1979 and with the first sales of nonlethal military equipment being announced a year later. Both of these moves were criticized by the Reagan Administration, which has become the longest presidency since the 1950s, and which will be discussed below. Has it broken free from the frequently confusing and occasionally disastrous pattern established by its predecessors? On what perceptions of American national interests do Reagan's policies rest and how coherent and realistic are these perceptions? How durable is the Reagan approach likely to prove? And, what problems is it likely to encounter?

REAGAN AND EAST ASIA

One may begin by summarizing some of the principal elements in Reagan's overall strategic appraisal of East Asia. The region is not viewed in isolation from the general policy objectives of the administration, especially in the area of defense, where the Reagan emphasis is very much on developing a capacity to respond flexibly to crises by moving forces from one zone to another when required.5/ Hence, the East Asian policy of the United States first must be understood against the background of the declared general purpose of the Reagan administration: to eliminate what it sees as "a decade's accumulation of doubts about U.S. staying power, constancy and readiness to support our friends" and to develop "a steadier and firmer approach to foreign policy problems."6/ Similarly, Secretary of Defense Caspar Weinberger has stated the broad objectives of American defense policy as:

1. Maintaining a collective defense posture that incorporates the strength of our allies.
2. Maintaining forward deployments that, combined with the forces of our allies, provide the first line of conventional defense in Western Europe, Japan and Korea.
3. Building a flexible force structure that supports our alliance commitments and forward deployments and provides us with a variety of options with which to respond to unforeseen contingencies in any region in which we have vital interests to defend.7/

Specific American objectives in East Asia and the Pacific also have been defined by Weinberger as follows:

> To maintain the security of our essential sea lanes and of the United States' interests in the region; to maintain the capability to fulfill our treaty commitments in the Pacific and East Asia; to prevent the Soviet Union, North Korea and Vietnam from interfering in the affairs of others; to build toward a durable strategic relationship with the People's Republic of China and to support the stability and independence of friendly countries.8/

Two further aspects of the broad Reaganite perspective on East Asia may be noted. First, the Pacific region as a whole is seen as having growing importance, in both relative and absolute terms, because of its economic development, the number of states in the region that share the United States' basic economic values and its political influence in the world. Secretary of State George Shultz drew attention, in 1984, to the most dramatic sign of the region's increased importance: "While our trade with the rest of the world last year grew by only one half percent, trade with this region grew 8%, reaching $135 billion. That means that over one-third of our total world trade is done with Asia and the Pacific--and it exceeds by nearly a quarter our overseas trade with any other area."9/ The second basic element in the administration's view of East Asia is that the Soviet military presence there is believed to have grown at a very rapid rate since the mid-1960s, while the American presence has fallen, so that a significant imbalance has emerged. Especially disturbing to the administration is a perceived imbalance in naval forces and in the nuclear equation in the Pacific.10/ The huge former American base at Cam Ranh Bay, in Vietnam, which is now exclusively under the control of the Soviets, is thought to have played a vital role in its naval build-up and is seen to pose a major threat to the vital sea lanes passing through the Malacca Strait and the South China Sea, as well as to the important American base facilities in the Philippines.11/ The Soviet Union is not seen as the only potential source of conflict in the region. A growing nervousness about North Korea is also apparent in Caspar Weinberger's 1982 report to the U.S. Congress that North Korea had "relentlessly modernized and expanded its military forces," and had become a "combat power that is deployed well forward." It had constructed "hardened air, naval and military facilities near the demilitarized zone," and "tunnels under the DMZ" and had placed "heavy emphasis on unconventional warfare forces."12/ Vietnam is also seen as a threatening factor in its own right, as well as by virtue of the important strategic facilities it has been able to provide for the Soviet Union.

American apprehensiveness concerning the Soviet military expansion in East Asia is in part a reflection of its overall strategic appraisal of a worsening global balance of power. Here, it must first be noted, that there is a considerable element of exaggeration in the Reaganite perception of the strategic balance. At current levels of military might on both sides it is virtually inconceivable that either could achieve a margin of power in its favor that would be politically meaningful, that could enable either to risk war or that could be employed for coercive diplomacy against the other. Furthermore, if accuracy, reliability, efficiency, flexibility and technical sophistication are included as yardsticks, as opposed to a simple head count of weapons, there is considerable doubt that the Soviet Union has overall superiority, especially if the nuclear weapons of France and Britain are counted on the NATO side.13/ Finally, Soviet influence in the world has not grown at anything approaching the rate of growth of its military power--in fact, for almost every significant advance, it is possible to point to a similar or greater setback.

What is true globally also has some validity for the regional picture. Soviet land and naval forces in East Asia have grown rapidly since 1965 while American forces have been reduced since the end of the Vietnam War. Moreover, the seventy Soviet Backfire bombers stationed in East Asia, its militarization of the occupied Japanese northern islands, the expansion of its fleet and its use of Cam Ranh Bay combine to improve significantly its capacity to project its power throughout Asia and the Pacific. The Soviet Union, however, also suffers from several fundamental strategic disadvantages in the region. Vladivostok, its main base, is an enormous distance from its industrial heartland and is highly vulnerable to a Chinese attack. Also, ships sailing from Vladivostok to the Pacific must pass through narrow waterways that could easily be sealed in the event of war. Petropavlovsk, on the Kamchatka Peninsula, the principal Soviet base for nuclear armed submarines, has no rail link with the rest of the Soviet Union and can easily be reached by U.S. bombers from the nearby Aleutians.14/ And, while Sino-Vietnamese hostility continues at its present level, Cam Ranh Bay's utility is strictly limited by the fact that it can only be supplied by sea and air from Soviet bases thousands of miles away.

The United States does face some genuine and serious security problems in East Asia, notwithstanding these qualifications. The very vulnerability of the Soviet Union actually may increase the possibility of a serious superpower confrontation breaking out in the region if, for example, Washington attempted to bring pressure on Moscow in response to a crisis elsewhere, or if the Soviets were panicked into a military response to a perceived provocation (as happened when they shot down the Korean airliner in September, 1983). The relatively few options open to the Soviet Union inevitably lower the nuclear threshold in East Asia, should it believe its position there to be seriously threatened. Moreover, its vulnerability might make it more prepared to contemplate high risk options. If successful, these options could significantly improve its overall strategic position, such as supporting an attack by North Korea on South Korea. Less serious difficulties for the United States are evident in its relations with its major allies and quasi-allies: the perennial issue of convincing Japan to undertake a greater share of the defense burden in the Pacific region; how far it should go in its relationship with China; what importance should be attached to human rights in its relations with the Philippines and South Korea; and, most generally, how to emphasize American determination and credibility in the region without at the same time encouraging the local powers to relax their own defense efforts.

THE UNITED STATES AND JAPAN

The Reagan administration has focused most of its efforts on developing its security relationship with Japan. This new emphasis did not come about immediately, as President Reagan's first Secretary of State, Alexander Haig, was rather more wedded to the Nixon-Kissinger notion of a great power triangle, which elevated China to a position of great strategic importance. Moreover, during the first two years of the Reagan presidency, the Japan-United States relationship was dominated by serious frictions over economic issues. These frictions stemmed from widespread suspicions in the United States that it had become the victim of an elaborate confidence trick by which Japan had somehow maneuvered itself into a position where it could maintain a $20 billion trade deficit. The effect was to endanger various American industries, while keeping Japanese markets closed to U.S. exporters. All this, including Japan's ability to undercut prices, was largely achieved in American eyes by the "free ride" it enjoyed in the defense area.

Despite these ominous perceptions of Japan, the Republican Party platform in 1980 had declared that Japan would be the "pillar of American policy in Asia"15/ and, beginning in 1983, a series of steps were carried out in an endeavor to improve the relationship. In this effort, American policymakers found an enthusiastic supporter in Japanese Prime Minister, Yasuhiro Nakasone. While visiting the United States in January 1983, he declared that Japan intended to increase its air defenses to a point where they could detect and prevent overflights by the Soviet Union's long-range supersonic Backfire bombers, gain control of the vital straits around Japan--thereby preventing the passage of Soviet submarines--and secure and maintain ocean lines of communication.16/ Other Japanese Prime Ministers had also promised much in the past, but somehow their promises had failed to materialize. However, Mr. Nakasone's remarks did provide an opportunity for the American side to reformulate the relationship, and a speech by Mr. Shultz on 5 March 1983 set out the new lines on which the Administration's policy would be based. Essentially the speech involved a subtle shift of emphasis in the American view of relations with China and Japan. Instead of being seen in global terms as part of a "strategic triangle"--a depiction which somewhat flattered China's actual military strength--China was now seen as having a primarily regional role, with a much greater importance to be attached to the U.S.-Japan relationship.17/

Apart from the different personal preferences of Haig and Shultz, four principal factors account for the new emphasis on Japan. First, its political and economic system is far more congenial to the administration than China's, and indeed preserving it is important to American interests. Second, China and the United States share only a narrow range of common interests, whereas the United States and Japan have mutual interests across a very broad spectrum, including the Third World and the Middle East, where Chinese and American perceptions often clash. Third, Japan is by far the more important of the two in economic terms. The United States and Japan together now produce more than one third of all the goods and services of the world.18/ Finally, whereas China in the longer term may be a major military power, Japan has the economic and technological capacity to turn itself into such within a few years of a decision to do so. While such a decision would not necessarily be a welcome one to Washington as it would probably destabilize the whole region, it draws attention to the fact that, for a relatively small expenditure on defense of 1.5 - 2.0% of GNP, as against 1% currently spent, Japan could play a major role in ensuring the security of the principal sea lanes in the region, probably the most basic American interest there.

Japan, however, is still some distance away from taking such a decision. Indeed there are serious inadequacies in its capacity to fulfill even the limited role of providing the first line of defense against a moderate attack. In 1982 Stephen Solarz, Chairman of the Sub-Committee on Asian and Pacific Affairs of the Congressional Foreign Affairs Committee, made a devastating critique of Japan's defense weaknesses, asserting that its unprotected radar sites and air bases and inadequate repair facilities would force all planes out of action within a few days of the outbreak of war; that much of the equipment of its ground forces was obsolete; that its naval forces lacked adequate electronic equipment, anti-submarine weapons, surface-to-surface and surface-to-air missiles and mine laying capabilities; that all Japanese forces suffered from shortages of ammunition and spare parts; that command and control capabilities were seriously inadequate; and that reserve units and mobilization procedures were virtually non-existent.19/ More recently, it was estimated that for Japan to fulfill its straits interdiction role, it would require 70 frigates and destroyers, 25 submarines and 125 P-3C patrol aircraft. These quantities are well above planned Japanese force levels for the 1983-87 period, and in May 1984 the National Defense Council of Japan formally acknowledged that it would not be able to meet its original timetable, deciding instead to postpone the date by which it would achieve the required force levels by three years, until 1991.20/

The American response to these delays has not been to bring political pressure to bear on Japan--a policy that in the past has proved to be counterproductive--but to adopt a more relaxed and patient posture, and to seek to make progress in other areas. Although the United States appears to accept Japan's new timetable, it intends to make sure that steady, if unspectacular, progress in modernizing Japan's Self-Defense Forces will be made over the next few years. It will also improve the capability of American airpower in the region by upgrading its base at Misawa from a support and surveillance center to a fighter base, with two squadrons of its advanced F-16 fighter bombers, and by arming its warships with Tomahawk cruise missiles.21/ It will furthermore lay increasing stress on what it terms "interoperability": that is, closer cooperation between the two forces in such areas as the standardization of equipment, collaboration in tactics and training, and the carrying out of joint exercises.22/ Finally, the United States will seek to encourage a closer relationship between Japan and South Korea, and more generally to associate Japan with Western positions on global issues. Frictions over various economic issues still exist and are likely to continue and, in the absence of any new crisis, are likely to play an increasingly important role in determining the overall American policy towards the region. Despite the friction, Secretary Shultz still felt sufficiently confident of the durability, strength and importance of the relationship to be able to endorse it in February 1985 in far more enthusiastic terms than had been heard for many years: "Our partnership with Japan is the keystone of American foreign policy in East Asia and the linchpin of our relationships in the region."23/

A NEW CHINA POLICY

The Reagan camp had signaled its intention to downgrade the relationship of the United States with China during the 1980 election campaign, and relations went through a highly troubled period for some three years. There were many reasons why this administration adopted a cooler posture towards China than its predecessors had. First, and probably of greatest importance, was its realistic perception that China was militarily and economically too weak and politically too unstable to be able to play the global strategic role that the more optimistic members of previous administrations had allocated to it. Not only was much of China's military equipment obsolete, but Beijing had made it clear that defense modernization was to be accorded a much lower priority than modernization in the key areas of industry, agriculture and technology. Second, China and the United States had little in common politically and except for the shared perception of the Soviet threat, found themselves at odds on a wide range of international issues. Moreover, from the perspective of America's Asian policy as a whole, too great a concentration on the China link carried certain dangers, since several Asian states viewed China with deep suspicion. Third, Reagan and some of his colleagues also shared an attachment to Taiwan that was based both on sentiment and more hard-headed factors: U.S. trade with Taiwan is at approximately three times the level of Sino-U.S. trade.24/ Finally, after eight years, the relationship offered little that could be exploited for domestic political benefit. These observations forced a reexamination in Washington as to what basic and enduring American interests were involved in its relationship with China.

Strategically, three fundamental interests may be identified. Most obviously, the United States must seek to ensure that its relations (or those of its allies) with China do not deteriorate to a point where it would once again be identified as a potential enemy. This gives the United States an interest in encouraging the continuation of the present moderation in China. A second, less crucial, U.S. interest is the economic one: China is not yet a very important American market, but economic issues, such as textile imports, have proved their ability to disrupt the relationship in the past, and a minimal American objective is to ensure that such frictions do not get out of hand. Continued improvement in current levels of trade with China and supporting its move towards a market economy should be in the interest of the United States. The third, and most complex set of American interests, concerns the security relationship between the two countries. Although China's strategic importance in the global balance of power may be less than some had believed in the 1970s, China is still highly significant in the regional strategic equation. Its value to the United States in security terms is large: as long as Sino-Soviet hostility continues, China will tie down large numbers of Soviet forces; the Sino-Vietnamese antagonism also provides a major constraint upon any Vietnamese tendency towards expansionism; China can play a multifaceted role in overall regional security by such means as guaranteeing Thai security, restraining North Korea, helping to monitor military activities in the Soviet Union, sharing information, permitting U.S. warships to call at Chinese ports, and cooperating with the United States and Japan in ensuring the security of the vital sea lanes along the Western Pacific.

When strains appeared in Sino-American relations during the first three years of the Reagan administration, part of China's response was to accept Soviet overtures towards a Sino-Soviet rapprochement. The administration, in turn, reacted by seeking to reassure China over the Taiwan question, notably through the joint Sino-American communique of August 1983, and to defuse other contentious issues, especially those relating to trade. But the administration appears to have calculated that there was not much risk of Sino-Soviet reconciliation proceeding to a point where it would seriously endanger the strategic balance in East Asia and that basic Chinese interests--such as the need for technical expertise and for some kind of commitment from the United States to its defense--would continue to dictate a policy of cooperation between the two countries. Indeed, it would not necessarily be against American interest that there should be some improvement in Sino-Soviet relations. The United States has no desire to be dragged into a conflict with the Soviet Union arising out of the Sino-Soviet antagonism. Moreover, a limited Sino-Soviet rapprochement might reassure them regarding their worst fears of the possible emergence of a United States-Japan-China axis and might provide them with some incentive to pursue a course of moderation in East Asia.

If such were the American calculations, they have been largely successful. China has felt free to criticize the United States over numerous issues since 1980, but this has not hampered a steady improvement in trade and actual relations and security cooperation. President Reagan, speaking in May, 1984, made this claim for his China policy:

> I have always recognized the importance of good U.S.-China relations. From the very outset of my

> administration I was determined to place this relationship on a more stable and enduring footing. I think we have succeeded. We have had some problems and some differences...but we have never stopped communicating with each other....We made substantial progress in working out some difficult problems and then proceeded to advance the relationship in a number of important areas--technology transfer, trade, student exchange, and so on....I told the Chinese leaders that we must continue to acknowledge our differences...but we agreed that there is much to be gained from mutual respect. And there is much to be gained...through stability and economic progress throughout the entire Pacific region.25/

Although this statement must in part be assessed in the context of the presidential election campaign, it does manage to convey the essence of the Reaganite approach to China: a shift in emphasis from grand strategy to more day-to-day issues and, in an overall regional context, an acceptance of the limits to the relationship.

THE PHILIPPINES AND SOUTH KOREA

As the only former American colony, the Philippines has a special significance to the United States. But since gaining independence, the primary importance of the Philippines has derived from the American air force installation at Clark Air Base and the naval base at Subic Bay, and from the complex of communication facilities of both. These bases were of crucial importance during the Korean and Vietnam wars. The naval complex--the largest such installation outside of America--has given the United States the ability to project its naval power in the Indian Ocean and Persian Gulf in response to crises in Iran and Afghanistan. In the Philippines, there has always been some opposition to these bases, but recently doubts about their retention have also been expressed in the United States. Some have argued that the bases are part of an obsolete "front-line-of-defense" strategy that nuclear missiles have rendered out of date.26/ A second line of criticism concerns the 900 million dollar "rent" paid by the United States for the bases. Others have suggested alternative locations for them in less volatile areas, but there are significant difficulties with each of these.27/

The most vocal American opposition to the bases came from those who believe that the perceived importance of the bases had drawn the United States into an unwelcome commitment to the increasingly repressive and corrupt regime of Ferdinand Marcos. Indeed, Jeane Kirkpatrick had provided an intellectual underpinning for the argument that the United States should support "strong man" rulers of the Marcos type as they alone were capable of sustaining social order against the communist challenge.28/ In the early years of his presidency, Reagan had clearly been influenced by this view of the Philippines. But after the assassination of Filipino opposition leader, Benigno Aquino, 21 August 1983, American policy moved towards a more ambivalent posture, with its uncertainty exacerbated by the divisions that had begun to appear on this issue between the State and Defense Departments. They took radically different views on the matter of how much pressure should be exerted on Marcos. The Pentagon adopted the position that essentially echoed that of Mrs. Kirkpatrick, while the State Department, in alliance with Stephen Solarz, the influential leader of the House of Representatives Asia-Pacific Affairs Subcommittee, favored a strategy of exerting pressure on Marcos to compel him to accept power sharing with Filipino moderates.29/

During 1985 the Reagan administration shifted significantly towards the State Department's approach, with Marcos receiving various warnings to further democratize the country, reform the military and pursue an open market economy. A key point in this strategy came in October when Senator Paul Laxalt delivered a personal message from President Reagan to Marcos that contained a strong warning of the necessity for reform. Hence, when "people's power" finally ousted Marcos in February 1986, the administration was well prepared to give the final push by making it clear to him that he should not expect any American support if he chose to resist by force a takeover by Mrs. Aquino.

Although the United States gained some credit with the new Aquino government for thus abandoning Marcos, several fundamental problems of American policy remain. The Philippines still faces extremely serious economic difficulties and an armed uprising led by the Communist New People's Army. Since the United States accounts for around half of all foreign investment in the Philippines, American banks are owed 60% of the Filipino commercial bank debt. And, since the United States is the principal source of aid and training the Filipino military, Washington's response to these problems clearly will be a critical factor in their alleviation.30/ Inevitably, whatever Washington offers will be deemed too little by Manila--indeed there already have been signs of friction over this issue. But the quantity of American aid is not the only, nor necessarily the most important, element in American assistance to the Philippines. Aid needs to be carefully and imaginatively targeted in ways that will help sustain the Philippines' precarious democracy and assist the process of professionalization and internal reform of the army, while simultaneously trying to undermine the appeal of the various factions of communists, Muslims and Marcos supporters who are threatening the Aquino regime from within.

The situation confronting the United States, in its relationship with South Korea, in certain respects is similar to the one it faces with the Philippines--a fact acknowledged by Stephen Solarz when he announced, in April 1986, that his committee would be turning its attention toward South Korea. "We'll be looking at the extent to which Korea could become the next Philippines, the potential for instability, the extent to which the U.S. should get involved in the drive for democracy and whether or not we should encourage direct election of the President."31/ Anti-Americanism in South Korea has been growing alongside violent opposition to the government. But Washington has tended to take the view that it should not emulate President Carter by linking American troop levels in South Korea to the country's human rights record. The American judgment is clearly that the security situation confronting the Philippines is quite different from the predicament of South Korea, which faces a relentlessly hostile neighbor who is only deterred from invading it by the certainty of an American response. Until the time that a general settlement of the Korean question can be reached, any moves by the United States suggesting any wavering in its support for South Korea seem likely to destabilize the Korean situation and the current administration appears determined to avoid this.

In Korea, the United States pursues a classic "carrot and stick" policy. On the one hand, it has given its support to South Korean efforts to seek to normalize its relationship with North Korea, and it has considered proposals such as the simultaneous recognition by the Soviet Union and China of South Korea and the American-Japanese recognition of North Korea. On the other hand, it has sought to enhance South Korea's security by strengthening the presence of its own force, assisting in the modernization of South Korea's military equipment and encouraging Japan to take a greater interest in the defense of South Korea.

CONCLUSION

The Reagan administration's East Asian policy has not yet been put to anything remotely close to the severe testing of some of its predecessors. How it will react to a major crisis cannot really be predicted with any certainty. Previous presidents have departed from general policy lines when confronted with a crisis and Reagan might be no exception. However, on the evidence of developments in East Asia in recent years, in contrast to its behavior in other regions, the Reagan administration has--by accident or design or both--arrived at a set of policies that seem appropriate to its interests, to the resources it can devote to the attainment of those interests, and to the actual situation in East Asia.

It is possible to quibble over many details. The legacy of bitterness left by the Vietnam War may have blinded Washington to the possibility that a more magnanimous policy towards Vietnam might have prevented it from being driven towards an exclusive dependence on Moscow. The Soviet threat in the region may be exaggerated. The administration at times also may appear insensitive and heavy handed to policy makers in Tokyo or Beijing.

But this administration's perception of its fundamental interests is far more clear-sighted and realistic than that of most of its predecessors in this century, as also is its understanding of Chinese and Japanese perceptions of their interests. It did not create the new prosperity of the Pacific region and in certain respects has been disadvantaged by it, but this has not prevented it from seeing clearly the importance of this prosperity for order in the region. As with many of its predecessors, it has hoped to see the countries in the region undertake a greater share of their own defense, but instead of holding out unrealistic expectations on China's ability, or nagging Japan into spending more than it is prepared to on defense, its approach on these matters with both countries has been subtle and far-sighted.

Finally, the Reagan administration has always seen that the crucial importance of deterrence is a clear American commitment to remain a major regional power. Many mistakes can still be made during Mr. Reagan's remaining years in office, but on the evidence to date he would be justified in regarding his achievements in East Asia as his greatest foreign policy success.

NOTES

1. For details, see J.D. Armstrong, "The Soviet Union and the United States," in The Soviet Union in East Asia, ed., G. Segal, (London and Boulder: U. of Colorado Press, 1983).

2. For an interpretation of America's Korean Policy that stresses the credibility factor, see W.W. Stueck Jr., The Road to Confrontation, (Chapel Hill: U. of North Carolina Press, 1981).

3. For a discussion of this idea, see J.L. Gaddis, "The Strategic Perspective: the Rise and Fall of the Defensive Perimeter Concept," in Uncertain Years: Chinese-American Relations 1947-1950, eds., D. Borg and W.H. Heinrichs (New York: Columbia U. Press, 1980).

4. On this point, see B.K. Gordon, "Asian Angst and American Policy," Foreign Policy (Summer 1982):47.

5. See W.T. Tow and W.R. Feeney, U.S. Foreign Policy and Asian-Pacific Security, (Boulder: U. of Colorado Press, 1982), p.3.

6. United States Information Service (USIS), 24 January 1987.

7. USIS, 23 February 1983.

8. Report to Congress on the Fiscal Year 1984 Budget, Fiscal Year 1985 Authorization Request and Fiscal Years 1984-88 Defense Programs, 1 February 1983, p.17.

9. Address before the Honolulu Council on Foreign Relations, 18 July 1984; Department of State Press Release, 19 July 1984.

10. Report of Secretary of Defense Caspar Weinberger to Congress, 8 February 1982, pp. II 20-21.

11. Jane's Defense Weekly, 12 August 1984, p.8.

12. Caspar Weinberger, op. cit., p. II 21.

13. For a recent, very detailed analysis of this, see The Defense Monitor, Vol. XIII, No. 6, 1984.

14. M. Klare, "Asia: Theatre of Nuclear War," South, November 1983.

15. International Herald Tribune, 20 January 1983.

16. Financial Times, 20 January 1983.

17. For a perceptive analysis of this speech, see R. Nations, "A Tilt Towards Tokyo," Far Eastern Economic Review, 21 April 1983.

18. The Guardian, 15 January 1983.

19. S.J. Solarz, "A Search for Balance," *Foreign Policy*, (Winter 1982-83):78.

20. *International Herald Tribune*, 14 May 1984.

21. See *The Economist*, 18 August 1984; and the editorial in the *Asahi Evening News*, 2 July 1984.

22. On this point, see C.C. Donnelly Jr. (Commander of U.S. Forces, Japan) "A Matter of Mutual Interest: The Japan-U.S. Security Relationship," *Speaking of Japan*, (December 1983).

23. USIS, 22 February 1985, p.4.

24. *U.S. News and World Report*, 17 September 1984, p.37.

25. USIS, May 11, pp.2-3.

26. This view was advanced by retired Admiral, Gene La Rocque, *Washington Times*, 13 August 1984.

27. See the discussion by former U.S. Ambassador to the Philippines, William H. Sullivan, "Relocating Bases in the Philippines," *The Washington Quarterly*, (Spring 1984): 114-119.

28. Jeane Kirkpatrick, "Dictatorships and Double Standards," *Commentary*, (July 1979).

29. Walden Bello, "Edging Toward the Quagmire: the United States and the Philippine Crisis," *World Policy Journal*, (Winter 1985-86).

30. R.J. Kessler, *U.S. Policy Toward the Philippines After Marcos*, The Stanley Foundation Policy Paper 37, (June 1986.)

31. *The Times*, 2 April 1986.

4

China's Influence in the Pacific Basin

Philip West

In strictly military and economic terms, China's role in the Pacific Basin is smaller than is often claimed, but it is greater in the sense that it has the ability to inspire fear and respect among outsiders, including the Western world and the Soviet Union. Despite the extensive discussion of China's global role today, there is little agreement on how to describe it. One common American preconception is the "hoary obsession with China as an emerging superpower." This obsession may be even greater in Southeast Asia and the Soviet Union. So subjective are outside perceptions of China's role today that one scholar concludes that China's "strategic significance is in the eye of the beholder."1/

Further complicating attempts to find a clear concensus about China's role is the dramatic and, at times, rapid change of images in the eyes of the same beholder. America feared and tried to contain China in the 1950s and 1960s, but it now regards China as a friend and at times an ally. The reverse pattern of China images is the case for the Soviet Union. Comparable shifts have occurred in the Japanese, Korean, and Southeast Asian perceptions of China, though less so perhaps for the Europeans. Chinese perceptions of themselves over the last half-century have also changed radically.

The components of China's global and regional roles do not easily add up to a coherent policy. The elements of that role are complex and can be conflicting, such as: China's preoccupation with its own security; conflicts arising from alternately pursuing pragmatic and ideological goals; ambivalent attitudes about the Third World; stresses created by central planning and a growing market orientation; ambivalence about ethnic Chinese living outside

China's borders; the mixed legacies of China's historical greatness, etc.2/

Of the many pieces in the mosaic of China's role in the Pacific Basin, this paper will focus on the two which the author believes to be the most useful for the discussions of the Eindhoven Conference. First, one must examine the usefulness of labeling China as a superpower, by comparing China's military capabilities with those of the two big superpowers. A brief discussion of diplomatic, economic, and educational issues as they bear on military questions will be included. Second, with the observation that the perception of power is a power of its own, the evolution of the images of China in the West as they bear on China's strategic role today will be explored. In earlier drafts of this paper, the author has used the phrase "tiger's bluff" as a metaphor for discussing China's role in the Pacific Basin. The metaphor was suggested with respect for the largely positive, though fearful, image of tigers in many cultures and for the admiration generally given to one who has the ability to bluff. There is no doubt that China is a great power and that it is a "tiger" to be respected and feared. Others bluff too, but China's ability appears distinctive. Between the tiger and the bluff, China's influence in the Pacific Basin is in fact very extensive, but in unconventional ways.

CHINA'S MILITARY CAPABILITIES

The confusion surrounding the uses of words like "strategic" influence and "superpower" may spring from an over-reliance on theories developed to categorize particular nations or organize particular hierarchies of power. These commonly accepted theories are not easily applied to China because they have been used to compare the relative strengths of nations similar in size and level of development in a conventional war. They were also designed to apply to balance of power situations in Europe before World War II and the Cold War that followed. Neither situation or period offers a suitable frame of reference for looking at China.3/ The claim that China has a major role to play in the Pacific Basin rests on its ability to frustrate the monopolization of power by the two superpowers and to inspire fear in the eyes of its neighbors. These roles are more defensive than offensive in nature, as a closer look at the figures for military manpower and the composition and quality of military services will show.

Figures published by the International Institute for Strategic Studies show that, in 1984, China's military forces, comprised of four million members in the armed forces and five million reservists, were very large. They were three times the number of the United States for the same year but still less than that of the Soviet Union. When one adds China's twelve million paramilitary forces, however, China's military manpower is nine times that of the United States and more than twice that of the Soviet Union. China's numerical strength in military manpower dwarfs that of all other countries in the world.4/

Impressive as these figures are, they mask important weaknesses in the composition ratio among the services in the armed forces. China's standing army in 1983 was roughly nine times that of its navy and seven times that of its airforce. For the United States the number of men in the airforce (and marines) is roughly equal to the army, while the navy is 70% as large. China's navy and airforce, measured in manpower in 1983, as compared to the United States, was, respectively, 60% and 70% smaller. Further weakening its combat capabilities is a decline in the size of the Chinese armed forces, by as much as 9% between 1979 and 1984. Over the same period of time, according to the International Institute, comparable manpower figures have increased by 6% in the United States and by almost 30% in the Soviet Union.5/

One explanation for the recent decline in military manpower is military modernization, in Deng Xiaoping's words, "improving the quality of the army" by reducing "overmanning." Large reserves of military manpower have also been placed in the service of industrial and agricultural development, while war production facilities have been subordinated to state construction.6/ Like the army, the navy is "aiding the nation's economic development" to the point of opening its harbors and airfields to civilian use. All navy factories in 1983 manufactured non-military products, accounting for 30% of the total output of these factories; navy planes are used in transporting civilian goods; and even the Huangpu Military Academy in Guangdong has been handed over to Guangzhou city to receive both Chinese and foreign tourists, after having been a military citadel for more than a half century.7/

Weapons improvement has also occurred. In the navy for example, modernization efforts since 1970 have increased the number of missile craft tenfold, from 20 to 200 and conventional submarine forces threefold, from 35 to 100. Professionalization has also been enhanced by the replacement of political study and ideological training in the military academies with courses and annual conferences on science and technology. China's modernization goals probably have also benefited the military. The shift of national attention to coastal and off-shore economic development in the Special Economic Zones and the modernization of port facilities and the shipping infrastructure in coastal cities have enhanced the navy's position and given it greater national attention. One indication of naval expansion was the sailing of an eighteen-ship task force in May 1980 to the vicinity of the Fiji Islands in support of two ICBM test launches from western China. In an otherwise terse summary of military developments for the year, the Chinese Encyclopedia for 1981 yielded a map the size of a half-page indicating the course of this maneuver.8/

Offsetting these modernization efforts is China's large store of antiquated weaponry. Numerically its offensive weapons are impressive, consisting of 5,000 aircraft and 1,500 military ships, considerably more than those of the Soviet Union or the United States. China's aircraft includes a large number of World War II planes, while the naval vessels include many small craft no larger than junk size. The contribution of this large number of small and old weapons to China's strategic capability is doubtful. China continues to produce its versions of the MIG-19 and the MIG-21 and is exporting aircraft to Bangladesh, Iraq and Pakistan, in search of foreign currencies.9/ However, according to Richard Gillespie, its air and naval strength is weakened by "antique weaponry," naval aviation "ill-equipped" to carry out extended sea missions, and its minesweeping capability is "badly out of date." The army is also weakened by a lack of mobility, logistical problems and shortages in armor and air defense. Faced with such problems, the one million PLA soldiers stationed on the Sino-Soviet border are tied down by half the number of Russian troops backed up by five times the number of tanks and armored personnel carriers.10/ The inclination to quantify, with disregard to quality or performance, may typify military bureaucracies generally. It is a tendency found among centrally planned economies like China.

How China will solve the major conflict between "guns and butter" is not clear. Before 1979, the military ranked third among the "four modernizations," behind agriculture and industry, but ahead of science and technology. Since 1979, however, the military has been placed fourth, and within the services, the airforce has been at the bottom. The combination of useless weapons and a declining status may lie behind the International Institute's characterization of the Chinese airforce as "inhibited by a shortage of aviation spirit" and the navy as an "ineffective offensive force except for inshore defense."11/ China's military authority is also weakened by continuing conflicts between central and regional commanders. Old officers--whom Deng chided, "If war should break out, would you be able to stay awake for three days and nights at a stretch,"--hang on to their positions, while "leftism" within the military continues to breed ideological opposition.12/

NUCLEAR AND SPACE PROGRAMS

Nuclear weapons, delivery systems and space programs may have a greater bearing on China's strategic role than the size and quality of its armed forces. China's nuclear capability is believed to amount to several hundred fission and fusion weapons, placing it third in the world. Its delivery systems in 1984, according to one estimate, included fifty MRBMs, sixty IRBMs and four ICBMs, while the first SLBM is now being trial tested.13/ Chinese space research, spurred by the "star wars" programs of the United States and Soviet Union, has received preferred attention in the last two years. China has already placed fourteen satellites into orbit and possesses an extensive capacity in spacecraft technology and remote sensing exploration. By utilizing Russian and American knowledge and experience, China may attempt to take the quantum leap from unmanned space instrument testing to the launching of a reuseable space vehicle. China's strategic capabilities in these three areas may put it ahead of other nations such as England, France, Japan and India, but it still remains far behind the two superpowers.

Another indicator of nuclear strength, which can be measured more precisely by using seismological techniques, is China's relatively low number of nuclear tests. The number of tests conducted between 1964, when China's first nuclear explosion was conducted, and 1980 is variously put between 21 and 26, less than Britain, a third that of France, and less than 6% that of the Soviet Union and 3% of the United States. Two nuclear tests were recorded in 1984. China's nuclear arsenal and delivery system give it a world status that such a capability alone can confer. It also has the impressive scientific expertise to expand these capabilities. But the size of China's nuclear programs is small when compared to that of the superpowers.14/

DECLINING DEFENSE BUDGETS

Perhaps the most telling indicator of China's departure from the model of the superpowers is the decline of its defense budgets since the late 1970s. Because China's defense budgets, like those of other socialist economies, typically exclude pay and allowances for troops, and research and development costs, actual outlays for defense are underreported and are not comparable to budget figures in the West. Nevertheless, published figures since 1981 are useful as indicators of proportion and of annual increases or decreases. It is possible that production of military goods has increased as a result of improvements in economic productivity, but if that is the case, China is not using this "slack" to increase military expenditures as other nations are doing. As Table 1 shows, the decline between 1979 and 1982 is marked not only in aggregate expenses for defense (more than 30%), but also in military expenses in per capita terms which show an even greater decline, and also as a percentage of the GNP, which is by far the largest decline of any major power. Even Japan has shown an increase in all three categories, to the point where total defense expenditures in 1982, in U.S. dollars, were higher than those reported by China. The nation with the largest increase that can be measured is in fact the United States, where per capita defense expenses have increased more than 50%. Figures for China's defense outlays for 1983 and 1984 show a continuing decline in real terms, dropping to U.S. $9 billion for both years. These figures also represent a percentage decline in the national budget of 15.8% and 13.1% respectively from the previous years. The defense budget in 1977 was, in fact, only U.S. $8 billion, although it represented that year 17.7% of the national budget.15/

Beyond differences in accounting practices, Chinese published figures for defense are not strictly comparable because they are compiled on the basis of exchange rates pegged on the U.S. dollar, rates which are constantly fluctuating. Moreover, because unit costs in military pay and support for an individual soldier in China are much less than in the United States, a larger army can be maintained at a relatively smaller cost. Nevertheless, the published figures do reinforce the image of China's relative military weakness, in actual outlays of money and more importantly in its declining budgets in all categories. If China were interested in becoming a superpower, or even in increasing its military role in the Pacific region, one might expect a rise rather than a decline in military expenses.

TABLE 1
COMPARATIVE DEFENSE EXPENDITURES, MILITARY EXPENSES PER CAPITA AND AS PERCENTAGE OF GNP, 1979 AND 1982

Country	Defense Expense (bil US$) 1979	1982	Per Capita (US $) 1979	1982	Percentage of GNP 1979	1982
China	14,598	9,464	15	9	6.8	4.2
U.S.A.	122,179	196,345	543	846	5.1	6.5
Japan	9,230	10,361	79	87	.9	1.0
Taiwan	3,197	3,556	183	193	7.9	7.8
France	22,668	22,522	424	415	3.9	4.2

Source: International Institute for Strategic Studies, London, 1984 pp. 140-141. Because the declared Soviet defense budget excludes a number of key elements such as military Research & Development, stockpiling, and civil defense, and because Soviet pricing practices are very different from those in the West, no simple figures can be given for Soviet defense outlays. Official figures of 17.05 bil. rubles for 1983 and 1984 equals about 4.8% of total government expenditures for 1983, 4.66% of that for 1984. Some Western estimates of the burden of military expenditures on the GNP range from between 10 and 20%.

MILITARY ALLIANCES

China's strategic role in the Pacific Region is further hampered by the lack of military alliances with any major power and by geopolitical vulnerability. In a day of modern warfare when sea and air lanes are the decisive geopolitical factors, China's large land area does not provide any significant strategic advantage. China's populated areas are protected by few natural frontiers, and its present land boundaries have been defined largely by Western colonial powers since the 19th century--to China's disadvantage. The population of much of the Chinese frontier by minority groups, who historically have mistrusted the Chinese, ties up much of China's military manpower in essentially defensive operations. China, according to John Copper, has "more nations on its border, more insecure frontiers and more controversies with neighboring states than any other large or small power."16/ China's besieged view of itself is borne out by a look at the map which reminds us not only of strategic vulnerability but also of boundaries shaped over the last 100 plus years by outside powers: The 880 mile boundary with North Korea (Japan, 1895 and 1910); the separation of Taiwan from the mainland (Japan, 1895, and the United States, 1950); Hong Kong (Britain, 1842, 1860, 1898); the 2,260 mile boundary with India, Bhutan, Nepal and Sikkim (Britain 1914); and the 4,150 mile boundary with the Soviet Union along Sinkiang Province and the Amur and Sungari Rivers (Russia, 1858, 1860 and 1864).

China also stands quite alone in military alliances. By contrast, both superpowers have extensive and broadly based alliances, giving to each a much larger strategic role in the world to play than their individual military size would suggest: the United States with NATO, and the Soviet Union with the Warsaw Pact countries. China has no such counterpart. In fact, China's alliances within the Pacific Region--its own backyard--are fewer than those of either the Soviet Union or the United States. China has a mutual defense agreement with North Korea dating from 1961, and friendship and non-aggression pacts with Afghanistan, Burma, Nepal (1960) and close military links with the Khmer Rouge faction in Kampuchea. But China's treaties with other countries are largely diplomatic arrangements with little strategic significance.

In sharp contrast, the United States has mutual cooperation and security treaties with Japan (1960), the Philippines (1951) and South Korea (1954). The United States also has military cooperation agreements with Australia and Thailand and continues to supply Taiwan with military arms under the 1979 Taiwan Relations Act. The Soviet Union has treaties of friendship, cooperation, and mutual assistance with Afghanistan (1978), India (1971), Mongolia (1966), North Korea (1961) and Vietnam (1978). The two superpowers occupy large military bases in the Pacific Region: the United States notably in Japan, South Korea and the Philippines, and the Soviet Union in Vietnam, with an air base in Danang and a naval base in Cam Ranh Bay. China has no military base outside of its own borders.18/

In sum, when the size, quality and trends within the Chinese military establishment are compared to those of the United States and of the Soviet Union, attempts to label China as a superpower can hardly be justified. Furthermore, when China's nuclear capabilities are examined more closely, assigning to China the label strategic power--that is the ability to destroy or cripple another major power or to deliver a second-strike, if attacked first, with nuclear weapons--is also hard to justify. Further complicating China's global and strategic role is the high degree of geopolitical vulnerability and diplomatic isolation that it feels and which explains, in part, its general defensiveness. Such vulnerability would seem to justify a greater military effort to guarantee national security than is now apparent. These observations lend evidence to Chinese claims that it does not wish to be a superpower and wishes to pursue an independent foreign policy. China's claims to have no hegemonic designs in the Pacific region are another issue.

THE ECONOMIC ROLE

China's influence in the Pacific Basin is affected by its expanding role in world trade, both as a supplier of goods and as a market. The degree and kinds of economic influence China can have in the region are questions that require some appreciation for the peculiar qualities of China's economic and demographic base.

By itself, China's GNP in the mid 1980s shows an impressive sixfold increase in size over the quarter century before. Compared to many other developing countries, China's average annual rate of growth of between 5 and 6% over the same years is an impressive accomplishment. Higher rates of growth in recent years, as high as 10%, and rates of 7 to 8% projected for China for the rest of the century, give China a potential power as a supplier and consumer of goods on the world market that is comparable to that of major European countries although still considerably less than that of Japan.

In per capita terms, of course, China today remains a poor country, largely because of the rapid increase in the size of its population over the same years, and static and even declining rates in productivity growth. Compared to other Asian countries, per capita income in China for 1984, stated variously as $260 or $500, was still a small fraction of South Korea's, reported as $1,600, and smaller yet than Taiwan's, reported as $2,483.19/ China's two-way trade with all countries in 1984 was $52.5 billion, representing an increase of 10 billion dollars over 1983. Compared to the previous 10 years, the 1984 figures show a large increase in China's role in world trade. Both the size of the amount and the increases are larger than the two-way Soviet and East European trade with the rest of the world. Still, when compared to other Asian countries, China's regional influence is small in aggregate terms and miniscule in per capita terms. Taiwan's total two-way trade for 1984 was about the same as China's; South Korea's was seven billion dollars more, while that of Japan was almost six times that of China.20/

One unique development in Chinese trade patterns is the informal or re-export trade with Taiwan and South Korea. It is a trade handled largely through Hong Kong and for each country amounted to approximately a half billion dollars in 1984 and nearly doubling that amount in 1985.21/ As a result of this informal trade, the ideological and political barriers that for decades divided this part of the Pacific Rim have begun to weaken. China's growing trade with the ASEAN countries is a separate question. The compliment between China's growing trade with the advanced industrial countries of Japan, North America and Europe is relatively smooth, but China's growing trade with the Asian NICs and the ASEAN countries may generate a competition not welcome by either side. Increased Chinese exports in the region may threaten specific markets dominated by specific countries: Singapore in its role as entrepot; Thailand, with its food-export markets; and other ASEAN countries with their light-manufacturing exports. Offsetting this potential threat is the lure of an expanded Chinese consumer market for Asian NIC and ASEAN exports produced where they have natural resource and skill advantages.22/ Under optimum conditions, China's trade volume by the end of the century can be expected to surpass that of all its Asian neighbors, except for Japan, but its overall economic influence in the region is likely to remain limited for many years.23/

Another factor affecting China's economic influence in the region is the composition of its workforce. Unlike Japan and the Asian NICs, the Chinese workforce remains largely agricultural, as high as 70%. Because of China's unique industrialization efforts, known generally as rural-small-scale industry and more recently as the rural and township enterprises, the rural domination of China's work force can easily obscure the progress China has made in industrialization. It is a pattern quite different from the more familiar one of the vast rural to urban migrations of other countries. Definite strides have been made in rural mechanization, as an estimated 70% of the rice crop is now planted by machine in some regions in China. As a whole, however, the rural economy remains heavily labor intensive.

Labor force patterns are related to China's strategic position in the region. Rural decentralization, the conscious policy of Mao Zedong, may still today provide China with a strategic advantage that allows it to flaunt threats and possible blackmail by any superpower. Moreover, except for the Soviet Union, China has one of the lowest percentages, 6%, of the urban population residing within its largest city, Shanghai. China's advantage in this regard stands in noticeable contrast to other countries such as South Korea, Mexico and even Indonesia, where the vortices of political and economic power make them vulnerable to sabotage or attack. The government's success in preventing greater rural to urban migration has also provided a remarkable degree of stability to China in the midst of rapid social and economic change.

China's potential as a market should also enhance its global and regional influence. Poor as China is, in per capita terms, especially in the rural areas, pockets of wealth are to be found. Many rural families have been able to accumulate considerable wealth, as reflected in recent years in the widespread housing boom, providing them with housing considerably better than that of their urban cousins, not only in China's large cities but also elsewhere in other countries of the Western Pacific. Some rural areas, notably in south and south central China, have also become major markets in recent years for the purchase of consumer goods from Japan and the Asian NICs. However dominant its rural orientation is, China has a very large urban population, put variously at two or three hundred million people, depending on how urban is defined. China can claim 78 cities with a population over 500,000, more than either the United States or the Soviet Union, and eight times that of Japan.24/ Differing definitions of urban dwellers and cities make simple cross-country comparisons suggestive at best. An urban dweller in Hangzhou, for example, may have only a fraction of the buying power of an urban dweller in Seoul or Taipei. As a potential world market, China's expanding influence as a market for other countries should continue to increase as middle-class values continue to spread, as its access to the world markets increases, and as consumer levels and expectations continue to rise. In assessing that increase, of course, China's influence must always be measured against the moving targets of other countries in the region.

EDUCATION

The idea that education plays a major role in creating national strength is commonly accepted and is particularly relevant to this discussion of China. For almost 80 years, since the abolition of the examination system of the imperial period, Chinese leaders of varying political persuasions have endorsed popular education. Education has been viewed both as a necessary component for creating national unity and for increasing economic production. During the Cultural Revolution of the 1960s and 1970s, Mao's fury against "liberal" or "capitalist-revisionist" education almost crippled the formal educational system, especially higher education. Since his death in 1976, the policy of regarding education as an economically productive force is once again firmly in place, as it was in the 1950s, while science and technology, now freed from political constraints, have become something of a cliche.

Despite these encouraging developments, when one looks at education in China today as a clue to national strength and economic power, one finds the size of the educational establishment to be frightfully low. Tertiary education in China, that is enrollments in higher education expressed as a percentage of the population between the ages of 20 to 24, is only 1%--among the lowest in the world. The Chinese leadership in the 1950s made great strides in increasing the numbers of higher education institutions and students enrolled therein, but these figures plummeted in the late 1950s, following the Anti-Rightist Campaign. Throughout the Cultural Revolution, however, science and technology, and even more, the social sciences and the humanities, were smothered in politics, resulting in devastating and perhaps irreparable damage to the system as a whole. Since the late 1970s, great attention has been placed on expanding higher education, but even the most optimistic projections of college level enrollments only will raise the tertiary education ratio to 2%, at best 3% by 1990. This rise and fall in the levels of higher education in China is presented in Figure 1. The secondary education ratio is much better, 44%, but still low when compared to other nations in the Pacific region. Literacy rates are hard to define and are variously put around 60% for China.

The correlations between education and economic development must be considered with care. Increased educational levels do not necessarily correlate with direct increases in economic development. The Philippines, for example, has a tertiary education rate of 26%, much higher than that of all of the Newly Industrialized Countries and almost as high as that of Japan, and yet it faces huge economic difficulties.25/ China indeed has experienced impressive economic growth, despite its low education ratios. In a relatively stable environment, nonetheless, strengths in science, technology and expanded research and development generally correlate with an improved performance over time.

Science and technology in China are now given preferred attention through increased spending on polytechnic universities and engineering schools, the introduction of science and technology curricula in military institutions, and the dominance of science and technology concentrations among the Chinese students studying abroad.26/ Public expenditures on education, as a percentage of the state budget have increased from a low of 4.24% in 1970 to 6.05% in 1979 to 10.03% in 1982. Furthermore, for the first time since 1949, educators feel politically secure enough to speak out against competing interests in heavy industry and other ministries in the central government.

Qualifications to these positive developments must be made. The current national commitment, as reflected in the national budget, is still far below the 15% of countries with whom the Chinese like to compare themselves. Also disturbing is the low level of productivity of higher educational institutions with extremely low faculty student ratios, in some institutions still as low as 3 to 1. Finally, in the effort to achieve major breakthroughs in science and technology, disproportionate amounts of state funds have been given to higher education at the expense of primary education. The ratio between them has been put as high as 75 to 1, compared to a ratio of 4 or 5 to 1 as the average for developed countries. Educators at the primary and secondary levels have expressed the fear that China's present system of education may produce a large gap between the masses and the elite; a concern that continually preyed on Mao Zedong's mind, but which has received minimal attention since the late 1970s.27/

In short, despite encouraging results in education, large questions remain. To what extent will the bureaucratism and the cynicism from the days when politics were in command continue to hamper national programs in science and technology? Are current efforts sufficiently strong to allow China to catch up with the moving targets of rival countries? As a continual reminder of the lag in China's education system, Taiwan, with one-fiftieth of China's population, has one-third as many college-level enrollees.

CHINA AND THE COLD WAR

One of the most remarkable developments over the last two decades has been the shifts of alignments of power in

Figure 1
The Development of Higher Education in China,
Trends and Projections, 1950 to 1990

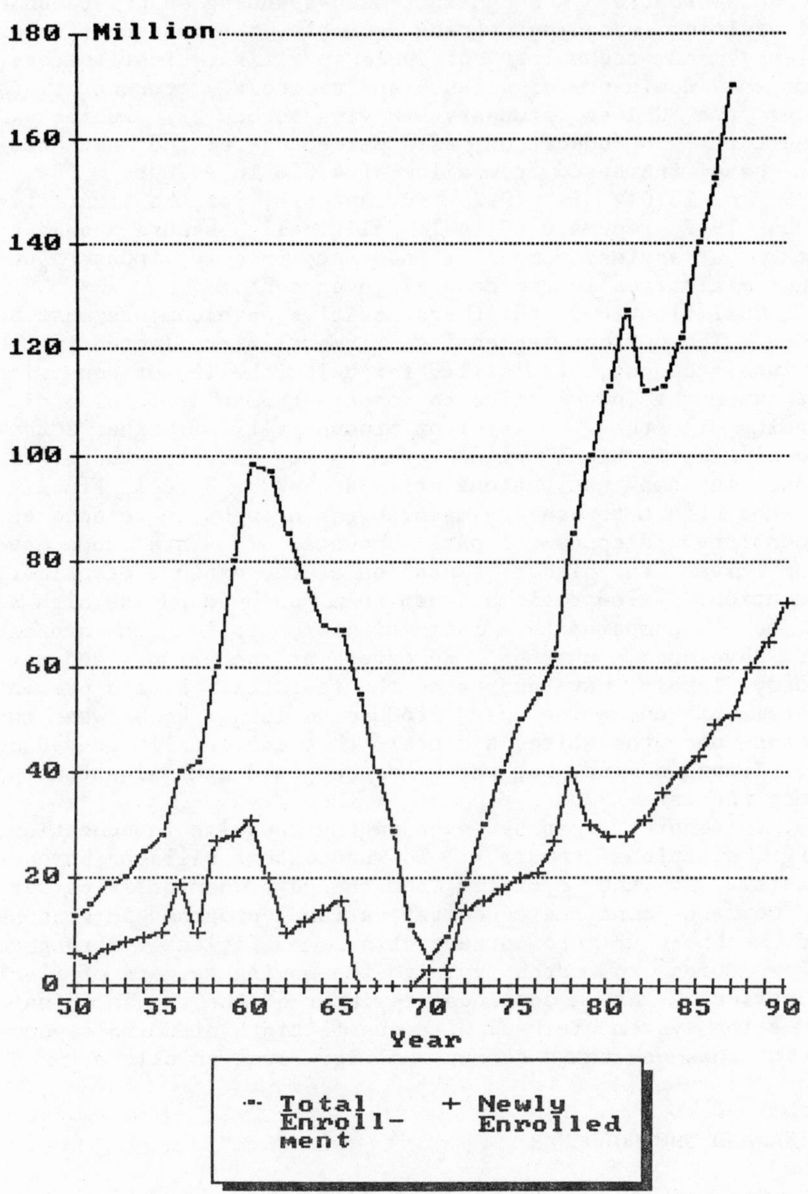

Source: Chinese Encyclopedia, 1981.

the Pacific Basin. The continued tendency to grant China the status of a superpower may be linked to the key role China has played in signaling these shifts: China is no longer an ally of the Soviet Union; it is now a friend of the United States. Its role on the Indochina peninsula is reversed from that of the early days of the Vietnam War. Its relations with the ASEAN countries are far different from the 1960s. And, economic goals are beginning to supercede ideological goals, as can be seen most clearly in its relations with Hong Kong, Taiwan and South Korea. The outcome of these complex political and diplomatic alignments is difficult to predict.28/ This paper will focus on one aspect of these shifts, that is China's role in the Cold War. This discussion bears more on American relations with China than European, but it anticipates the later discussion of Western perceptions of China in general.

Prevailing Western views from the 1950s to the 1970s portrayed China as a destabilizing and hostile force to the international order. The swift military takeover by the Communists in 1949 established a new political order which, in a few decisive moves, brought to an end almost all expressions of Western and Japanese humiliation that had become the hallmark of China's modern experience with the outside world. Violence also characterized the social revolutions taking place in the family, villages, towns and cities. The Korean War confirmed, in American minds at least, China's image as a hostile force. And the aggressive label given by the United Nations General Assembly to China for its behavior in the Korean War in the spring of 1951 became the cornerstone for official American thinking about China for over two decades. China's diplomatic behavior in the early years of the Cultural Revolution confirmed in the popular mind the image of China's threatening role. Until recently, the Cultural Revolution has also marked in Western minds this pattern of defiant behavior.

China's stance against a world order it saw then as hostile to its own was an extension of the revolutionary experience of the Communist rise to power and the ideology and politics of its ally, the Soviet Union. From another perspective, however, China's defiance contributed to stability in the region because the consolidation of revolutionary power produced a degree of political unity that had eluded China for half a century. The Communist Revolution finally brought both civil strife and foreign aggression to an end.

Postwar instability in the 1950s, however related to the Communist Revolution, may be seen as part of the struggle to create a new order in the wake of Japan's defeat. As an extension of its occupation of Japan or its commitments to the governments in South Korea, Taiwan and Vietnam, the American military presence from the late 1940s into the mid-1970s, in Chinese eyes at least, was for many years the major contributor to political instability in the Pacific region.

Despite a decade now of political stability and of a conservative political profile, images of revolutionary defiance still linger and may explain the difficulty China has had in attracting foreign investments from the West. Although the number of foreign investments has increased from 20 in 1980 to 1,300 in 1985, Japan's, the United States', and Western Europe's combined share of investments has declined from a high of 32% in 1981 to 14% in 1984. The common cultural bond with China may explain Hong Kong's expanded share in foreign investments, from 55% in 1980 to 82% in 1984. The cultural bond may help overcome the barriers of bureaucratism and legal uncertainties that heighten political risk.29/ An unacceptable risk in one culture may be quite acceptable in another.

To return to outside images of China's political instability, an attempt by one side to establish order in that area of the world can easily be perceived as a force for disorder in the eyes of another. In similar ways, though from opposite ends, the Cold War in Europe was projected by Americans and Chinese onto the Pacific Basin from the 1950s to the 1970s. In the hothouses of McCarthyism in the United States and Resist America Aid to Korea Campaigns in China in the early 1950s this extraction onto the Asian scene created some expressions of hostility greater than the European original. For more than 20 years the U.S. government barred American companies and their foreign subsidiaries from all trading activities with the PRC, with the objective of inhibiting China's economic and political development and of contributing, possibly, to the downfall of the Chinese government. China responded in kind. The American embargo on China was more severe than American restrictions on trade with the Soviet Union and Eastern Europe at the time.30/

Two developments largely altered China's role in the Asian Cold War. The first was the Sino-Soviet dispute which by the mid-1960s began to overshadow China's conflict with the United States. The other was growing pressure from American businesses to drop the embargo and through diplomatic recognition open up trade relations within

China. At the time that these shifts were occurring, the outcome was not at all certain. On the eve of the gradual lifting of the embargo--July 1969, when Americans were allowed to purchase $100 of Chinese goods for personal use--Richard Nixon would define the American role in Asia as the "dynamic detoxification" of the "poison from the thoughts of Mao" and compare China with the "explosive ghetto elements in our own country" where "aggression has to be restrained."31/ In February 1972 President Nixon was in China, posing with Mao. These twin forces offered the prospects of rapprochement that would soften the bitter legacies of both the Korean and Vietnam Wars, the stranglehold of the Cultural Revolution on Chinese society and politics, and the impasse over Taiwan.

China's political impact on the Pacific region at this watershed in Sino-American relations is as hard to assess as the impact of Richard Nixon's initiatives, and the American political role in general. To continue to suggest that political instability in the Pacific region rests more with China than with other powers in the region risks being little more than unreflectively ethnocentric. It could be argued that arms sales alone contribute as much to global and regional instability as any other particular policy, domestic or foreign. For example, between 1966 and 1973, the period of China's greatest political instability in the world, its total arms exports in constant 1972 dollars were reported to be U.S. $1.78 million. American world arms exports in the same years were U.S. $33.21 million; Soviet sales were U.S. $19.4 million, and French sales were U.S. $2.77 million.32/ Although China's arms exports today have increased, the instability generated by these sales is likely much smaller than those of the Soviet Union or the United States.

Since China's admission to the United Nations, its behavior has become more predictable and conservative. When asked about China's political stability by a group of American professors in 1983, Deng Xiaoping bristled: "The United States brags about its political system, but the [American] President says one thing during the election; something else when he takes office; something else at midterm; and something else when he leaves. The Americans say our policies are unstable, but compared to theirs, ours are much more stable."33/ Deng's comments are a reminder that assessments of political stability, like the question of strategic significance are very much in the eye of the beholder.

IMAGES

If China's military power is not that of a superpower and if its economic base, its trade volume and its programs in science and technology, even under the most optimistic projections, remain far behind the moving targets of other powers in the Pacific, why is its influence still so large? One clue to the question is China's ability to inspire awe and fear. This power is linked to China's own sense of historical greatness, even when it has been politically and militarily weak, and to the willingness of outsiders to believe in that greatness. Outside awe of China differs from nation to nation, and it may be interrupted periodically by attitudes of contempt, especially in the modern West. Whatever the twists and turns in outside images, China's ability to inspire awe and fear remains strong today.

At mid-century China was a "sleeping giant" that had awakened and dared to call the mightiest power in the world then a "paper tiger." The tiger image was a favorite of Mao's. Outsiders came to know it best in 1946 when he discussed the United States with Anna Louise Strong and dismissed "all reactionaries" as "paper tigers." Tiger images are complex and contradictory. There are "real" tigers as well as "paper" tigers, and they can change from one into the other. From a "strategic point of view" enemies, in Mao's words, were "paper tigers," but in "tactical thinking" they were "real tigers which can devour people."34/ The tiger's confidence can be expressed as contempt for the mighty. Again, quoting Mao: "We must do as Mencius says: when speaking to the mighty, look on them with contempt."35/

To continue the tiger image, Mao attacked the "bureaucratic arrogance" of cadres who thought they were tigers and to whom he asked, "Do you think that nobody will really dare to touch the arse of tigers like you? They damn well will!" China, in Mao's earthy touch, was often like a tiger, arrogant in its historical greatness and yet weak and vulnerable like a paper tiger. In January 1958, in launching the Great Leap Forward, he said: "We say that our country has such an enormous population, it has such a vast territory, abundant resources, so many people, 4,000 years of history and culture...We have bragged so much about this, yet we cannot compare with a country like Belgium."36/ Even in weakness, internal struggle and self-criticism, Mao and the Chinese people were able to project confidence and inspire respect.

LEGACIES

The outsiders' widespread awe of China began with the Mediterranean travellers of Marco Polo's day. They had visited Persia and India, but they reserved their superlatives of description for China. Writing about China as he did, Marco Polo faced a credibility problem, but Europe eventually became convinced of the "populous and magnificent" reality of Cathay.37/ Within two centuries the printing of books facilitated the spread of Marco Polo's awe of China to all of Europe.

European awe of China reached a peak in the Enlightenment. Jesuit missionaries, beginning two centuries earlier, focused the energies of the Counter Reformation onto East Asia. Encouraged by successes in winning converts in the highest circles in East Asia, they wrote reports back to Europe as enthusiastic as Marco Polo's account, but in greater detail. European readers of these reports were impressed with the "immense vigor and fertility" of Chinese culture, in contrast to the "immobility and imperviousness" of European culture at the time.38/ Size of population alone was a major factor, with 150 million in China at the founding of the Qing dynasty (1644-1912), compared at the time to less than 20 million in France and 10 million in England and Wales. China's huge populace was ruled under one emperor and a uniform code of behavior. European awe of China was so powerful that it obscured critical assessments of the corruption and chaos at the end of the Ming dynasty and the brutality of the Qing consolidation of power in the 17th century. Later expressions of awe would blot out other weaknesses and tragedies in China. By the 18th century many Enlightenment thinkers had come to look upon China with admiration as a model of morality, social relations, and politics. Voltaire, for one--and there were many others-- asserted that the Chinese "empire is in truth the best that the world has ever seen."39/

With the onset of the Industrial Revolution, the pervasive Western awe of China gradually gave way to expressions of contempt. Protestant missionaries, and those from Catholic orders as well, came to mirror little of the Enlightenment's admiration and saw China as backward and "heathen," reflecting perhaps a greater change in the West than in China. Marx supplied a secular version of this contempt in his endorsement of 19th century European imperialism in Asia, through its shattering of traditional social and religious structures and through its attack on the "subjugation of man to external circumstances instead of elevating man to be the sovereign of circumstances." As the father of "progressive ideology"--to anticipate Solzhenitzyn's contempt for China--Marx scorned the Asians' "brutalizing worship of nature," and he saw the passing of the traditional order as the necessary condition for revolutions in Asia.40/

Soon after the turn of the 19th century, Chinese leaders themselves, responsive to the contempt of religious and secular voices in the West, began to scorn their own past. China's feeble struggle against Japan in the Pacific War strengthened the self-contempt and outsiders' contempt as well. The Guomindang's ineffectual war efforts that infuriated General Joseph Stillwell in the early 1940s would become an "enormous practical joke" to the Chinese people.41/

Even in its most inglorious moments of disorder in the first decades of this century, the awe-ful legacy of China would not completely give way. Tolstoy criticized China, not for its weakness but for its nationalism. Bertrand Russell exhorted Chinese youth in the 1920s to avoid the mistakes of Western industrialization and not to turn their backs on tradition. G. F. Hudson closed his study of European relations with China, published in 1931, with a warning against the "instruments of suffering and death" of modern science and with an appeal to the "principle to which the Chinese have held more steadfastly than any other people, the principle that the study and understanding of social man should be the premier subject of education and the indispensable preparation for political responsibility?"42/

China's borrowed contempt was not indiscriminate. Drawing upon the sensibilities of the "little tradition," nationalist leaders fused mass energies with mass anger and launched a mighty revolution, described thus in Mao's words: "To destroy the rule of imperialism, feudalism and bureaucrat-capitalism in China took the Chinese people more than a hundred years and cost them tens of millions of lives before the victory in 1949. Look! Were these not living tigers, iron tigers, real tigers? But in the end they changed into paper tigers, dead tigers, bean-curd tigers. These are historical facts."43/ The giant tiger of China in this half century admits to both the awe of the Enlightenment and the contempt of Marx, but fused with the power of the masses, it has impressed outsiders who still grope for ways to explain its influence.

Bluff, in part, but not all bluff. The rollback of American troops in North Korea in the winter of 1950, the ability in the first five-year plan to unify China and build a solid industrial base, standing up to the Soviet Union with defiance, Chinese guerilla tactics and back-up in Vietnam, defeating American troops equipped and protected with the best arms that money could buy--all these, as Mao would say, are "historical facts." The tiger was real. American awe, then contempt, then bewilderment, quickly changed to fear. In frustrated anger, Americans turned on themselves over the question, "Who lost China?" The Korean War confirmed the reversals of American images. In early 1951, 64% of a national poll indicated a "favorable impression" of the Chinese, only 21% unfavorable. This was a legacy of missionary stories and Pearl Buck at first glance, but at a deeper level, legacies too of Marco Polo and the Enlightenment. By 1955, in an identical poll, "favorable images" dropped to 45%, while "unfavorable" ones rose to 40%. American image-makers in the 1950s candidly admitted: "Before the Korean War, I think most Americans thought of the Chinese as a kindly people. Now there is an association of cruelty."44/

Many outside were also angry at China's "conquest" of Tibet, at its support of revolutionary movements in Southeast Asia, and even at its overkill response to Vietnam in 1979. These military actions confirmed images that China had limited respect for its neighbors. Struggle and violence against the "individual" inside China confirmed images of struggle and violence against the "free world" outside. Cold War images died hard. If China was not a superpower, the fear still was that she might behave irresponsibly and aggressively. Joining the outsiders' awe of the past and her awesome abilities to unify the inside and defy the outside today, China leads uncritical and unreflective outsiders to grant her more power and influence than she may really have.

Perhaps the most surprising twist among Cold War legacies today and one which offsets Washington's rapprochement with Beijing is the great fear of China in the Soviet Union today. The Chinese tiger in Russian eyes is real, but the tiger's bluff, either as ideology, conscious contempt, or unconscious history, appears to be the more powerful. The keen articulation of Russian fear is not confined to official statements. It can also be found in the passionate words of Russian writers in the 1970s, words that create a surprisingly powerful image of fear.

The fears of the Russian writers are directed at the size of China's population and spring from a conviction that China's leaders have both succumbed to and succeeded to the "disease" of communist ideology. Andrei Amalrik's pessimistic essay, "Will the Soviet Union Survive Until 1984?" (1969) predicted a war with China would break out between 1975 and 1980 and begin the demise of the Soviet regime. His images of China were: "Eternal expansionism," "rise of a fearsome 'revolutionary curve,'" and "colossal superiority in numbers." The advantages that Russian soldiers held in the past were "toughness, endurance, and an undemanding nature," qualities that have gradually given way to the weaker forces of Russian "civilization." To Russia's disadvantage, those qualities are still in abundance in China.

Amalrik believed the United States would side with Russia in a war with China because they "are white and the Chinese are yellow," but he was convinced that in the end China would win the "guerilla war." Amalrik saw the Chinese "villages" and the "villages" of the underdeveloped world encircling the "cities" of Russia and the developed world. Most threatening was the "village" of the subconscious, characterized by "organization and unity," overpowering the "city" with "ever greater isolation of the individual." This development "gladdens the heart of Mao Tse-tung, but the inhabitants of the world's cities...have reason to worry about their future."45/

Alexander Solzhenitsyn was no less fearful of China. In his "Letter to the Soviet Leaders" (1974) he saw the "West on its knees" and war in China as inevitable. That war was "bound to cost us 60 million souls at the very least, and as always in wars, they will be the best souls." In that war the "very last root will be exterminated," bringing to a climax the annhilation of the Russian people which began in the 17th century with the extermination of the Old Believers. Solzhenitsyn appealed to the Russian leaders to give up their ideology, the communism--as Stalin did during World War II--and "let the Chinese leaders glory in it for a while...Let them grunt and heave and instruct humanity, and foot all the bills for their absurd economics, and let them support terrorists and guerillas in the southern hemisphere, if they like."46/ These fears have been muted somewhat with Mao's death and the end of the Cultural Revolution, but little if any serious attempt has been made in the subsequent decade to offer a set of counter-images.

Given the military balance in the world today, it is hard to see how Russian writers today could write so fearfully. The explanation must rest with deep feelings and perceptions which center on the plunder of the West by the

Mongols in the 13th century. Hordes, whose root word is the Mongol "ordos," and the "colossal superiority in numbers" of Chinese soldiers mobilized in guerilla warfare overshadow the judgment of a more detached assessment. Spared for the most part from this plunder, Western Europe in the same period was introduced to the opposite imagery of Marco Polo. The legacies of 13th century China to the West are indeed complex. Awe can be respect, or it can be fear.

A fear of China also pervades the Pacific region. It is most keenly felt in Vietnam, whose conflicts with China go back for centuries. ASEAN nations are also highly fearful and grant to China a strategic role in the Pacific region that is greater than military and economic factors alone would suggest. The fear in the ASEAN case is a combination of anxieties about the role of the Overseas Chinese in these countries, of lingering revolutionary ideology that threatens the market orientation of these countries, and of China as an earlier model for Vietnamese behavior in the Indochina Peninsula. ASEAN countries and China converge in their support for the Khmer Rouge in Kampuchea, but that common ground is small. South Korea's fear of China is well-known, although it has been blunted by the covert trade with China and new economic cooperation and cultural exchanges between the two countries. Whether North Korea has a fear of China which might, like South Korea's, rest on China's historic and sometimes brutal dominance of Korea, is not implausible.

Of all the Asian countries, Hong Kong has the greatest reason to fear China, and yet recent agreements between London and Beijing over the future of Hong Kong have allayed those fears somewhat.47/ Taiwan's fears are also highly understandable, but the problem of reunification with the mainland, although by no means clear, has been softened by informal contacts and by both sides pursuing common goals through covert trade. In Northeast Asia, Japan may be the least fearful. When fear is discussed in Sino-Japanese relations, it is typically Chinese fear of Japan, based on the brutal experiences of the Pacific War.

To all neighboring nations, the Chinese tiger inspires some degree of fear, but the tiger's bluff is perceived through historical and cultural lenses very different from the West. Trade and technology transfers may have softened it in recent years, but the fear remains, despite China's eagerness to join the Pacific Basin community, its relatively weak offensive capabilities, and declining outlays for defense.

As a fillip to the awe Westerners have had towards China, a recent survey showed China ranking highest in the perceptions of those nations whose influence in the world is likely to be greater thirty years from now than it is now. The survey was conducted by Gallup International for the International Institute of Geopolitics and a conference it held in May 1984 on the theme "The Challenge of the Pacific: Western Hopes and Fears." An average of 1,000 adults were interviewed in each of ten countries. The results of five of the most highly industrialized among them, Japan, the United States, West Germany, France and Great Britain, were tabulated according to a formula calculated by subtracting the percentage of the total who thought the influence would be less from the percentage of those who thought the influence would be more. Though not a measure of the amount of influence but rather of the increase in influence, the results bear out the point of this paper. Out of a possible raw score of 500, if all interviewees in all five countries were to indicate that a particular country's influence would be greater thirty years hence, China scored 333, the United states 274, Japan 261, the USSR 232, West Germany 162, France 33, and Great Britain -10.48/ China's particular arrangements of power and influence in the Pacific Basin are reinforced by an enduring image by outsiders, more powerful than a more empirical analysis might suggest.

The term "superpower" should be limited to discussions of two countries, the Soviet Union and the United States, whose strategic influence in the Pacific Basin and elsewhere are much larger than China's. This is not to deny that China is capable of inflicting military harm on its Pacific neighbors. Furthermore, although China's economic influence in the region is relatively weak compared to that of Japan and the United States, the potential to increase that power is high. Where China's influence is the highest, however, is in its ability to create the images of power through its historical greatness, its cultural richness, and its huge population "having lived together time out of mind in the same place."49/

NOTES

1. See Steven I. Levine, "China in Asia: The PRC as a Regional Power," and Jonathan D. Pollack, "China and the Global Strategic Balance, " in <u>China's Foreign Relations in the 1980s</u> ed., Harry Harding (New Haven: Yale University Press, 1984) pp. 139 and 169. Another useful reference,

with an extensive bibliography is Samuel Kim, ed., China and the World: Chinese Foreign Policy in the Post-Mao Era (Boulder: Westview Press, 1984).

2. Ibid.

3. John Franklin Copper, China's Global Role, An Analysis of Peking's National Power Capabilities in the Context of an Evolving International System (Stanford: Hoover Institution Press, 1980) p. 7.

4. The Military Balance (London: International Institute for Strategic Studies, 1984), and the Asia 1986 Yearbook (Hong Kong: Far Eastern Economic Review, 1986) p. 21.

5. The Military Balance, pp. 140-141.

6. Ibid.

7. "Navy Seeks to Expand Civilian Endeavors," China Daily, 11 January 1985.

8. One indication of naval expansiveness was the sailing of an 18-ship task force in May 1980 to the vicinity of the Fiji Islands in support of two ICBM test launches from Western China. In an otherwise terse summary of military developments for the year, the Chinese Encyclopedia for 1981 yielded a half-page size map indicating the course of this maneuver. See Bruce Swanson, "China's Emerging Navy," China Business Review (July/August 1984):26, and the Zhongguo baike nianjian, 1981, p. 169.

9. Madelyn C. Ross, "China's Air Defense," The China Business Review (July/August 1984):31-33.

10. Richard E. Gillespie, "China's Ground Forces," The China Business Review (July/August, 1984):36-37.

11. "Navy Seeks to Expand..."

12. Far Eastern Economic Review (hereafter FEER) (February 21, 1985):24-25; and the Asia 1984 Yearbook (Hong Kong: FEER, 1984), pp. 22-23.

13. Bradley Hahn, "China in Space," China Business Review (July-August, 1984):13-16.

14. Asia 1986 Yearbook, p. 16.

15. Asia 1984 Yearbook, p. 22.

16. Copper, China's Global Role..., p. 17.

17. The map referred to was published by Current Scene: Developments in Mainland China and is reproduced in Copper, China's Global Role..., p. 17.

18. Asia 1984 Yearbook, p. 16.

19. World Development Report, 1985 (World Bank) Tables 1, 2 and 3, and the Asia 1986 Yearbook, pp. 6-7.

20. Directions of Trade Statistics Yearbook, 1979-1986 (Washington, D.C.: International Monetary Fund, 1986) pp. 137-139, 241-243, 248-249, 394-395, and the Asia 1986 Yearbook, pp. 8-9.

21. "The Door Opens Wide" FEER (28 February 1985):97.

22. "Threat or Challenge," FEER (28 February 1985): 98-89.

23. Asia 1986 Yearbook, p 16.

24. World Development Report, 1986, pp. 240-241.

25. Stanley Rosen, ed., Chinese Education, Educational Investment in the PRC (Armonk, New York: M.E. Sharp, 1985), p. 3. For a stimulating essay on "scientism" and the politicization of science in china, see Richard Baum, Scientism and Bureaucratism: The Cultural LImits of the Four Modernizations, Lund University Research Studies Discussion Paper Series, no. 145 (1981). Also see World Development Report, 1984, Table 24.

26. Thomas Fingar and Linda A. Reed, An Introduction to Education in the People's Republic of China (Washington, D.C.: Committee on Scholarly Communication with the PRC, 1982) pp. 16-21.

27. Rosen, Chinese Education..., p. 6.

28. Another excellent study of China's global role is Richard H. Solomon, ed., The China Factor: Sino-American Relations and the Global Scene (Englewood Cliffs, N.J.: Prentice-Hall, 1981).

29. China Business Review (May/June 1986):77.

30. A. Kapoor, Foreign Investments in Asia, A Survey of Problems and Prospects in the 1970s (Princeton, N.J.: The Darwin Press, 1972), p. 138.

31. "Asia After Vietnam," Foreign Affairs (October 1967):123.

32. U.S. Arms Control and Disarmament Agency, World, Military Expenditures and Armst Trade, 1963 to 1973, (Washington, D.C., 1975), pp. 85, 90, 115, 119.

33. Louisville Courier Journal, 2 January 1985.

34. Mao's speech on December 1, 1958, is reproduced in Stuart Schram, ed., Quotations From Chairman Mao Tse-tung (New York: Bantam, 1967), pp. 39-40.

35. Stuart Schram, ed., Chairman Mao Talks to the People, Talks and Lectures, 1956-1971 (New York: Random House, 1974) p. 82.

36. Ibid., pp. 14, 33.

37. G. F. Hudson, Europe and China, A Survey of Their Relations from the Earliest Times to 1800 (London: Edward Arnold and Company, 1931), p. 162.

38. Ibid., p. 309.

39. Ibid., pp. 312, 322.

40. Shlomo Avineri, ed., Karl Marx on Colonialism and Modernization (Garden City, N.Y.: Doubleday, 1968), pp. 132-133.

41. Graham Peck, Two Kinds of Time, Life in Provincial China During the Crucial Year, 1940-1947 (Boston, Mass.: Houton Mifflin, Sentry Edition, 1967), p. 99.

42. Hudson, Europe and China, p. 329.

43. Schram, Quotations, p. 40.

44. Harold Isaacs, Scratches on Our Minds (Cambridge, Mass.: MIT Press, 1957), pp. 218-219.

45. Andrei Amalrik, Will the Soviet Union Survive Until 1984? (New York, N.Y.: Harper and Row, 1970, pp. 45-67.

46. Alexandr I. Solzhenitsyn, "Letter to the Soviet Leaders," in East and West (New York, N.Y.: Harper and Row, 1980), pp. 82-91.

47. FEER, (4 October 1984).

48. John K. Fairbank, "The New China and the American Connection," Foreign Affairs (October 1972):31-32.

5

Security in the Pacific Basin: The Role of Japan

Reinhard Drifte

The European neglect of East Asia is the result of several factors: postwar economic retrenchment policies and concentration on rebuilding the European economies; the decolonization movement; and efforts to strengthen European political unity and economic cooperation. In addition, the preoccupation with the East-West conflict in Europe has diverted one's attention away from security problems in East Asia and their far-reaching consequences for global peace. A look at Japan's role in the security of East Asia, from a European perspective must begin with general observations.

Changes in East Asia are now forcing Europeans to adjust their views of this region. Economically, they realize that there is a major shift of attention to the emerging markets and production centers of Japan and the Asian NICs (Taiwan, South Korea, and Hong Kong). This shift is most dramatic in the realization that the United States now trades more with East Asia than with Europe. Western Europe is particularly upset about Japan's trade balance surplus. On the security level, European consciousness of East Asia's importance is less acute. They recognize that China is turning against the Soviet Union, Europe's major adversary, but they are even less capable than the United States of playing the so-called "China card."

Other changes affecting European consciousness of the Pacific Rim are concerned with Japan: its growing understanding of large security issues, especially the Soviet military buildup in the Far East and the arms race on the Korean Peninsula; its realization that economic might must be more nearly matched by political and military might; its ambition to be recognized as more than an economic superpower, and the constant prodding by the United States to do more in the field of military security. Japan now better understands the interdependence of the security of all nations.1/ All these changes have caused the Japanese to devote more efforts to national as well as regional security and render the Japanese-American military alliance more intimate and more effective. This paper will look at Japan's changed perception of East Asia and what new role it might play in security matters in the Pacific Basin.

JAPAN'S CHANGED PERCEPTION OF SECURITY IN THE 1970s

Throughout the 1950s and 1960s and into the 1970s, the United States was willing to shoulder a major part of Japan's external defense without any reciprocal demand for Japanese defense efforts, thus allowing Japan to concentrate on its economic rehabilitation and expansion. Over the first two decades, the Korean war took place close to Japan, but the American intervention was made without asking the Japanese for troops. This long ensuing experience of external peace under American protection, coupled with a feeling of geographical remoteness, fostered a wave of pacifism and a low level of threat perception. The Japanese developed an attitude which assumed that nothing could happen to the country if the nation kept a low international profile and concentrated on economic issues. Such an attitude was also encouraged by Japan's Asian neighbors and even by public opinion in the United States which was, and still is, wary of a strong military power in Japan.

In the 1970s, Japan's perception of its East Asian security environment and the global strategic balance changed dramatically. The new assessment is shared not only by the Self-Defense Forces and the Self-Defense Agency, but also by the Foreign Ministry and a majority of public opinion, even including a growing number of opposition politicians.

Several developments and events account for this change. The oil crisis in 1973 and again in 1979 demonstrated Japan's vulnerability and dependence on global events. In 1975 the United States withdrew from the Indo-China peninsula and limited itself to offshore retrenchment, while the military vacuum was soon filled with Soviet-backed Vietnamese troops. The fall of Saigon increased perceptions, if only briefly, of the danger of a North Korean attack on the South and the reunification of the Korean Peninsula by force. President Carter publicly announced his intention to withdraw all American ground troops from South Korea. Japan began to fear that the United States might withdraw completely from Asia at the same time that the Soviet Union was increasing its military presence in East Asia.

JAPAN AND THE SOVIET UNION

The change in Japan's perception of its security environment is mainly due to the Soviet Union's increased military power and its apparent willingness to use it. The Soviet Union now deploys modernized strategic land and air launched missiles along the Trans-Siberian railway and has turned the Sea of Okhotsk into a sanctuary for strategic submarine forces. The number of Soviet SS-20 launchers now exceeds 160, and it is not clear how many are deployed against Asia. Out of a total 194 Soviet army divisions, about 40 divisions (370,000 men) are reportedly deployed east of Lake Baikal. The vastly increased airforce in East Asia is made up mostly of modern MIG-23, MIG-27 and Sukhov-24, with total operational aircraft numbering about 2,220. Whereas the airforce and the army are deployed primarily against China, except for about 80 long-range Backfire bombers, the Soviet Pacific Fleet is a potential threat to Japan. This fleet includes 90 major surface vessels and 135 submarines. Two out of the three existing Soviet aircraft carriers are deployed in the Pacific. What has particularly annoyed the Japanese is the redeployment of ground troops on three of the disputed islands to the north of Hokkaido which are now occupied by the Soviet Union, and the continuous construction of military installations there since 1978. The invasion of Afghanistan and the shooting of the Korean airliner has further damaged the image of the Soviet Union in Japan.

Political and economic relations between the two countries are at an all time low. Japan has probably become the only country in the world that the Soviet Union, in the recent past, has directly threatened with nuclear annihilation. The Soviets seem especially worried about strengthened Japanese American security cooperation. Soviet propaganda focuses particularly on the deployment of American F-16s at Misawa in northern Honshu and on the cruise missiles on the ships of the U.S. 7th Fleet that uses Japanese harbors. Unfortunately, the Soviet Union does not understand how much its own increased military presence has contributed to these developments.

The key in understanding the framework of the Japanese-Soviet relationship is the strategic connection each has with the United States. The Chinese challenge, against which the Soviet Union devotes considerable military effort, compounds its concerns. It does not see Japan as an independent actor in a multipolar world, but rather as a tool of the American world strategy. This perception is enhanced by the strengthening of the Japanese-American security link and Japan's refusal to comment positively on the Soviet proposal for CBM in the Far East.

Japan's adherence to a bipolar world view finds expression in its conviction that a militarily strong United States is sufficient to guarantee stability and security in East Asia, and that its international diplomacy must be subordinated to that arrangement. In this view, American requests, whether they concern the opening of Japan's domestic market to American imports or increasing Japan's own defense efforts, must be met to some extent if continuous support from the United States is to be safeguarded. This bipolar world view is nolens volens strongly supported by Japanese public opinion, which prefers to leave concrete defense efforts to the Americans. Both Japanese leaders and public opinion consider the United States sufficiently strong and are less alarmed by the Soviet threat than the American public. At the same time, however, Japanese leadership finds it useful to refer to the threat in order to raise the public's defense consciousness.

The issue of the SS-20s is a case in point. It was only in 1982 that the Japanese government began to voice public opposition to the deployment of SS-20s in East Asia. But this protest had more to do with hurt national pride than with real concern about security. The Japanese feared the possibility of the transfer of SS-20s to East Asia as a result of arms-control agreements and Asian perceptions that Japan was overly linked to the West as shown by Nakasone's participation in the Williamsburg summit in 1983 and his signing the declaration on INF. In contrast to Europe, in Japan there has never been the fear of being decoupled from the United States as a result of the deployment of SS-20s. In addition, since there has been no question of the deployment of American nuclear missiles on Japanese soil, public opinion has never been aroused to the pitch level that it has reached in Western Europe.

Also, in contrast to Europe, Japan's low degree of concern about its present poor relations with the Soviet Union gives the latter less political leverage than say it has over the Federal Republic of Germany. The decline of detente in Europe, where Bonn has to bear in mind the interests of Germans in the German Democratic Republic when determining its policy with Moscow, finds no parallel in

Japan where there are no longer any of its citizens living on the Northern territories claimed by the Soviet Union. The Japanese can therefore permit themselves to remind the Soviets constantly of their territorial claim. Also, Moscow no longer has any economic leverage on Tokyo. Trade was down to U.S.$4.1 billion in 1985, although this figure is higher if it includes the U.S.$1.5 billion Japanese-Soviet trade handled by third-party countries. The dream of a Siberian bonanza has evaporated in the light of experience and changed economic conditions: there are safer and cheaper supplies of raw materials available from other countries, and the present glut of oil and natural gas makes Soviet supplies less attractive. The annual fishery agreements, formerly a permanent bone of contention, are now much more quickly concluded, since catch quotas have been substantially reduced and the USSR needs hard-currency earnings.

Under these circumstances, Japan can distance itself from the Soviet Union as there are not many incentives worth the effort and it does not have much confidence that any breakthrough can be attained. Similarly, the Soviets are unable to make any meaningful gesture toward the Japanese, having maneuvered themselves into a deadlock over the issue of the Northern Territories. Even so, some movement has come into Japanese-Soviet relations with the visit to Japan, in January of 1986, of a Soviet foreign minister, the first in ten years. Both sides agreed to resume their negotiations on a peace treaty which included a discussion of the Northern Territories. A long-term trade agreement could not be finalized, but a meeting of the Japan-Soviet joint economic committee took place in April 1985 and on the occasion of Foreign Minister Abe's visit to Moscow in the middle of 1986, a cultural exchange agreement was concluded and the Soviet Union declared its willingness to allow the Japanese to resume ancestral grave visits on the Northern Territories.2/

JAPAN AND CHINA

Japan never considered the People's Republic of China to be a direct threat to its security. At most, Japanese leaders were concerned with the possibility that the Chinese might foment internal turmoil. Chinese nuclear armament was perceived as a possible means to intimidate Japan, and it was used by some Japanese as an argument against Japan's adherence to the Nuclear Non-Proliferation Treaty. But it was always clear that the American nuclear umbrella was sufficient as a shield. Since August 1978, Japan and China have not only become closely linked economically, but they have also concluded a treaty of peace and friendship. Japan and China also have no large outstanding problems, comparable to the Taiwan question in the Sino-American relationship. China no longer considers Japan a threat to its security and even welcomes its efforts for self-defense and the Japanese-American security treaty. Japan sees in China an important counter-weight against the Soviet Union and a stabilizing power of the region. The abrupt change in the Chinese attitude has considerably weakened the Japanese opposition parties' rejection of an increased Japanese military role in the Pacific. Moscow is understandably concerned about the possibility of an emerging Anti-Soviet linkage among China, Japan, and the United States.3/

The security dimensions of the Sino-Japanese relationship have intensified as can be seen in the increased exchanges of military personnel and information. In July of 1984, Zhang Aiping was the first Chinese Minister of Defense to visit Japan, and his Japanese counterpart is expected to visit China before too long. Although there are no outright sales of Japanese weapons to China, the expanded economic relationship contributes indirectly to the modernization of China's armed forces through the influx of Japanese dual-purpose items, such as electronic and high technology goods. Developments in space and nuclear technologies are also affected by this expanding trade. In July of 1983, Japan and China agreed to expand their military exchanges, in the fields of education, training and other matters involving personnel. In order not to arouse undue suspicion, the Defense Agency announced in December of 1984 that such exchanges should center on education, training of personnel and information but not on operations and military technology.4/

JAPAN'S ROLE ON THE KOREAN PENINSULA

The security of the Korean Peninsula is also of great concern to Japan. For several years the Japanese have sought support from the Chinese in order to reduce tensions on the peninsula, including asking China to use its influence with North Korea. China understands Japan's concern very well. In 1980, Japan was quite surprised by Hua Guofeng's firm conviction that North Korea would not attack the South. Since then Hua's statement has been reconfirmed. The stability of the Korean peninsula now figures prominently on all Sino-Japanese meeting agendas. The issue is further heightened by China's decision to open itself to limited contacts with South Korea. In a recent meeting with a Japanese delegation, Chinese officials admitted that they sometimes have differences with their North Korean allies. Foreign Minister Wu Xueqian expressed to his Japanese counterpart the hope that President Chun Doo Hwan's visit to Japan would contribute to easing tensions on the peninsula, thus practically endorsing the visit. Japanese Foreign Minister Abe has also spoken of Japan's function as a bridge between China and South Korea.

It is difficult to predict how far China will go without losing its influence with North Korea. It also very much depends on North Korea's flexibility in opening itself to the outside world. Beijing actively supports this opening and has even urged Japanese business to react positively to Pyongyang's invitation for joint ventures. Until recently, the United States was for Japan the only guarantor of external stability on the Korean Peninsula. The mission of a portion of the American troops in Japan is to serve as an active deterrent against an outbreak of war in Korea. In a sense then, Japan is shouldering a part of the Korean security. Since South Korea and Japan have a security treaty with the United States, both countries cooperate in the maintenance of a joint air defense identification zone. For domestic reasons, however, the Japanese government was until recently extremely reluctant to discuss in public the security of Korea and its importance to Japan. The warming up of the bilateral relationship between Tokyo and Seoul under Prime Minister Nakasone, is now publicly acknowledged in joint communiques and declarations. There is no direct military cooperation, but exchanges of military officers regularly take place. Japan's most substantial contribution to the security on the Korean peninsula, apart from diplomatic moves, lies in its support of the American military commitment to South Korea and the large trade between them.

THE JAPANESE-AMERICAN MILITARY ALLIANCE

The changing strategic environment on regional and global levels has prompted Japan to render its relationship with the United States closer and more effective. It is here that the changing role of Japan in East Asian security is developing most spectacularly. The United States now has 46,000 troops in Japan and is making use of 118 separate military facilities. Until very recently, joint maneuvers took place only between the navies of the two countries, and no joint planning for emergencies or relief occurred because the subject was too politically sensitive. Given Japan's explicit and complete dependence on the United States military for its security, such a situation was most peculiar.

The improvement of Japanese-American military cooperation has taken place on many levels, one of them being reciprocity. The United States has consistently asked Japan to do more for its own defense by increasing its defense budget. After many years of criticizing Tokyo for not doing more, Washington stated in 1984 that it was satisfied with the ongoing Japanese defense build-up. Any more criticism, it appeared, would be counterproductive. The Japanese are now spending U.S.$1 billion per year for the support of American troops in Japan. In per capita terms, these expenditures are greater than those made by West Germany. In addition, this financial support is above and beyond the rental payment for property and improvement of American facilities in Japan.

The flow of Japanese arms-related or dual-purpose technology to the United States has been another level that demanded reciprocity. In view of a growing trade deficit with Japan and the advances of its technology, the United States was no longer willing to accept a one-sided flow of military technology under Japanese co-production schemes. In January 1983, after lengthy negotiations and much stalling on the part of the Japanese, the Nakasone government finally agreed to allow the export of military technology to the United States and the joint development of new weapon systems up to the prototype stage. In November of 1983, an Exchange of Notes on Transfer of Japanese Military Technologies took place, and in December of 1985 the Detailed Arrangements for the Transfer of Military Technologies was signed.5/ In the summer of 1985, the United States also requested the first item of Japanese technology, a homing device developed by the Technical Research and Development Institute of the Defense Agency, in conjunction with Toshiba. This particular request has also drawn attention to the fact that the United States expects Japan to help with research on the Strategic Defense Initiative. Japan was invited to conclude a government agreement on this subject in 1985, along with West European and other Western countries. Although three Japanese government missions have gone to the United States, the last one in April of 1986, which included representatives from Japanese industry, no agreement is yet in sight. The major stumbling block is the reluctance of industry (fear of losing control over important technologies of the future) and public opposition to SDI.6/

The upgrading of American forces and of their equipment in Japan has strengthened the Japanese-American military alliance on another level. The best known case concerns the deployment of two squadrons of F-16s in Misawa in Northern Japan. This project was started in 1985 and is expected to be completed, ahead of schedule, in 1986. The United States and Japan will share the cost of the facilities equally. In Japan there has been opposition to this deployment because the aircraft, with their ability to reach the eastern provinces of the Soviet Union, are considered to be offensive weapons and therefore are likely to invite Soviet retaliation in case of a conflict. This argument is used against any steps to strengthen the efficiency of the Japanese-American security treaty. A further step in upgrading the strength of American forces has been the deployment of SH-3H Sea King helicopters on the Yokosuka-based aircraft carrier Midway and the United States' decision, in 1981, to deploy Tomahawk cruise missiles on units of the Pacific 7th Fleet. These steps are criticized in Japan because they would violate its three non-nuclear principles of not possessing, not producing and not permitting entry of nuclear weapons into Japan.7/

A third level concerns the planning of more joint military exercises and the degree of Japanese-American cooperation in case of a crisis or conflict. This cooperation was given a major boost in November of 1978 when guidelines established for such cooperation were approved by the U.S.-Japan Security Consultative Committee. Among others, the guidelines called for joint operational plans, including emergency planning, common procedures for cooperation in communications and logistic support, as well as more joint training.

In 1980, the Japanese Navy participated in the RIMPAC exercise that included the United States, Australia, New Zealand and Canada. It was Japan's first participation in a multinational exercise with states other than the United States. Since then, it regularly has taken part in these biannual maneuvers. Bilateral military exercises now also include the army and air force.

A study on how to cope with an armed attack against Japan was completed in 1981. That same year, the United States and Japan finally agreed to initiate a study concerning Japanese support for American forces in the Far

East in case of an emergency. This issue is highly sensitive in the context of Japanese domestic politics. Such support through transport and other logistics supply is seen by many as involving Japan in a war to which it was not an original party. The most likely scenario however, is that a war could result from a resumption of fighting on the Korean peninsula. Both the Japanese and the American governments argue that in such a case Japan's security would also be at stake and it would, therefore, have an interest in helping its American ally.

SEA LANE DEFENSE

A fourth level of improvement is the greater regional military role that Japan has been given in the defense of sea lanes in the West Pacific. On the occasion of his visit to Washington in 1981, the then Prime Minister Zenko Suzuki promised that his country would assume greater responsibility for the defense of sea lanes extending 1,000 nautical miles from Tokyo. Caspar Weinberger, Secretary of Defense, made it clear in March of 1982 that this expanded role for the Japanese Navy would allow the American Navy to commit more forces to the Southeast Asian and Indian Ocean theatres. In contradiction to previous official interpretations that it cannot send troops overseas, under this new arrangement, Japan would contribute to the military security of regions as far as the Middle East. Resistance to this arrangement is softened by the fact that Japan, more than the United States, is dependent on oil from the region.

For an island nation like Japan, which is highly dependent on sea transport for the import of raw materials and the export of manufactured goods, concern about the security of the sea lanes would seem only natural. However, an increased role in protecting those lanes, at the request of the United States, has aroused greater adverse reaction in Japan than other measures taken to strengthen the Japanese-American military alliance. Soviet retaliatory strikes are feared not only because of the increased offensive capability of a more powerful navy but also because of the specific mission that the United States wants to assign to it. In August of 1982, the United States reportedly presented concrete plans which called for Japan to undertake air defense operations over the Straits of Soya (width 23nm), Tsugaru (width 10nm) and Tsushima (width of eastern channel 27 nm, Western channel 23 nm). These plans also called for Japanese operations over the sea lanes in an emergency situation, in which the United States would conduct offensive operations against the Soviet Union. The United States clearly wants Japan to interdict Soviet use of these key straits through which the major part of the Soviet Navy would have to transit in order to operate. After a difficult start, in March of 1983, due to the inability of the Defense Agency and the Foreign Ministry to agree on their scope, these joint American Japanese studies are now well underway.

The Japanese also realize that in case of a major superpower confrontation, it would be strategic for the United States to strike the Soviet Union where it is the most vulnerable. A possible scenario, for example, might involve a major confrontation in the Middle East with the United States seeking to block the Soviet Pacific Fleet in its East Asian harbors and striking from Japan at Siberian airfields. Therefore, the expansion of the Japanese-American naval cooperation touches the very core of Japan's proclaimed "defensive defense" concept. There is also much debate in Japan about the feasibility of a sea lane defense up to 1,000 nautical miles. Even naval experts like Osamu Kaihara question whether such a mission is realistic. These doubts concern the feasibility of such a task not only with the present Japanese naval force but also with a much more powerful one. In the meantime, great efforts are being undertaken to remedy the present shortcomings of the Japanese Navy and to improve anti-submarine warfare. Until now, Japanese ground forces received the greater share of the defense budget. This is changing now. In September of 1985 the National Defense Council and the Cabinet endorsed a new five year buildup plan (59 Chugyo) at a cost of approximately Y18.4 trillion or about U.S. $86 billion. Of this amount, $22 billion has been allocated for equipment procurement. The Maritime Self Defense Force (MSDF) will get $8.68 billion (39.3.%), the Air Self Defense Force (ASDF) $7.58 billion (34.3%), and the Ground Self Defense Force (GSDF) $5.83 billion (26.4%).8/

Finally, the adverse reaction of other Asian countries inhibits an enlarged Japanese naval defense role. Should its navy reach the shores of the ASEAN countries, Japan's leaders would be unable to convince their neighbors that it is not their objective to become a great military power. Former Prime Minister Suzuki's original announcement on the defense of Japan's sea lanes up to 1000 nm is sufficiently ambiguous to worry its neighbors. The Defense Agency interprets this line of defense to be measured from Tokyo.9/

Asian concerns have been heightened recently by yet another outbreak of the textbook crisis where the Ministry of Education used its influence in the education system to downplay Japan's aggression against its Asian neighbors during World War II.

CONCLUSIONS

The above analysis cannot produce a clear-cut judgment of Japan's role in East Asian security since too many elements are still unclear. The Japanese now recognize the need for an expanded role in the security of the region. In order to avoid a narrowly military response, the government has singled out what it considers "strategically important countries," namely South Korea, Thailand and Pakistan, as prime recipients of Japanese economic aid. However, American pressure on Japan to do more for its own defense as well as for that of the region will force Japan's leaders to decide whether they want their armed forces to be merely a vehicle to assure the American commitment to their nation's security or whether they should acquire a denial capability to deal on their own with limited and small-scale aggression. In either case, Japan's military role cannot be comparable to that of the war years, but it has already expanded far beyond that prescribed by its constitution. It is far larger than that tolerated by Japanese public opinion from the 1950s through the 1970s, much greater than that commonly perceived by Europe, and more powerful and perhaps more threatening than that preferred by the Soviet Union.

NOTES

1. For a detailed discussion of European-Japanese security interest see Reinhard Drifte, "The European Community and Japan," Journal of International Affairs, 37 (Summer 1983) and reprinted in Japan's New World Role, ed. Joshua D. Katz and Tilly Friedman-Lichtschein (Colorado: Westview Press, 1985).

2. The Daily Yomiuri, 18 April 1986. Japan 363 (12 June 1986).

3. For a detailed analysis, see Reinhard Drifte, "China and Japan Since 1976" in The End of an Isolation: China after Mao, ed. (Dordrecht: Martinus Nijhoff Publishers, 1985).

4. The Daily Yomiuri, 9 December 1984.

5. For text of the documents see Office of the Under Secretary of Defense for Research and Engineering, Japanese Military Technology. Procedures for Transfers to the United States, (Washington: Department of Defense, 1986).

6. For more details see Reinhard Drifte, Arms Production in Japan: The Military Application of Civilian Technology, (Boulder, Colorado: Westview Press 1986).

7. G. Jacobs, "Japan Views the Tomahawk Deployment," Asian Defense Journal (October, 1984). For technical details on this weapon see article by Ronald O'Rourke, Navy International, (July, 1986).

8. Flight International, 2 November 1985.

9. Far Eastern Economic Review, 12 June 1986.

PART TWO

Economic Development in the Pacific Rim Countries

6

Transitions from Less-Developed Country to Advanced Nation Status: Case Studies of the Asia Pacific and Brazil

Lawrence R. Klein

CONCEPTUAL ISSUES

Countries are commonly classified in groups according to their individual stages of development. In the broadest terms there are classifications of developed and developing countries. At times, the latter have been called underdeveloped, undeveloped, less developed, emerging, southern, third world and other names. The World Bank has adopted the term LDC (Less Developed Countries) and it separates these into low income, lower middle income, upper middle income and high income oil exporters. Other international organizations have different classification schemes and names.

By contrast, the countries at the other end of the spectrum are called developed, industrial or OECD (Organization for Economic Cooperation and Development), or the industrial West (plus Japan, Australia and New Zealand). Another group of countries consists of the socialist or centrally planned ones, and some of them may well be called developing, China being among the most notable.

These considerations indicate the thrust of this paper with respect to the taxonomy of country groupings, but there is more substance in the question of determination of how different economies end up in the various classifications. The principal concern in this essay is to inquire whether some countries may soon be moving from the developing to the developed category, reflecting considerable forward strides in their economic progress.

A striking success story of the present generation, has been the upward classification of Japan since the end of World War II. A respected colleague from a Japanese university enthusiastically informed this author, in 1963, that Japan was being reclassified as a developed nation because its per capita level of production was approximating that of Italy. In April of 1964, Japan was admitted to membership in the OECD. Not only did it achieve recognized advanced nation status in one generation, but it also rose to become one of the top economic performers in the OECD, far surpassing Italy's performance in a short time period.

In 1950, Robert Summers and Allan Heston estimated that Japan's per capita real product (gross domestic product = GDP) was just 17% of that of the United States.1/ By now its per capita GDP is practically three-fourths of the corresponding U.S. figure.

At the low level of 17%, Japan clearly should have been classified as _developing_ if one looks at the relative per capita GDP status alone. Many third-world countries, widely thought of as LDCs, presently have a much higher standing relative to that of the United States. But, the authors of the study cited suggest that other indicators, especially the share of manufacturing or total industry output, would place Japan as an advanced industrial economy long before 1963, possibly as early as 1950. According to World Bank estimates, 13% of Japan's GNP originated in agriculture in 1960, but 45% originated in industry. By now the agricultural share has fallen to less than 5%, with the main compensatory upward movement being in services. Other significant indicators, such as life expectancy (70 years in 1960) and infant mortality rate (30 per 1,000 live births in 1960) were much more favorable than figures from countries that were obviously classified as _developing_.

Nevertheless, Japan has set an example. Other countries are asking whether they too can become fully recognized as _developed_, since they are growing as fast as Japan did after World War II. Many countries are setting targets for the year 2000. In what follows, information will be assembled to help the reader decide whether other countries can cross this barrier before the end of this century.

NEW CANDIDATES

Some developing countries appeared to be at a very favorable stage on their paths of economic progress right after World War II, but have failed either to live up to growth expectations or simply remained in a relatively stationary position.

When Japan was ranked at 17% of the U.S. norm, Argentina was estimated at 41%, Uruguay at 47%, and Venezuela at 38%. By 1960, Japan had largely recovered from wartime destruction and reached a level of 33%, but Argentina at 41%, Uruguay at 48% and Venezuela at 42%, had not moved significantly upward in comparative rankings. Now the situation is about the same. As of 1980, Argentina was placed at 40%, Uruguay at 41% and Venezuela at 46%. The last mentioned country probably gained some advantage on the basis of its oil wealth, but, by and large, the whole group did not achieve comparatively higher living conditions, and they continue as developing countries while Japan challenges the United States as this century draws to an end.

For a variety of reasons, some countries do not appear to be gaining acceptance in the club of advanced industrial nations. Many others look to the Japanese model, see that they (meaning the Japanese) have made the jump, and wonder if, by following various aspects of that model, they can become developed?

In seeking to identify countries that have a good chance of crossing the classification barrier, some interesting cases come to mind. Without being exhaustive, attention will be focused on South Korea, Taiwan and Brazil, commonly classified as Newly Industrializing Countries (NICs). The first two come from a part of the world that is close to Japan both ethnically and geographically. They are in the Pacific Far East, also known as the Pacific Basin or Pacific Rim.2/ In many respects, they do seem to be following the Japanese model. Much the same could be said about other countries in the Pacific Basin, including the city-states of Singapore and Hong Kong, which may qualify equally well with South Korea and Taiwan as NICs and have as good a chance of becoming advanced nations in the near future. But, in this paper the discussion, although somewhat arbitrarily, will be limited to those two particular cases.

The third country, Brazil, is very differently situated. Its recent economic history is quite different from that of such Latin American neighbors as Argentina, Uruguay and Venezuela. Brazil shows a real growth potential, as opposed those just mentioned which started in a very favorable position many years ago but have advanced very little or not at all. Also, due to the immense area that it incorporates, it is less dependent on trade than many other LDCs or NICs, and its large primitive region holds down some national economic averages.

These three countries did not show unusual economic progress during the 1950s or early 1960s. Brazil and Taiwan showed strong growth tendencies in the early 1960s, fell back again, but revived in the latter part of that decade, which coincided with an economic take-off in Korea that was sustained for all three during the 1970s. This is all the more remarkable in that these countries are significant oil importers and some of their best gains were realized at a time when they experienced adverse terms of trade. Although the setback in American growth may have helped them improve their relative status (to the United States), they did make impressive gains in their own right.

In the present decade, they continue to have bright economic prospects, even though all three have very special and different kinds of difficulties. Taiwan faces political instability in its relationship with the People's Republic of China; the burden of servicing extraordinarily large debts continues to be borne by Brazil, and South Korea faces a hostile northern border. Both Brazil and South Korea have had recent economic setbacks of large proportions, but are showing good signs of recovery, especially in Korea where recent economic performance statistics have been among the strongest in the world. It should be mentioned also that South Korea has large debts. Although they are not as great as Brazil's and not as burdensome in terms of maturity or accommodation, they are nevertheless quite large.

The United States, serving as a world norm in this discussion, slowed down from about a 4% growth to a 3% one after the oil embargo period. There are some optimistic estimates that it may regain its 4% path for the rest of this decade or century, but the general consensus is that it will continue at about 3% for the next 10 to 20 years.

The three NICs under consideration are all candidates to grow, on an average, at rates between 5% and 10% annually. To a large extent, these countries have population expansion fairly well under control. The issue is this: can any or all of these countries sustain a high growth rate during the next 15 years, one significantly above that of the United States, and reach advanced nation status? As Japan did in the early 1960s, can they cross the borderline, the Italian standard, which seemed to be a crucial level for Japan's achievement?

STRATEGIES FOR ADVANCEMENT

Many ideas have been put forward to explain Japan's development early in this century and since the end of World War II. These fall under the headings of: dualism, inequality in income distribution, population restraint, high educational standards, high health standards, a strong work ethic, a low defense budget, American aid, service as the offshore supply center for the Korean War, dismantling of Zaibatsu, and protectionism. All the items listed are worthy of elaboration and justification in the context of growth, but for the main explanation for the achievement of advanced status in modern times, export-led growth with good quality technology in the framework of channeling savings into productive investment, should be cited. The work ethic, a light defense burden, and American assistance in reconstruction after the war were also major factors. Between pre- and postwar Japan there were significant movements towards modernization, exemplified in a shift towards best quality in manufacturing output.

Can similar traits be seen in the three NICs that are examined in this essay? Certainly the Taiwanese and South Koreans have had ample opportunity to observe and emulate many positive Japanese characteristics such as export promotion, high work standards (both in effort and quality), support of education, population restraint, good health care, and development of manufacturing. Taiwan and South Korea, like Japan, depend on raw material imports and fuel imports to turn goods into finished manufactured products. Japan rose to pre-eminence through quality production of textiles, electronics, optics, vehicles, ships, steel, chemicals and pharmaceuticals. Now, as Japan is shifting more towards the production of ever-sophisticated goods, it is possible to observe Taiwan and South Korea, together with a few other countries, moving in to fill a gap in world supply of the kinds of goods that Japan produced so successfully in the 1960s. They are following in Japan's footsteps and developing some of their own specializations. Korea is a world leader in construction, while Taiwan is the center of one of the world's largest producers of PVC. Up to now, these two countries have not done well as efficient producers of motor vehicles, but there are some new ventures that may change that image.

The strategies of Taiwan and South Korea now are to continue to expand the standard production of electronics, optics, textiles, apparel, petrochemicals and the like, but they are also trying to enter the world of high technology where they may be able to leapfrog and achieve advanced status quickly, without waiting for residues from Japan. With well educated and trained workers, they should be able to promote new technologies in microelectronics, bioengineering, health care delivery systems, information (software), and other new lines of activity. Taiwan is having some success in attracting foreign capital to a major science park by offering tax incentives, research and development protection, and a highly skilled labor force. Already some 30 or more multinational enterprises have made a commitment to invest in the science park.

South Korea has taken on the 1988 Summer Olympics. This will surely provide an incentive to supply goods and look attractive to the rest of the world. In addition, there are some interesting joint ventures in vehicle production taking place, and foreign equity capital is being sought. This latter point should be emphasized because it is far different from the loan pattern of the 1970s, which entrapped many of the most promising LDCs. The Korean Fund was oversubscribed to last summer and now is listed on the New York Stock Exchange at a premium of 30-40%. The success of this venture, as with the Olympics, will be important in showing how the country can participate on the fast track of the world economy.

The Brazilian case is quite different. It was an economy known in world circles for its exports of such primary products as coffee, cocoa, cotton and iron ore. It is well endowed with natural resources except for any known deposits of oil, but its determination to carry out an alcohol program for motor fuel has been impressive. Brazil has a large domestic market and is a sophisticated producer of cars and other manufactures, but a substantial thrust was provided by a shift during the 1960s from a heavy reliance on primary exports towards manufactures. Few nations have ever achieved lofty economic status by concentrating on producing or exporting primary products. The Asian NICs specialize in the exporting of manufactured goods, construction and the provision of some services--finance, shipping, information and other software. Brazil continues to export coffee, iron ore and other primary products, but manufacturing is now much more important.

In Brazil there are many productive Japanese and other immigrants, but the population as a whole does not seem to measure up to some of the skills, intellectual achievements and work effort found in Taiwan and South Korea. Brazil is also fortunate to have a relatively light military burden, unlike the one borne by both Taiwan and South Korea.

SOME TENTATIVE PROJECTIONS

The United States, serving as a norm, is a moving target. The Wharton World Forecast estimates real per capita growth between 1980 and 2000 at just under 2.0%, actually at 1.992%. For Italy, the corresponding figure is 1.94%. This leaves the relative position of Italy as compared to the United States just about unchanged.

According to the World Bank, Korea's per capita growth rate from 1960 to 1982 was 6.6%, while Brazil's was 4.8%. The official economic and social development plan of Korea estimates growth for the next few years at 5.9%. Taiwan grew at 6.3% (per capita) for the twenty-year period between 1963 to 1983. If these three countries could maintain per capita growth rates of 5.0% for the twenty-year period from 1980 through 2000, they could come close to the Italian figure. Taiwan would be about as close as Japan was in 1963. Actually, it is not an impossible pace for these NICs to maintain, given their past performance. An upside figure would be 7.0%, which exceeds past performance over extended periods of time, but still is not an impossible target.

At 7.0%, there is little doubt that they would achieve advanced status, even if the United States reached a 3.0% per capita growth rate, but this would represent a very difficult goal to maintain for such a sustained period of time. The relevant figures are given in the accompanying table.

TABLE 1
PROJECTIONS OF REAL PER CAPITA GDP
(1975 international prices)

	1980	2000
	Growth at 2.0% per capita	
United States	8,089	12,020
Italy	4,661	6,805
	Growth at 5.0% per capita	
Taiwan	2,522	6,691
South Korea	2,007	5,325
Brazil	2,152	5,709
	Growth at 3.0% per capita	
United States	8,089	14,609
Italy	4,661	8,418
	Growth at 7.0% per capita	
Taiwan	2,522	9,760
South Korea	2,007	7,767
Brazil	2,152	8,328

PROMOTION OF GROWTH IN THE DEVELOPING WORLD

As sustained rates averaged over business cycle swings and turns, 5% to 7% per capita is in the high range, requiring very good performance. On what does such an achievement depend, and what can developing, as well as developed, countries do in order to meet this goal? The outlook, as a whole, for developing countries is not particularly bright; it is just mediocre unless the developed countries perform at rates that are a good deal above the consensus projection. Of course, only the most favorably situated LDCs are discussed in this essay and there is every reason to believe that they will exceed the average.

The most important ingredient for a growth and development policy is self-help, and that is clearly visible in the developing countries being examined, especially Taiwan and South Korea. Self-help means promoting education, capital formation, productivity growth, efficiency in economic organization, and maintenance of a work ethic. Of course, there always will be concern for North-South relationships and some degree of capital transfer to promote southern progress, but this source tends to be unreliable, erratic and usually conditional. Given the present state of LDC debt, especially in Brazil and South Korea, it is not a dependable source of growth promotion.

Something that the LDCs can do, in addition to promoting self-help, on an individual basis, is to encourage more South-South trade, including some capital transfer. South-South trade looks unusually attractive in the Pacific Basin because so many of the countries interested have mutual complementarities among raw materials, primary energy, and industrial facilities. The educational network is highly developed, and ethnic ties help to avoid confrontation at the political/strategic level. Peaceful relations have not always been in place, but they have prevailed over much of the area during the last two or three decades. The tensions that do exist are held in a state of abeyance.

The developing world as a whole would benefit if swords could be turned into plowshares, meaning that military related imports or domestic military activities, when they exist, harm productive peacetime pursuits. The scarce financial capital devoted to defense expenditures does not provide durable facilities or human resources that are capable of generating a future income. Stable growth or levels of GDP of an additional one-half point or more could be achieved if defense imports were cut back by 1% or 2% of GDP and replaced by capital goods imports.

In the context of a world program to seek better growth in the OECD countries, capital transfers to the LDCs, bringing the transfer rate to a target of 0.7% of GDP in the developed part of the world, would do much to put the countries under consideration on paths that would indeed lead them to a higher status. In response to the inevitable question--how does one pay for the transfers?--the answer could be: through a fund created by multilateral disarmament. In a research paper that studied the world impact of coordinated fiscal-monetary policies, coupled with multi-lateral disarmament (among the big powers) amounting to cuts of U.S. $26 billion, transferred in capital goods exports to LDCs, it was found that about one-half percentage point could be added to the LDC growth rate without holding back any growth in the developed countries.3/ In fact, under the terms of a well-rounded policy, the OECD countries would initially gain in GDP and be at a sustained higher level of activity.

Many scenarios can be conceived that would help the developing countries in their quest for a better life, and it is in the self interest of the advanced nations to see that this happens. There are risks, however. The successful advancement of any LDC depends very much on the world economic environment, that is largely built around the economic performance of the OECD. OECD growth at 2.0% per capita is a good baseline case and has a reasonable chance of success. It is much less likely that 3.0% can be achieved, but that should not to be ruled out, a priori. But is there a possibility that a deep economic crisis could occur or that average performance could be very dull and disappointing? There is a chance of such a downside risk. The danger areas are possible default on LDC debt, or at least on large portions of it. In some cases the debt situation is not fully known. There have been many surprises in the past few years, when debt problems turned out to be more serious when scrutinized closely than had been anticipated at the outset. Likewise, huge money-center banks have turned out to be more vulnerable than had been previously thought. Loss provisions for non-performing loans have not been fully allowed for in the accounting statements of many banks. In the past few months there have been surprises at Bank of America, First Chicago and Crocker National. When these are added to the fully anticipated troubles at Continental Illinois and Seattle First National, one realizes that the banking system is fragile. Since debt default and bank exposure with non-performing loans go hand-in-hand, the combination of these two sources of trouble may occur all at once. The uncertainty generated by such circumstances would put financial markets in disarray and cause a breakdown in trade and general economic activity. An exodus of foreign capital from the United States would be induced, with a crowding out in capital markets and the probability of high and rising interest rates.

A different kind of danger, with a downside risk, is the potential rise of protectionism. In the United States, nontariff barriers have already been put to work through quota and other quantitative restrictions on shoes, cars, textiles, motorcycles, TV sets and steel. Many of these are aimed directly at Pacific Basin countries, including Japan, but also at Brazil. The latest round of steel barriers is expressly designed to restrain American imports from Korea and Brazil, among other exporting nations. These restrictions make export-led growth all the more difficult. Also, it hampers attempts by Brazil and other heavily indebted countries to earn foreign exchange currency with which to pay their debt. As far as growth is concerned, it contributes to a slowing down among LDCs because imports are the main determining factor for world trade, and the LDCs must try to capture their share of global trade volume.

It is noteworthy that protectionist tendencies that have broken out in the U.S. Congress have come to focus on four countries--Japan, South Korea, Taiwan and Brazil. They are the ones most upsetting to American producers in competing lines of activity and serve as targets for protectionism, possibly due to their success in enhancing output and bringing higher levels of living to their respective constituents. It is not surprising, then, that these countries have had some of the most impressive growth performances and that they might duplicate Japan's feat of moving up to advanced nation status.

SOME THOUGHTS ON CHINA

So far, the discussion has focused on LDCs and their relation with the OECD countries. There are three major blocs of nations; which is why there is a "third world." The missing bloc consists of the aggregate of Centrally Planned Economies--the Soviet Union, the Peoples' Republic of China, six countries of Eastern Europe, Albania, Cuba and other Asian socialist countries, such as North Korea and Vietnam.

For the most part these countries will be passive, small actors on the world economic scene, not initiators.

China, however, is different. Currently China is a star performer among the CPEs. Fast growth, during the past three years, has given some credibility to its target of quadrupling real GDP between 1980 and 2000. There is now some talk of catching up to the Western countries.

As of 1980, China's per capita GDP has been placed at 14% of the U.S. position in the Summers-Heston tables (see Table 2). This ranking, although highly controversial, can be defended. It now places China at about the relative standing (if compared to the United States) of Taiwan, South Korea and Brazil in the early 1950s. If the real GDP in China were to quadruple between 1980 and 2000, it would have to grow at the average rate of 7.2%. Allowing for a population growth of 1.0%, this would mean a per capita rate of a bit more than 6.0%. Some countries have been able to grow at this rate for sustained periods of time. Taiwan and South Korea are outstanding examples. China only fell slightly short (by one percentage point) of this target between 1960 and 1982, according to World Bank estimates. Chinese population growth was formerly much faster than the 1.0% rate projected for the rest of this century, and if this rate is not maintained, the overall economic plan may be thrown out of harmony.

The main point, however, in the present analysis is the competitive position of China vis-a-vis the NICs who are trying to gain advanced nation status. In some conventional lines, especially textiles, apparel, toys and bicycles, China is a formidable competitor, with low prices and good quality. In more sophisticated lines--electronics, optics, motor vehicles and pharmaceuticals--it is not yet competitive but may become so. At the high technology end of the spectrum, China is a receiver and not a supplier. There is an indefinite catch-up period lying ahead. China is a customer and supplier of raw materials to Japan, the United States and other advanced countries. Its trade with Hong Kong is obviously significant. Trading with China could be a positive growth factor for some partners, but with the NICs which are striving for new success, the relationship is more likely to be competitive.

TABLE 2
RELATION OF PER CAPITA GDP,
FIVE COUNTRIES COMPARED TO THE UNITED STATES
(Relatives: U.S. = 100)

Year	Japan	Taiwan	Korea	Italy	Brazil
1950	17	10	9	31	14
1951	19	12	10	31	14
1952	20	11	10	32	14
1953	21	12	11	34	14
1954	22	12	11	36	15
1955	23	12	12	36	15
1956	24	12	11	38	15
1957	26	12	12	40	16
1958	28	13	12	43	17
1959	29	13	11	43	17
1960	33	13	12	46	18
1961	38	18	12	49	19
1962	38	14	12	49	18
1963	41	14	12	51	17
1964	44	15	12	49	17
1965	43	15	12	47	16
1966	45	15	12	47	15
1967	49	47	13	50	15
1968	53	17	14	51	16
1969	58	18	16	52	17
1970	64	20	17	56	18
1971	64	21	18	55	20
1972	66	21	17	53	20
1973	67	22	18	54	21
1974	67	23	20	56	24
1975	68	24	21	54	25
1976	66	26	22	54	25
1977	67	26	24	53	24
1978	68	27	26	52	24
1979	70	29	27	54	25
1980	72	31	25	58	27

Source: R. Summers and A. Heston.

TRENDS VS. CYCLES

In targeting economic objectives for the year 2000, a nation must engage in trend analysis. In general, economic development planning must take a long view and work out the trends. The short-run cycles of recession and recovery, at rates far different from the prevailing trend, cannot be ignored because cycles sometimes shape the trend, and countries can be thrown off track for a number of years by extreme crises.

During the recent world-wide cyclical recession from 1979 to 1983 or 1984, the Pacific Basin countries have performed outstandingly well, sometimes reaching growth figures of 10% (not on a per capita basis). Brazil has also fared well, but had a definite set-back during 1982-84 due to the imposition of austerity measures to deal with its international debt crisis. This set-back, however, should be viewed as temporary, and it should be able to exploit its rich potential in due course. Brazil has very good prospects For the long term trend, in spite of some recent poor years.

The Pacific Basin countries (apart from the Philippines) enjoyed extremely good growth during 1984. The United States incurred an unusually large trade deficit which was reflected in strong export-led growth by a number of Pacific Basin countries, including Taiwan, South Korea and China. These three countries continue to have excellent prospects although they faced economic difficulties in 1985 when exports to the United States began to falter. South Korea and Taiwan will both experience significant declines in their growth rates. China's program of domestic economic reform is responsible for its continued dynamism, and is affected only moderately by the world economic slowdown in 1985. But it has experienced a swing from trade balance to trade deficit. Much of China's precious stock of foreign exchange has been used up in carrying out liberal reforms, such as building special economic zones. Reserves are estimated to have fallen drastically, and this signals a future slowdown in growth.

China, therefore, will experience a temporary lull in economic progress that will be cyclical. In the long term, the future still looks bright for South Korea, Taiwan and Brazil, all of which have a shot at the goal of becoming advanced nations by 2000. China's economic perspective remains very favorable, and its target of quadrupling production between 1980 and 2000, remains viable, if not assured.

NOTES

1. R. Summers and A. Heston, "Improved Comparisons of Real Product and Its Composition, 1950-1980," The Review of Income and Wealth (30 June 1984):207-262.

2. This geographical region has attracted a great deal of attention, much of it on the Bloomington campus of Indiana University partly through the East Asian Studies Center's sponsorship of a conference, held May 3-4, 1984 in Indianapolis, on the growth prospects of the Pacific Rim, as one of the most promising areas of the world economy.

3. C. Andrea Bollino and Lawrence R. Klein, "World Recovery Strategies in the 1980s: Is World Recovery Synonymous to LDC Recovery?" Journal of Policy Modeling 6 (2/1984):175-207.

7

The Japanese Economy: Consolidation or Continued Expansion?

Karel G. von Wolferen

The answer to the question in the title is not obvious. There are dynamic forces pushing the Japanese economy ahead. It must put up with conditions and attitudes which form a more formidable collection of drag-anchors than is probably realized abroad. Consolidation--in the sense of solidifying a position which has already been achieved so as to provide the opportunity for national relaxation--has never been a voluntary Japanese goal. However, foreign circumstances may force Japan to adopt it. The Japanese themselves generally think that the only alternative to moving ahead is to fall behind.

Some seemingly indispensable factors for long-term prognoses of the Japanese economy, particularly political ones, are not treated in Japanese economic discussions. Genuine debate on desirable policy is rare to begin with. Economic discussion, amongst the experts and in the media, generally does not move beyond the familiar categories established by decades of bureaucratic-corporate monitoring of progress along a course which was decided in the 1950s. In the absence of what could be called a national debate, and in the presence of too many imponderables, making prophecies on the Japanese economy is even more hazardous than usual. The author hopes to be forgiven for leaving the question mark where the editor placed it. In the meantime, however, there are many things relating to this subject that can be discussed.

WHAT KIND OF ECONOMY?

To begin with, when one speaks of the Japanese economy, one is dealing with a phenomenon which, although by now has been very extensively commented upon in the West, still causes tremendous conceptual difficulties, and not only among foreigners. No general agreement exists as to what constitutes this phenomenon.

For example, Japanese bureaucrats, politicians and company officials emphatically maintain that theirs is a free-market economy. This view is in direct conflict with what half a dozen well-known Japanese economic thinkers told the author in recent conversations. Almost to a man they contended that the subservient function of the Japanese market mechanism is insufficiently understood by foreigners. Ironically, dominant opinions among foreign economists and officials tend to be exactly the reverse of those of their Japanese counterparts. On the one hand, most foreign emissaries, negotiators and politicians commenting on Japan have been taking it to task for not reciprocating the hospitality it has enjoyed in the markets of the international free trade system. On the other hand, Western academic economists, especially those of the conventional neoclassical persuasion, appear horrified at the suggestion that Japan, although formally classified as a member of the club of "capitalist free-market" nations, does not in fact belong in that club. While Japanese officials have interests to protect and Western politicans have discovered a way to make political hay out of the issue, many of these Western economists have stuck their heads into the sand against this peculiar Japanese threat to a set of theories already heavily undermined by factual evidence from the real world.

If Japan cannot, without reservation, be included in the category of Western capitalism, does it then belong to a category of its own, as quite a few commentators have implied? The author thinks not. The quick rise of South Korea and Taiwan as industrial states enables one to look at the Japanese "economic miracle" afresh and to discover that even when shorn of its cultural and psychological specifics, it constitutes a model that can be pursued by (at least some) others. The South Korean and Taiwanese economies appear to be driven by a phenomenal force similar to that of Japan, even in the absence of exceptional "harmony," life-time employment, and other aspects often cited as reasons for the Japanese success.

An insightful commentator on the political economy of East Asia, Professor Chalmers Johnson of Berkeley, has isolated this category of industrial nations and labeled it Capitalist Developmental State (CDS). Because of the undeniable successes of the East Asian CDSs, Marxist-Leninist theory has become distinctively less plausible a guide for economic development to politicians and intellectuals in less developed nations of non-communist Asia. The examples of South Korea and Taiwan probably also help stimulate the revisionism of the Chinese pragmatists. The Asian examples of Soviet-style centralism have shown, like examples elsewhere, that you do not achieve improvement in the standard of living with class struggle and the centralization of economic power.

The most eloquent theoretical objection to government interference in the economy known to the author is by Friedrich von Hayek. Hayek's explanation, reduced to its essentials, holds that planners at the center can never know enough about the circumstances in the many ramifications of the economy to make judicious decisions. Therefore, according to Hayek, centrally planned economies always fail in establishing prosperity. How have Japan, South Korea and Taiwan, whose governments consider manufacturing and trade as very much their business, improved the living standard of their peoples? First of all, they have never considered private entrepreneurism as antagonistic to their goals. Contrary to the communist approach which equates entrepreneurism with original sin, or the European welfare state's socialist approach whose regulations obstruct the entrepreneur, the CDS encourages and stimulates the private sector.

The manner in which Japan, South Korea and Taiwan have found a way around the Hayekian obstacle is crucial to understanding the CDS. The central bureaucrats never attempt to gain absolute power over the non-governmental corporations. They guide the economy while using the entrepreneurs as their antennae. In the CDS, the center knows what is happening at the periphery through constant monitoring of the experiences of capitalists trying to find new ways of making money. The economy prospers because areas of industry that show promise are stimulated by central policies favoring investment. Those areas which appear to have reached a dead end are more easily abandoned by policies forcing reorganization.

The model of the CDS is a model for rapid industrial development. Whether the bureaucratic-entrepreneurial partnership will flourish after the industry faces market saturation at home and inhospitable export markets abroad has not yet been demonstrated. The question in the title of this chapter coincides, in large measure, with the question as to whether the CDS model has a future once a certain level of development has been reached. A related question concerns the survival of the international free trade system as it struggles to accommodate the CDS.

GOVERNMENT/PRIVATE ENTERPRISE PARTNERSHIP

As for Japan, it is very difficult to imagine that its partnership between the state and private enterprise will ever break up. Japan pioneered the CDS model a century or so ago by transferring state industries into private hands during the Meiji period, after state entrepreneurism had brought a lot of governmental corporations to the verge of collapse. Kim Jae Ik, who was (before his death in Rangoon) the chief economic adviser to South Korean presidents Park Chung Hee and Chun Doo Hwan, told the author once that Park Chung Hee had the Japanese Meiji period in mind when he instructed Nam Duck Woo, the "architect" of the South Korean economic miracle, to design the mechanism for rapid growth.

A comparison with the current stage of CDS development in South Korea is helpful for viewing the Japanese political economy in perspective. Whereas in South Korea there can be no doubt as to where one can find the government and who the entrepreneurs are; in Japan it is not possible to locate a center, an ultimate organ where "the buck stops." Japanese society is best imagined as a system of mutually balancing components (incorporating mutually balancing subcomponents), each with a remarkable, in Western experience often inconceivable, degree of autonomy. We may call this the Japanese "System." It is impossible to extricate the State from the System for purposes of analysis.

The government line, also adopted by the top business organizations in Japan, is that today the various forms of governmental guidance (if acknowledged at all) carry much less weight with the private sector than they did in the past. Even though this contention is habitually accompanied by a demonstration that current tariff regulations make Japan about the freest market in the world, this does not result in a sudden transfer of Japan into the category of Western free market economies. What is true on paper, in Japan, quite often and rather more frequently than in the West, is not true in practice. What has given the Japanese CDS set-up durability is the erasing of dividing lines between private and public sectors. The power relationships which are likely to remain very significant for the further developments in the Japanese economy have evolved into something far more intricate than the term "bureaucrat-businessman partnership" suggests.

The bureaucrats, the politicians and the top businessmen are sometimes the same people, generally highly dependent on each other, and they belong, for all intents and purposes, to the same club. The ubiquitous antagonism at the top rarely, if ever, separates the formal organs of state and the industrial organizations, but exists rather between overlapping groups cutting across institutional boundaries with the politicians functioning as go-betweens.

Whereas South Korean companies are, to a large extent, still in the hands of the entrepreneurs that founded them, management in the large Japanese corporations tends to be highly bureaucratized. The obvious question is whether under these circumstances the Japanese CDS is not gradually losing its vitality. In order not to lose the entrepreneurial spirit of their companies, South Korean technocrats, under the tutelage of the late Kim Jae Ik, have begun to carry out a program of liberalization. South Korea's top economic planners tend to speak passionately about a lessening of bureaucratic control. But when one persists in discussions, it is difficult to escape the impression that they view a free market not as a final goal, but as a means to confront weaknesses in the economic system. In Japan there have been uncountable instances that demonstrate that the market pressure of competition functions as an instrument of policy. Without disparaging the real effects of past Japanese liberalization efforts in various fields, it has not led to a dismantling of the actual CDS apparatus.

Loss of vitality is an openly stated concern of Japan's bureaucrats and the groups of experts they hire for writing reports on future prospects of the economy. There are other problems which raise the question of whether the Japanese CDS apparatus, while advantageous for a fast growing economy, will be able to deal efficiently with future contingencies. The mechanisms necessary for the rapid industrial expansion in the 1950s and 1960s are still largely in place. But, domestic and international circumstances would seem to demand a re-formulation of national priorities. The System has so far shown that it is incapable of effectively addressing this issue.

JAPAN'S ECONOMIC GROWTH

For roughly another decade and a half the Japanese economy is likely to enjoy moderate growth at a somewhat higher rate than the average for the other industrially advanced nations. That appears to be the general opinion among informed observers. The productive population ratio will for some time remain relatively high. The decline in the savings rate is expected to remain slow. Due to investments in labor and energy saving facilities, the machinery and service industries are likely to be growth sectors. A continuing shift to smaller machinery will contribute to the steel industry's further decline in importance. Much is expected from the new industrial sectors utilizing advanced technology that is currently enjoying much attention. Japan pours much effort into the development of semiconductors, optical fibers, biochemistry, ceramics and other new materials, and the so-called fifth generation computer. Over the past five years or so there have been few ceremonial speeches by top businessmen and few white-papers and reports by bureaucrats which have left out a reference to the "new information age" or the "knowledge intensive" future.

Expectations of economic growth generated by these hi-tech areas follow from the often demonstrated Japanese ability to apply and commercialize state of the art technology to the assembling and processing industries. Many European and American inventions have been transformed into commercially viable products exclusively by Japanese firms.

An acute concern, noticeable in discussions about the newer sectors, that Japan may be left behind provides an extra driving force. Bureaucratic stimulus for research in the above-mentioned areas has helped reintroduce the old fashioned catch-up fever. Investments in these fields are being justified as necessary for competition with the United States. Entrepreneurism is certainly not dead in Japan. It has always survived in the small workshops of the subcontractors and sub-subcontractors, which have served as shock absorbers underneath the giant conglomerates, cushioning the effects of recessions. It is now visible in a number of adventurous small firms making products or parts which are becoming indispensible, but are unlikely ever to be mass-produced. These are dubbed venture businesses, although they are not backed up as broadly by venture capital as are American venture businesses. A number of talented engineers, tired with the social restrictions associated with the seniority system in the large firms, have struck out on their own.

A structural change is currently underway about which the planners are not undividedly optimistic. Companies left behind by hi-tech are going bankrupt. Whether the hi-tech areas can repeat what the textile, heavy, and chemical industries have done for the rapid growth of the economy remains a question. At the moment, the hi-tech industry appears too fragmented to arrange communal priorities. And whereas much publicity abroad gives the impression that Japan is ahead or almost ahead in most of the new areas, there is in fact much that is being left undone.

If there is wide agreement on anything, it is that further growth of the Japanese economy will depend on the introduction of new products. A Japanese consumer market, highly sensitive to fads and fashion, eagerly absorbing novelties and gadgets, has in the past played a decisive role in the evolution of successful products fit for export. However, consumer spending seems to have reached a plateau. It constitutes roughly half of the GNP, as compared with 75% in the United States. The Japanese businessworld does not yet consider higher salaries as an investment for maintaining a consumer market highly conducive to the development of new products.

Some characteristics of the Japanese political economy which in the past were lauded as partly responsible for the "economic miracle" could, in the long run, turn out to be draw-backs, as well. The very weak and mostly ceremonial union movement is an example. By guaranteeing a disciplined, relatively undemanding workforce, it gave an obvious advantage to companies expanding their market share with borrowed money and only the slightest (if any) profits. A stronger labor movement today would most probably turn employees of highly profitable enterprises into stronger consumers.

The financial structure, as a whole, may turn out to have become anachronistic. Japanese households save roughly one fifth of their disposable income. Tax incentives and underdeveloped social security provisions will help encourage continuation of this highest savings ratio in the world. It has facilitated the large capital formation necessary for rapid expansion. Japanese corporations, with their notoriously low equity ratios, used to be heavy borrowers. Since the late 1970s, however, a capital market has begun to function and high profits over the past few years have rendered the successful segments of the manufacturing sector awash with surplus funds.

This money could be invested in badly needed projects for improvement of the Japanese infrastructure, which has lagged far behind as industry expanded. Instead of tackling that challenge, however, Japan has become the world's biggest exporter of capital. Japanese, with a long term perspective, consider this risky and not economically justifiable, mainly because the exported capital is largely invested in American government bonds rather than in production facilities.

Artificially low interest rates are one reason for the flight of capital out of Japan. Interest rates, which are considerably lower than they would be if fixed by the monetary supply and demand mechanism, played a major role in the Japanese CDS during its days of glory. They naturally led to excessive demand for funds, and this in turn resulted in the need for credit rationing by which the bureaucrats could select the industries to be supplied with funds. This influence on the direction of lending and industrial investment, completely divorced from the market, has sometimes led to misallocations. The problem today is that during the years of expansion an elite class of borrowers was created, represented by the large companies belonging to the conglomerates. These continue to be favored over other potential winners in industry.

Countering this tendency's negative effects, the System planners wage campaigns to popularize new industrial pursuits. The above-mentioned slogans about "information age" and "knowledge intensive" industry are good examples. The dedication with which these slogans are inserted into writings and speeches even when there is no clear reason why they should be mentioned at all, is reminiscent of the campaigns with which the Chinese Communist Party cadre used to be informed of the direction in which it was supposed to move. The Japanese System needs to be imbued with a sense of urgent necessity before its components make way for any new measures that are out of the ordinary.

The protectionism inherent in the CDS has created some areas in the Japanese economy which are in bad shape. Agriculture is a notorious example. For political reasons, rationalization is bound to be extremely slow. Other old-fashioned industries run by old-fashioned companies which have never had to be effective because of political protection are drag-anchors as well. Attention has recently been fixed on one example which the Reagan administration has singled out for American competition: the plywood industry. The entire retail sector is a drag on the economy. Japan has a much larger number of shops and small stores than is "rational" in a modern economy. Its distribution system is vast and highly parasitic. But streamlining it would do away with Japan's largest haven for the would-be unemployed, as well as with an important instrument with which large corporations maintain control over smaller ones.

The most important aspect of this situation is that there is hardly any serious discussion in Japan about any of the above-mentioned problems. The System lacks conceptual agility. Contrary to what outsiders may imagine, Japan has very few professional economists, and among those there are perhaps but a handful capable of formulating original perspectives helpful to speculations about the future.

The perspective used by the bureaucrats as background to their numerous pronouncements on economic matters has changed surprisingly little since it was formed in the early 1960s. Essentially based on experiences with the business-cycle of the 1950s, it has had some correctives added to it in response to obviously deviating developments. The Japanese CDS is in many respects still on the "high growth" course set out for it in the 1950s. A decade ago the slogans spoke of a switch to "stable growth," but, in retrospect, these seem to have been launched as part of an adjustment to unstoppable external conditions. Japan had not planned for a slow down in economic growth in order to attend to new national priorities.

Today, economic thinking among bureaucrats, business representatives, politicians with official representatives, and politicians with official responsibility for it, tends to be a mixture of the obvious and the above mentioned sloganizing. The greatest problem, mentioned by about everyone who says anything at all about the future, is Japan's aging population. Stuck with the conventional set of assumptions about what is and is not desirable, this problem is mostly thought of in terms of extra costs for companies under pressure to raise their retirement ages to sixty or even older.

Back to positive factors which spell further growth: Japan has demonstrated a very striking capacity to adjust fairly rapidly to such altered conditions as are perceived by the bulk of the entire System. The oil crisis was a good example of a dramatic change the System was able to respond to. It did so with fuel-conservation technology innovations and modified patterns of usage that brought consumption down from a rate which had been growing faster than the GNP, to one which has remained under it ever since.

Japan will also retain a degree of flexibility which in the West was lost some time ago. Its workforce will probably accept sacrifices and put up with considerable discomfort if it is made to understand that new economic policies make these necessary. This readiness is due to an underdeveloped welfare system and a highly restricted labor market. Japan still belongs to those countries in which the struggle for existence has not yet been separated from the economic process.

THE CDS AND THE OUTSIDE WORLD

The main obstacles to relatively high growth over the long term appear to be not so much purely economic factors, but political ones. Efficient management of national resources requires the formulation of new priorities. The internally divided bureaucracy appears to be incapable of doing this. Some recent cases in which strategically placed big-name politicians have been called in to set up armistices in territorial wars between various ministries (caused by promising new industries), indicate the need for more input from the side of the politicians. When Yasuhiro Nakasone formed a commission for Administrative Reforms (Rincho), he cited the need for a drastic revision of government institutions, the revolutionary possibilities of information technology, and the fact that the urge to catch up with the West no longer stimulates Japan. Since then Nakasone, by becoming prime minister, had an opportunity to add other organizations to the Rincho as part of an attempt to increase political influence over the bureaucrats.

The effect of Nakasone's efforts has been marginal, as would surprise no one acquainted with the power relationships of the Japanese System. In the 1950's a major political decision was made to make industrial expansion the national goal. Since then politicians have not interfered with the bureaucratic elite assigned to carry out that policy. The de-facto one party system of Japan guaranteed that there would be no disturbing confusion from messy parliamentary and democratic processes. But it also meant that politicians were abdicated from responsibilities which in Western democracies are crucial for major policy adjustments. Japan's political world is an anachronism when viewed against the apparent needs of the System today. Parliamentary representatives are largely chosen for their pork-barrelling skills, and leave the introduction of bills and arguments on the budget almost entirely to the bureaucrats, except if one or the other affects their own constituency.

The area in which political mediation is most needed and where it has most glaringly fallen far short of being effective is in the area of <u>international relations</u>. In its dealings with the outside world the Japanese Capitalist Development State faces probably its biggest future challenge. Most discussions about the future of the Japanese economy with intelligent observers of the current situation end up with the major question as to whether there will be a continued acceptance of Japanese exports.

The lion's share of Japanese economic growth since the second oil crisis has come from exports. The friction this has caused with its trading partners is generally known. By far the most important relationship is with the United States. There the idea has recently been gaining ground that the Japanese economy is growing only because of an upturn in the American economy and that the relationship has become parasitic. Notwithstanding its achievement of economic development, Japan appears to systematically block American products from its markets.

Many categories of Japanese exports are already under some form of curtailment, and further arrangements to protect threatened industries in the West can be negotiated relatively easily. Cartelization is, after all, a familiar method of the Japanese CDS. But rather than work out a more systematic arrangement for a division of labor, the American side appears determined to gain improved access to the Japanese market. As this is bound to fail in any but a marginal sense, there is likely to be a great deal more friction. The term friction has by now become an euphemism for sentiments which in certain American quarters have become very hostile toward Japan.

Japanese authorities and their unofficial spokesmen in the academic and business communities contend that whereas the primary and tertiary sectors require further deregulation, the secondary sector of manufactures is as open as can be. Again, what is true on paper is, in this case, not true in fact, as the System erects nontariff barriers about as fast as it removes others. Rhetoric about further efforts to open the market to foreign manufactures implicitly contradicts the official contention that the market could not be more open, and at the same time continues to give rise to expectations which are not fulfilled.

Frustration with Japan on the part of its trading partners is exacerbated by a growing awareness that no officeholder, from the prime minister on down, is able to hold the System to any agreements one has reached with him. The System will grudgingly respond, but always with little and very late, if it is subjected to simultaneous pressure on many of its parts. It reacts only if imbued with the certainty that the status quo will lead to damage.

It would seem that a new set of political decisions is needed for adjustment to a world that finds it increasingly difficult to live with Japan. Prospects for such political decisions to be made are not encouraging. In the meantime, Japan has become an easy scapegoat for economic problems in the U.S. and elsewhere in the West, problems which are quite unrelated to the inaccessibility of its market. In the late 1970s the trade dispute with the Western countries was transformed from an economic into a political problem, without the Japanese System being sufficiently aware of the change. Even though Western countries have become partly dependent on Japanese equipment for their manufacturing capacity, the emotions involved may well outweigh sensible economic reasoning. Recent political rhetoric, especially from the United States, begins to carry the suggestion that Japan is somehow morally deficient.

Thus far the postwar Japanese CDS has met severe challenges with an effectiveness that has repeatedly surprised the pessimists. The most relevant question today is whether the Japanese System will by its actions be able to defuse the gathering anger of the American Congress. Possible American legislation directed against Japanese economic practices is likely to have a snowballing effect resulting in the contraction of world trade. The answer to the question whether in the long term the Japanese economy will move further ahead will therefore probably depend on whether the Western world will risk the collapse of the international free trade system, by attempting to slow it down.

8

The Economic Development of the ASEAN Countries

Janamitra Devan

ASEAN'S DYNAMISM

Southeast Asia is one of the most vibrant regions in the world today. Of particular interest is the Association of Southeast Asian Nations (ASEAN) which, over the past decade, has become the focus of attention of economists, political leaders, and social scientists alike. ASEAN comprises six nations: Indonesia, Malaysia, Singapore, Thailand, the Philippines, and its newest member, the oil-rich sultanate of Brunei. From its inception in 1967 in Bangkok, to the early 1980s, the Association has charted impressive growth rates and equally impressive social and structural changes. More recently, however, ASEAN's economic performance can be described as one undergoing dynamic restructuring.

This paper sets forth the patterns of economic development of the ASEAN countries by focusing on a few key economic variables. In particular, the paper examines principal sectoral compositions and changes (agriculture, industry, services), direct investment flows, and trade.1/ Additionally, the paper compares and contrasts these key variables with three major economic blocs--the EEC, USA, and Japan--by examining the areas in which inter-regional relationships have affected ASEAN. The paper then concludes with a discussion of trends and implications for the 1980s and provides an overview of the major non-economic variables that affect economic development in ASEAN.2/

AN OVERVIEW OF THE ASEAN PHENOMENON

Before proceeding further, a cursory glance at certain facts and figures is in order. By any criterion, the ASEAN countries are diverse. Indonesia, with a population of 162.2 million, dwarfs Singapore's population of 2.5 million and Brunei's population of 0.2 million.

Socially and culturally ASEAN countries comprise numerous ethnic groups and sub-groups. The Malayo-Polynesian populace is the largest ethnic group forming large proportions of the population in Indonesia, Malaysia, Brunei and the Philippines. In the Malayo-Polynesian grouping are hundreds of sub-groups. Interspersed with it are also ethnic Chinese and sub-continental Indians. The Chinese are in the majority in Singapore (75%), and comprise 35% of the population in the Federation of Malaysia. Thailand, to the north, is also ethnically diverse and complex, though less so than elsewhere in ASEAN. Besides ethnic heterogeneity, a vast array of religious differences exists: from Buddhism in Thailand, Catholicism in the Philippines, to Islam in Indonesia, Malaysia and Brunei, and a mixture of Buddhism, Islam, Hinduism, and Christianity in Singapore.

Perhaps the greatest diversity within ASEAN is found in the economic sphere. On one end of the spectrum there is Indonesia with the lowest per capita GNP (US $488, see Table 1), and, on the other end, oil-rich Brunei has the smallest population and the highest per capita GNP equal to US $20,810. This dissimilarity in per capita figures illustrates the vast differences in stages or degrees of economic development making Common Market goals difficult to attain in the immediate future. It also is indicative of the ambitious concept of regional cooperation that is ASEAN's _raison d'etre_.

Despite this diversity, each ASEAN country has some features in common that are striking and boasted about. In the 1970s, when most of the rest of the world was strenuously trying to record even marginally positive growth rates, every ASEAN country, for instance, attained significant economic growth rates (ranging from an average 6.2% in Thailand to 9.2% in Singapore). Indeed, ASEAN then had the fastest growing regional economy in the world. Given ASEAN's large population, and in spite of recent setbacks (mostly due to external circumstances), the region's economy can be expected to continue growing as (and if) greater sections of the market are tapped.3/ The consumption market, in this respect, stands out.

As can be seen from Table 1, consumption and per capita GNP growth figures have similarly increased in magnitude throughout the 1970s, indicating the advent of consumerism in ASEAN societies. Thus, increased production and trade potentials are likely. Enhanced consumerism was supported

TABLE 1
THE ECONOMIES OF ASEAN

Country	Population (millions) 1984	Area (000 Sq. Km.)	GNP (US$ bil.) 1982	GNP (US$ bil.) 1984	Avg. (%) GNP Growth (1970-80)	Avg. (%) Real Growth GNP (1979-83)
Indonesia	162.2	1,919.0	87.2	78.87	7.8	6
Malaysia	15.3	329.7	24.9	30.62	8.0	12.2
Philippines	54.5	300.0	39.4	32.19	6.4	3.8
Thailand	51.7	514.0	36.3	40.63	6.2	5.0[1]
Singapore	2.5	0.6	14.2	18.05	9.2	8.8
Brunei	0.2	5.8	4.1	4.16[1,2]	NA	11.0[2]
ASEAN SUBTOTAL:	286.4	3,069.1	206.09	204.52		

Country	Per Capita GNP (1982) US$	Per Capita GNP (1984) US$	Per Capita GNP Growth (% Per Year) 1960-81	Per Capita GNP Growth (% Per Year) 1981-84	Private Consumption Growth (% Per Year) 1979-81	Private Consumption Growth (% Per Year) 1981-84	Gross Domestic Investment Growth (% Per Year) 1979-81	Gross Domestic Investment Growth (% Per Year) 1981-84
Indonesia	576	488	4.1	-7.7	8.9	-3.7	14.0	1.0
Malaysia	1,694	2,004	4.3	9.2	7.3	10.1	10.4	8.7
Philippines	764	603	2.8	-10.6	4.8	-2.5	10.1	-16.3
Thailand	729	806	4.6	5.3	6.2	3.8	7.5	0.6
Singapore	5,680	7,139	7.4	12.9	6.8	7.1	7.2	13.4
Brunei	20,450	20,810[1]	NA	1.8[3]	NA	NA	NA	NA

1. 1983; 2. GDP (not GNP); 3. 1982-1983; NA: Not Available. Several pieces of information were reported in local currency terms. These were converted to U.S.$.
Sources: Key Indicators of Developing Member Countries of ADB, Supplement, Economics Office, Asian Development Bank, Vol. XVI, October 1985. The World Bank, World development Report 1983. Far Eastern Economic Review, Asia Yearbook 1983, 1984, 1985. International Monetary Fund, Financial Statistics Yearbook 1983. Economist Intelligence Unit, Quarterly Economic Review, Annual Supplements and Quarterly Reports.

additionally by large domestic investment growth rates in each ASEAN member country. The domestic investment growth rates, ranging from Indonesia's 14% average growth rate (over the last decade) to Singapore's 7.2%, implied that the region was gearing itself to be more competitive in a larger range of economic activities. The investment growth rates are even more conspicuous when compared with those registered by the United States (1.9%) and Japan (3.1%) during the same period. These statistics seem to point to the conclusion that ASEAN could maintain and carry the momentum of the 1970s into the rest of the 1980s and perhaps into the 1990s. However, the potential for heightened productive activities and consumption patterns is likely to slow down given the lethargy more recently experienced by most of the ASEAN member states. The current slow growth atmosphere is largely due to external circumstances such as the fall in price of commodity and primary produce on which ASEAN has been dependent. More recent statistics show declines of investment and consumption growth rates in all member states except for Singapore. In Indonesia, the investment growth rate fell to 1.0% during 1981-1984, while that of the Philippines contracted dramatically by 16.7%. Contractions also have occurred in consumption spending for both Indonesia and the Philippines, while continued growth has been experienced in Malaysia and Singapore. Consumption in Thailand has certainly slowed down. Therefore, serious difficulties loom ahead. To better understand ASEAN, the key variables mentioned earlier need to be considered.

THE DEVELOPMENT OF ASEAN--KEY VARIABLES

Sectoral Concentrations

From Table 2, one may quickly discern that the sectoral concentration in ASEAN as a whole is evenly distributed between agriculture and industry. Since 1960, there has been a gradual movement away from agriculture to industry and service, as shown by the sectoral proportion figures of the GDP. This has been true for all of ASEAN except Brunei and Singapore which, due to land and resource constraints, do not have an agricultural base. Again, with the exception of Singapore and Brunei, the other states' manufacturing is oriented to national and regional markets and has been characterized, through the 1970s at least, by moderate import substitution policies. These manufacturing centers are all relatively labor-intensive, taking advantage of cheap and abundant labor. Singapore recently has made the move away from a labor-intensive, industrial framework to one that is technology and capital-intensive so as to accommodate a more skilled workforce.

Although the industrial sector's contribution to GDP has increased, the workforce is still largely concentrated in the agricultural sector in Indonesia, Malaysia, the Philippines, and Thailand. In each of these countries the largely rural population is engaged in small-scale agricultural

TABLE 2

SECTORAL APPORTIONMENT OF WORKFORCE (1960, 1977, 1981) AND SECTOR PROPORTIONS OF GDP (1960, 1970, 1982)

	Indonesia			Malaysia			Philippines			Thailand			Singapore		
	1960	1977	1981	1960	1977	1981	1960	1977	1981	1960	1977	1981	1960	1977	1981
Employed Workforce (millions)			59.1			5			18			24.4			1.1
% Agriculture	75	60	55	63	44	50	61	51	46	84	77	76	8	2	2
% Industry	8	12	15	12	20	16	15	15	17	4	8	9	23	32	39
% Services	7	28	30	25	36	34	24	34	37	12	15	15	69	66	59
GDP			1982			1982			1982			1982			1982
% Agriculture	54	31	26	36	26	23	26	29	22	40	27	22	4	2	1
% Industry	6	34	39	18	29	30	28	35	36	19	29	28	18	35	37
% (Manufacturing)[1]	8	9	13	9	18	18	20	25	24	13	20	19	12	25	26
% Services[2]	32	35	35	46	45	47	46	36	42	41	44	50	78	63	62

Note: Data for Brunei is mostly unavailable. However for 1981, out of a workforce of .7 million, 3% were in agriculture, 18% in industry and 79% in services.

1. Manufacturing is a part of the industrial sector, but its share of GDP is shown separately because it typically is the most dynamic part of the industrial sector.

2. Services include the unallocated share of GDP.

Sources: ADB, Key Indicators, October 1985; World Bank, World Development Indicators, 1979, 1983, 1984.

production. With no major inputs in the rural sector, agricultural productivity increases on the whole have not been substantial, while the rural population explosion and rural poverty have continued to depress agricultural development. Productivity also has been low due to the slow introduction/implementation of mechanization programs.4/ A case in point is the decline in agricultural productivity in Malaysia in the face of a large increase in the agricultural workforce (see Table 2). From a policy perspective, both Thailand and Malaysia have implemented land reform programs in the rural sectors that have been at least partially effective. However, the Philippines and Indonesia have been slow in reforming the latifundia inherited from their colonizers. This is a major reason for the slackness in productivity, as well as for the income inequalities in these countries.

In the industrial sector, since 1960, there have been marginal increases in the employed work force. However, industrial productivity has been high. It is clear that, in deciding development priorities, the ASEAN countries have given greater emphasis to fine-tuning the industrial sector. And, although agricultural development was not deliberately neglected, the lack of concrete steps to enhance output has certainly put ASEAN at a disadvantage.

Service industries have also grown in all of the ASEAN economies, especially in Indonesia. However, most of these are domestically oriented, except for Singapore which has moved on to internationally oriented service industries (e.g., financial and management consulting services).

On the whole, sectoral trends have leveled out, and, in the next decade or so, efforts at intensification in the existing sectors will probably be seen. Even though ASEAN is generally self-sufficient in agricultural produce today, if intensification efforts are sucessful in this sector, it can be expected to grow as a net-exporter of such produce. Besides internal motivation, a major force behind ASEAN's economic spurt has come from the foreign sector. To illustrate this, the impact of foreign direct investments in the ASEAN region will be examined.

Direct Investment Flows

One indication of the growth and development potential of a region is the magnitude of direct investment that flows into it. Table 3 provides some information on this trend within ASEAN from two major economic blocs (the

United States and Japan) from 1976 to 1980. What is striking about these figures is that the United States, although maintaining a relatively large flow of direct investment into ASEAN, has seen low proportions of its total direct investment going to ASEAN. Japan, however, consistently has had a high proportion of direct investment flow in ASEAN. Through 1985, this trend remained unchanged.

The major nations investing in ASEAN are: the United States, followed by Japan, the newly industrialized nations of Hong Kong, South Korea and Taiwan, the EEC, and Australia. American investment, until 1979, was strictly directed to the Philippines and Indonesia, while Japanese investment, though largely directed to Indonesia, was present to varying degrees among other ASEAN countries even before 1976. The United States recently increased its investment share in all ASEAN countries, particularly in Singapore and Malaysia, but it has not been able to keep up with the fast flow of investments into ASEAN from other countries.

The forms of investment flows have altered significantly in the last decade. Flows into ASEAN from private banking sources have grown more rapidly than those emanating from international agencies such as the Asian Development Bank and the World Bank.5/ Additionally, traditional forms of direct investment from transnational corporations, while by no means slack, have taken new forms. These include international subcontracting, turnkey operations, licensing agreements, management contracts, and joint ventures, to name only a few.6/ All these new forms of foreign direct investment not only involve the transfer of capital, but they also include transfers of technology, marketing strategies, and management techniques--packages which the governments in ASEAN are actively pursuing.

TABLE 3

U.S. AND JAPAN, DIRECT INVESTMENT FLOWS INTO ASEAN AS A PERCENTAGE OF THEIR TOTAL DIRECT INVESTMENT IN MILLIONS U.S.$

Country	1976	1977	1978	1979	1980
U.S.	2,306 (1.7)	1,035 (1.4)	2,248 (1.3)	4,066 (2.2)	4,752 (2.2)
Japan	1,044 (30)	636 (23)	917 (20)	595 (12)	926 (20)

Source: Extracted from Oborne and Fourt, 1983, pp. 56-57.

ASEAN has benefited tremendously from the increased volume of investment flows over the past decade. Perhaps this is one reason why there has been a rapid increase in the export sectors of these countries. ASEAN is still very much a major source of important primary commodities like tin, rubber, palm oil, and coconut products. Moreover, as mentioned earlier, labor inputs are cheap while the infrastructure and communication networks are reasonably well developed. This supportive environment has attracted and maintained the flow of direct foreign investment into the region. The spin-off effects of direct foreign investments have also benefited the ASEAN countries. These include feeder industries which propel these countries into higher-technology production.

Trade

ASEAN has been aggressive in yet another area, trade, which has directly contributed to the Association's dynamic rise. The ASEAN economies are the world's newest open ones and exhibit high ratios of foreign trade to GNP as seen in Table 4.

TABLE 4

ASEAN'S FOREIGN TRADE

Country	(1) X as % of GDP (1984)	(2) X Growth (1970-81)	(3) M Growth (1970-81)	(4) X Growth (1981-84)	(5) M Growth (1981-84)
Indonesia	26.1	6.5	11.9	-4.6	1.5
Malaysia	50.4	6.8	7.1	11.8	7.1
Philippines	34.6	7.7	2.6	-5.9	-9.0
Thailand	17.7	11.8	4.9	4.5	5.3
Singapore	85.0	12.0	9.9	3.9	1.6

X: Exports of goods and non-factor services

M: Imports of goods and non-factor services

Source: ADB, Key Indicators, 1985; Statistical Yearbook of Indonesia, 1981, 1984; Yearbook of Statistics, 1982, 1985; World Development Report, 1983; The Asia Yearbook, 1983.

ASEAN's total merchandise exports were more than U.S. $68 billion in 1982. The share of manufactures as a percentage of total exports ranged from 55% in the Philippines to 1% in Indonesia.7/ Comparing export growth rates of ASEAN in the 1970s (column 2 of Table 4) with those of the United States (average of 6.5% per year) and Japan (average of 12% per year), reveals ASEAN's increasing competitiveness and adeptness at marketing its products in the international arena.

On the import-consumption side, ASEAN was not less conspicuous throughout the last decade. Imports also grew rapidly in the rest of ASEAN, apart from the Philippines. Total merchandise imports were U.S. $71.9 billion in 1982. In the same year, China's imports were U.S. $22 billion. The ASEAN "market for foreign goods," in essence, is approximately three-and-a-half times larger than that of China, about half the size of Japan's, and is growing more rapidly than both.8/

Furthermore, the basket of ASEAN's imports, is also revealing. Capital goods account for more than 60% of ASEAN's total imports (ESCAP, 1982). This implies that the consumption pattern of the ASEAN countries is not merely to absorb short-term non-productive goods, but to also absorb long-term capital goods whose benefits are yet to be seen.

Exports and imports grew quickly in the 1970s and early 1980s, but not lopsidedly. The cumulative balance of payments of Indonesia, Malaysia, and Singapore (from 1978 to 1982) has been positive. Thailand and the Philippines have had negative balances, but, as witnessed in the past two years, only the Philippines continues to have serious problems with its BOP (exacerbated by the assassination of President Marcos' political foe, Benigno Aquino, in 1983). There is no doubt that ASEAN has been aggressive in trade. However, the scale has been tipping.

In the past few years, due to external shocks and worldwide recession in key trading countries, the ASEAN nations generally experienced slower export and import growth. As columns 4 and 5 indicate, Indonesia's export growth took a dip into negative growth due to falling oil prices, while the rate of import growth in Singapore was vastly reduced. The massive reduction in the Philippines in both exports and imports can be squarely blamed on the internal political upheaval that the country had been undergoing. Recovery in the Philippines is subject to a successful transition of power. The Marcos regime hindered recovery by massive mismanagement and interference of state enterprises. These recent setbacks in ASEAN have not shadowed the impressive economic growth and trade that ASEAN has had with the outside world. Provided that the restructuring processes that all ASEAN members are undertaking evolve unhindered, the potential for continued growth is still present. One of these potentials is closer to the home front.

Intra-ASEAN trade has been relatively meager. Although it has expanded in absolute (volume) terms, it has not as a percentage of trade. In essence there are still many barriers to intra-ASEAN trade. Table 5 depicts this clearly. Intra-ASEAN trade data from the years 1970, 1976, and 1982, show how the volume of trade has increased. Each country's exports to another, as a percentage of the country's total exports, besides being small in general, have increased only minimally. In fact, in some areas the export shares have decreased. This immediately calls to attention that even though ASEAN has made long strides in many areas, trade liberalization, though worded formally, is not one of them.9/ Preferential trading arrangements have been cleared gradually over the past few years by the ASEAN government in order to generate more intra-ASEAN trade.10/ Since one of ASEAN's goals is to reduce its excessive dependence upon advanced countries, greater intra-regional trade is the most effective strategy to follow. Although a number of reasons can be given to explain this relative stagnation in intra-regional trade, three of them stand out.

First, the major productive capabilities of ASEAN are primarily destined to be consumed outside the region (e.g., rubber, tin, palm oil and coconut), as the intra-regional capacity for the absorption of these products is still too small. Second, import-substitution policies among the larger ASEAN countries have resulted in priority being given to imports of capital and intermediate goods which are not supplied in great quantities by the region itself. Third, past foreign aid and loans from developed countries have often been tied to imports from donor countries.11/ Other reasons include the present limited knowledge about trading opportunities among ASEAN members, the inadequacy of regional transport and shipping facilities, and the weaknesses of existing financial services for intra-regional trade. These limitations are essentially due to the institutional biases that each country developed during the colonial days (except Thailand, all other members of ASEAN were previously colonized), when various trade supporting services and financial structures were created mainly to foster trade with Western countries.

TABLE 5

INTRA-ASEAN TRADE, EXPORTS AS % OF TOTAL EXPORTS 1970, 1976, 1982

(U.S.$ MILLIONS)

From/To (A)	Year	(B) Indonesia	Malaysia	Philippines	Singapore	Thailand	Brunei
Indonesia	1970	--	36 (3.2) -	26 (2.3) -	172 (15.5) -	0 (0) +	0
	1976	--	23 (0.3) *	90 (1.1) -	644 (7.5) -	2 (0.02) +	0
	1982	--	61 (0.3)	207 (1.0)	1,050 (5.2)	32 (0.2)	0
Malaysia	1970	11 (0.6) -	--	29 (1.7) -	364 (21.6) -	15 (0.9) +	10 (0.6) +
	1976	23 (0.4) -		80 (1.5) -	967 (18.3) +	68 (1.3) +	37 (0.7) -
	1982	39 (0.3)	--	117 (1.0)	3,033 (25.7)	348 (3.0)	32 (0.3)
Philippines	1970	2 (0.2) +	0 (0) +	--	7 (0.7) +	3 (0.3) *	0 (0) *
	1976	12 (0.5) -	5 (0.2) +	--	56 (2.2) *	7 (0.3) *	0 (0) +
	1982	55 (1.1)	17 (3.6)	--	111 (2.2)	14 (0.3)	4 (0.1)
Singapore	1970	NA	340 (21.9) -	4 (0.3) +	--	51 (3.3) -	25 (1.6) -
	1976	NA	1,005 (15.2) +	52 (0.8) +	--	197 (3.0) +	97 (1.5) +
	1982	NA	3,669 (17.7)	323 (1.6)	--	799 (3.8)	359 (1.7)
Thailand	1970	16 (2.3)	40 (5.6) -	1 (0.1) +	49 (7.0) -	--	0 (0) +
	1976	154 (5.2) -	126 (4.2) +	30 (1.0) -	202 (6.8) *	--	4 (0.1) *
	1982	142 (2.0)	379 (5.4)	33 (0.5)	477 (6.8)	--	9 (0.1)
Brunei	1970	0	83 (82.2) -	0 (0) +	1 (1.0) +	0 (0) *	--
	1976	0	74 (6.3) -	2 (1.7) +	20 (1.7) +	0 (0) +	--
	1982	0	1 (0.03)	71 (2.2)	203 (0.4)	17 (0.5)	--

+ Implies an increase in exports from A to B (in percentage terms)

- Implies a decrease in exports from A to B (in percentage terms)

* Unchanged (in percentage terms)

Source: Directory of Trade Statistics Yearbooks, 1970-76 and 1983.

In essence there are still many obstacles to be removed before the free-trade potential is actually reached among the ASEAN countries. But similar efforts towards a freer trade, experienced in other regional cooperation schemes among developing countries, show that the attainment of genuine cooperation is not an overnight process. Much rhetoric likely will be spilled before full cooperation can be achieved. While intra-ASEAN trade has been slow to take off, extra-ASEAN trade has been prolific, albeit not vis-a-vis all parties.

Whereas ASEAN has been looking aggressively beyond its boundaries, the major market economies of the world in general are not looking beyond their backyards. Table 6 examines some trade-intensity ratios. Based on this formula, ASEAN's export and import-intensity ratios are shown vis-a-vis three of its major trading partners--the United States, Japan, and the EEC--and the rest of Pacific Asia. What can readily be seen is that Japan is by far the most intensive trading partner of ASEAN in both the export and import sectors, followed by the rest of the Asian Pacific, the United States, and lastly the EEC.12/ What can also be seen is that there has been a steady improvement in, or at least a maintenance of, the import and export intensities of ASEAN in three trade sectors--ASEAN-United States, ASEAN-Japan, and ASEAN-Rest of the Pacific Asia--while the relative importance of the EEC to ASEAN, though remaining steady, has not been significant.

In examining the trade-intensity ratio in more detail, the figure of 0.33 in 1982 shows that exports to ASEAN from the EEC as a proportion of total exports to ASEAN were smaller than exports from the EEC as a proportion of world exports. There is a twofold implication to this ratio. One is that the EEC has not been making significant inroads into the ASEAN region, and the other is that the EEC has not been able to compete effectively for ASEAN market imports.

In the same way, the ASEAN-EEC export-intensity ratio of 0.25 in 1982 suggests that ASEAN has not made significant inroads into the EEC market for imports. The implication of this gain is twofold. Either ASEAN has not been able to compete effectively for the EEC import market, or biased trade barriers in the EEC have curtailed potential exports from the ASEAN to the EEC. Since ASEAN's export-intensity ratios have consistently been greater than 1 vis-a-vis the other three markets, one is compelled to believe that EEC protectionism and trade barriers are probably the cause of the low ASEAN-EEC export-intensity ratios. In a similar vein, since ASEAN's import-intensity

TABLE 6
EXTRA-ASEAN TRADE-INTENSITY RATIOS

ASEAN'S Trading Partner	1970 Am	1970 Ax	1976 Am	1976 Ax	1982 Am	1982 Ax
United States	0.97	1.24	1.13	1.56	1.10	1.07
Japan	3.63	4.33	3.17	3.92	2.60	3.78
EEC	0.43	0.39	0.36	0.38	0.33	0.25
*Rest of Pacific Asia	2.82	1.79	2.49	1.91	1.91	2.05

*Includes Australia, New Zealand, Hong Kong, South Korea, Taiwan and China.

Source: Statistics from International Monetary Fund, Direction of Trade Statistics Yearbook, 1970-76 and 1983.

Note: The figures in this table are indicators of the intensity of exports (imports) from (into) ASEAN to (from) each of the countries (regions) categorized above. The formula was suggested in Sautter, October 1980.

ratios have been consistently higher than 1 with respect to the United States, Japan, and the rest of Pacific Asia (except for 1970, when the ASEAN-U.S. ratio was 0.97), the ASEAN-EEC import-intensity ratio being less than one can be attributed more towards the EEC's inability to compete effectively for the ASEAN market than the protectionism that exists in ASEAN.13/

ASEAN Infrastructure

Having briefly examined the key elements of the economic development of ASEAN over the past ten to fifteen years, one can see that major structural changes have occurred. Traditional sectors such as agriculture have remained an integral part of ASEAN's development, but non-traditional sectors (industry and services) have grown and taken on more sophisticated forms. The strengthening that has resulted is due to the emphasis the ASEAN governments have placed on technology imports (mainly in the form of foreign direct investments) and on a rapidly expanding trade sector. What have not been discussed in ASEAN's developmental spurt, but which are nevertheless important contributions to its overall success, are the support areas of education, manpower planning, infrastructural development and rural development, among other things. In each of these areas ASEAN has made significant progress. This is not to say that problems do not exist or are negligible. Income redistribution, for example, has had mixed results in urban areas as opposed to rural areas.14/ Furthermore, to a great extent ASEAN has yet to eradicate poverty among large sections of its population (although Singapore and Malaysia have made significant progress in this area), and health services, while improved, remain wanting by Western standards. Given the improvements that might be expected in these support areas, what are some trends and implications for the rest of the 1980s? To answer this, one must consider the non-economic variables of economic development as well, and in particular, the political variable.

ASEAN'S FUTURE

All things considered, ASEAN's future development pattern looks promising. ASEAN will continue to emphasize industrialization; however, changes will have to be made in the agricultural sector. As mentioned earlier, agricultural productivity, being one of the lowest sectorally, will have to be improved in order to meet local requirements. Also, the growth of its population is still a problem. Aside from Malaysia and Thailand, the agricultural productivity of Indonesia and the Philippines has not been impressive.

Provided there are sufficient incentives, foreign direct investment should continue to grow. These incentives fall under two major categories. One incentive comes from the consideration of foreign investors to exploit the local market (except in Singapore and Brunei, where markets are relatively small). The other incentive comes from the ability of foreign investors to continue exploiting the local raw material supplies. Both motivations have been consistent with the import-substitution policies and the economic goals of ASEAN host governments.15/ Barring political upheavals, and provided incentives remain unchanged, direct foreign investments can be expected to continue flowing into ASEAN. The only conceivable change in foreign direct investment would be in the form of ownership, since there is an increasing tendency towards joint ventures. In what follows, future trade patterns will be discussed .

As the more industrialized countries of the Pacific Rim (especially the "Newly Industrialized Countries," NICs, of Hong Kong, Taiwan, South Korea and Singapore) substitute for the traditional industrial nations in the export of capital goods equipment and to ASEAN, one possible new pattern of ASEAN trade will become increasingly evident. Unless the traditional industrial countries (particularly the United States, Japan and the EEC) maintain their comparative advantage in that export sector, there is a strong possibility of the Asian NICs taking over as the foremost suppliers of capital goods to the ASEAN countries.

Trade in the ASEAN countries, except for Indonesia, and of late, the Philippines, could be enhanced further if the terms of trade keep improving, as they did throughout the 1970s despite the high price of oil. Both of these countries are facing problems with their balance of payments, resulting in several devaluations of their currencies and the subsequent deterioration in their terms of trade as relative prices of their exports decline.

The trade potential of ASEAN vis-a-vis Japan, the EEC, and the United States is mixed. The Japanese will continue to figure prominently in trade relations with ASEAN, while the United States and the EEC, by all indications, will register declining volumes of trade with ASEAN. The Japanese have several "built-in" advantages in trade with ASEAN. Geographical proximity gives the Japanese a tremendous advantage in terms of transportation costs. ASEAN, in a sense, is the "hinterland" of Japan, just as Latin America is to the United States. The Japanese economy, being resource poor, is also heavily dependent on ASEAN for imports of its necessary raw materials, and being capital rich, is dependent on ASEAN as an investment outlet for its surplus capital.16/ In addition, the Japanese have been aggressive in their marketing efforts in the ASEAN countries and consequently have captured larger market segments in ASEAN. They have taken great pains in determining the appropriate nature of ASEAN requirements (e.g., providing products and technology which are right for its scale of operations) and by patiently establishing the goodwill necessary for business practice in the unique cultural and social settings of the ASEAN countries. Perhaps most importantly, the Japanese have made great efforts in ASEAN simply because they are after long-run market shares rather than short-run profits. Once they have persuaded their hosts, they also try to obtain the encouragement from the ASEAN governments.

The United States and the EEC, however, have been slow in taking advantage of the ASEAN market. It remains to be seen whether the United States and the EEC will be viable competitors for the ASEAN market in the late 1980s. If they are to pose any serious challenge to the Japanese, then several steps need to be taken. One is the need to know the local markets, which includes knowledge of ASEAN economies, government plans and policies. An understanding of how to deal with indigenous ASEAN businesses is also required, since any form of business depends to a large degree on its rapport with local suppliers, agents and subcontractors. A foreign business could be seen as a competitor, and thus be resented. So the approach the foreign business has to take is one of caution--"not to tread on the other's foot"--so to speak. Further, foreign businesses have to realize that labor-management-government relations in all ASEAN countries are very unlike those in their own countries. In effect, the relationship is threatened. If the United States and the EEC are able to successfully tap the ASEAN market, then there is no doubt that its economic development will be hastened in the 1980s. However, this depends on one other non-economic variable.

An important factor in the development of ASEAN economies is politics. ASEAN performed well in the 1970s because the political leadership was, in general, quite stable. Many scholars may dispute this, since Indonesia and the Philippines (until recently) are run by autocrats, Brunei by a monarchy, Thailand by an uneasy coalition of civilian and military leaders, and Singapore and Malaysia by groups of elite technocrats intolerant of opposition. However, the scholars who dispute this invariably resort to Western standards of democracy in judging the ASEAN countries. The fact is that these standards do not apply to the ASEAN framework, where for the majority of the people consensus rather than confrontation is the name of the game. As long as the political machinery can deliver the goods, the people of ASEAN are generally tolerant and accept authority without too much griping. When the goods stop flowing however, as happened in the Philippines recently, and as happened in Thailand and Indonesia in the 1960s, then the political processes begin to falter. Virtually all of the countries in ASEAN are undergoing some form of transition of power or social and economic restructuring.

Problems in Singapore are on the rise because of the inability of the second-tier leadership to gain complete support of a more educated workforce, and clamoring for greater degrees of freedom has caused disaffection. Racial tension is still very much in evidence in Malaysia where the large Chinese population is apprehensive of economic policies that favor the majority Malay population. Thailand and Indonesia have the constant threat of a military junta taking over. Brunei faces increasing difficulties in coping with rapidly falling oil prices. And in the Philippines the rule of the law faltered rapidly, ending the Marcos regime amid a largely ineffectual and corrupt bureaucracy and a resurgent communist movement, which now threatens the Aquino government with seemingly insurmountable problems.

If the transitions of political power are smooth in all ASEAN member states, then there is no doubt that their economic development will surge ahead into the 1990s. The potential is evident.

NOTES

1. The choice of direct investment flows and trade as key variables in the development of ASEAN follows from the emphasis that the ASEAN governments have placed on rapid industrialization and export growth.

2. The non-economic variables of economic development, such as the perceived external threat from Vietnam, the dynamics of ASEAN politics, and the behavior of ASEAN businesses, are a perennial problem for the economist probing economic issues, and undoubtedly play important roles in the explanation of economic development. However, for the purpose of this paper, the <u>ceteris</u> <u>paribus</u> cliche regarding these non-economic variables will hold for the most of this discussion. The author apologizes for this profusely.

3. No doubt, the large ASEAN population can be a disadvantage as well, expecially if current population growth rates grow unbridled. In tandem with growing labor productivity currently experienced, a large population in ASEAN would result in high unemployment in the future. See also Linda Lim, "Prospects for U.S. Business in Southeast Asia," <u>Southeast Asia Business</u> 1 and 2 (Spring/Summer 1984): 2-6.

4. There is a strong economic case to show that the introduction of partial mechanization into the agricultural sector would raise productivity in traditional agricultural sectors. See Herman Southworth, ed., <u>Farm Mechanization in East Asia</u> (New York: Agricultural Development Council, 1972). This, however, is inconclusive. As observed in several developing countries with large populations, the rapid introduction of mechanization programs also caused greater rural unemployment and distress. The problem therefore, is far from being resolved.

5. Note that in absolute value, international organizations are still ahead of private sources of investment flows. See Michael W. Oborne and Nicholas Fourt, <u>Pacific Basin Economic Cooperation</u> (Paris: OECD Development Center Studies, 1983), p. 31.

6. For details on these new forms of direct investment see Charles Oman, <u>New Forms of International Investment in Developing Countries</u> (Paris: OECD Development Center, 1984).

7. Given the growth in fixed capital formation, ranging from 15.9% in Indonesia to 7.6% in the Philippines over the period 1963-1979, the growth in manufactures as a percentage of exports is surely to increase <u>ceteris paribus</u>. Therefore, countries like Indonesia were expected to increase their export capabilities once the gestation period was over, <u>or</u> after domestic requirements were taken care of. (Indonesia, one notes, has a large market within its own borders.) However, recent setbacks in commodity prices negated the expected increases in exports.

8. Lim, "Prospects for U.S. Business...," p. 2.

9. As seen in Table 5, the only consistently sizable shares in intra-country trade is the Singapore-Malaysia trade category. The figures however are not representative because a large percentage of trade between these two countries involves re-exports since Singapore acts as the port of entry and exit for products headed to and from Malaysia. As a word of caution, low trade percentages do not necessarily imply that free trade does not exist. As the ensuing discussion shows, there are other reasons for low trade percentages pertaining to intra-ASEAN trade.

10. The ASEAN governments have already agreed on extensive trade liberalization schemes, involving thousands of products, with tariff concessions ranging from 10% to 30%. The present trade preference agreement operates in such a way that if one country enjoys a concession from another, then all other member countries automatically have the concession too. Tariff concessions, in addition to being handled on a product-by-product basis, now encompass the broader across-the-board approach based on certain criteria of eligibility and exclusion lists.

11. John Wong, <u>ASEAN Economies in Perspective</u> (London: Macmillan Press, 1979).

12. There is some bias in the intensity ratios which one should be aware of. Take ASEAN's intensity ratio vis-a-vis Japan for instance. It is Indonesia which, being the major oil-producing country in ASEAN, exports to Japan intensively. Indonesia's exports, therefore, make it seem as though ASEAN's export intensity is higher than its import intensity vis-a-vis Japan (as seen in Table 6). Actually, Japan imposes many restrictive import policies for which the members of ASEAN have tried negotiating reversals with little success.

13. The above explanation does not imply that the EEC-ASEAN trade link is an insignificant one. The EEC-ASEAN link has been significant in terms of the shares of EEC's exports to ASEAN and imports from ASEAN. All the intensity

ratios say is that the relative weight of EEC-ASEAN trade has not been significant with respect to each region's links with the rest of the world. The analysis does purport, however, that there is much room for improvement in trade ties between the EEC and ASEAN and, for that matter, with the United States too.

14. John Wong studied the problems in income distribution and found, using Gini ratios, improvement in income distribution in rural Indonesia, urban Philippines, urban Thailan, and Singapore. He found deterioration in urban Indonesia, rural Philippines, rural Thailand, and Malaysia. Wong, ASEAN Economies in Perspective, p. 197.

15. Only in Singapore, where the strategy is one of export-promotion industrialization, did foreign investors come in to take advantage of export potentials in line with government goals. For further information on motivations for foreign direct investment, see Wong, ASEAN Economies in Perspective, pp. 88-92.

16. The Japanese also rely on many of the ASEAN countries for their "indirect" exports to Western markets.

REFERENCES

Asian Development Bank. Key Indicators of Developing Member Countries of ADB. Supplement, Economics Office, Asian Development Bank, Volume XVI, October 1985.

Economist Intelligence Unit. Quarterly Economic Review, Annual Supplements and Quarterly Reports.

The Far Eastern Economic Review. Asia Yearbook, 1983, 1984, 1985.

International Monetary Fund. Financial Statistics Yearbook, 1983.

International Monetary Fund, Direction of Trade Statistics Yearbook, 1970-76, and 1983.

Lim, Linda. "Prospects for U.S. Business in Southeast Asia." Southeast Asia Business 1 and 2 (Spring/Summer 1984):2-6.

Nair, Devan C.V., ed. Socialism That Works... The Singapore Way. Singapore: Federal Publications.

Oborne, Michael West, and Fourt, Nicholas. Pacific Basin Economic Cooperation. Paris: OECD Development Center Studies, 1983.

Oman, Charles. New Forms of International Investment in Developing Countries. Paris: OECD Development Center, 1984.

Sautter, Christian. "Le Japan et l'Asie-Pacifique." Economie et Prospective 4 (Octobre 1980).

Southeast Asia Business 1 and 2 (Spring/Summer 1984):55 pp. (Quarterly Newsletter published by the Southeast Asia Business Education and Resources Program, Center for South and Southeast Asian Studies, University of Michigan).

Southworth, Herman, ed. Farm Mechanization in East Asia. New York: Agricultural Development Council, 1972.

Statistical Yearbook of Indonesia. Jakarta, Indonesia: Biro Pusat Statistik, 1981, 1984.

United Nations. Yearbook of National Statistics, 1980.

West, Philip. "The Pacific-Rim: An Overview." Strategic Planning and the Pacific Rim, Second Annual Pacific Rim Conference held at Indianapolis, May 3-4 1984.

Wong, John. ASEAN Economies in Perspective. London: Macmillan Press, 1979.

World Bank. World Development Report, 1983.

World Bank. World Development Indicators, 1979, 1983, 1984.

Yearbook of Statistics. Singapore: Department of Statistics, 1982, 1984.

9

The Economic Development of the Newly Industrialized Countries in East Asia

Rong-I Wu

The rapid economic development of the Newly Industrialized Countries (NICs) in East Asia (Hong Kong, The Republic of China [Taiwan], Singapore and South Korea) have attracted a great deal of attention from all over the world. This is due to the following two reasons: developing countries are eager to learn from the developmental experiences of the Asian NICs; while industrial countries may see the Asian NICs as growing competitors in both domestic and international markets. Economic development, however, is a process of long-term transformation. Two or three decades of development is probably not long enough to form any conclusive observations. Therefore, this section intends to emphasize the following two aspects: first, the strategic factors in the economic development experience of Hong Kong, Singapore, South Korea and Taiwan during the past two or three decades; and second, the problems of both domestic adjustment and increasing protectionism in the international market as a result of their high degree of trade dependence. The study will conclude with an evaluation of the economic development strategy of the Asian NICs and its implications for world development.

DISTINCTIVE FEATURES OF ECONOMIC DEVELOPMENT IN EAST ASIA

Rapid Growth

The most distinctive feature of the development of Hong Kong, Singapore, South Korea, and Taiwan in the past two decades is the rapid growth of their economies as compared with other developing countries. Average annual growth rates of the per capita Gross National Product (GNP), from 1965 to 1984, were 5.2% in Hong Kong, 7.8% in Singapore, 6.6% in South Korea, and 7.0% in Taiwan, while those of low income developing countries (with an average per capita GNP of U.S. $260 in 1984) and middle income developing countries (with an average per capita GNP of U.S. $1,250 in 1984) were only 2.8% and 3.1% respectively during the corresponding period (see Table 1).1/ The per capita GNP doubled in ten years with a compounded rate of growth of 7%, and it quadrupled in twenty years. Thus, the per capita GNP of Hong Kong and Singapore rose to U.S. $6,330 and U.S. $7,260, respectively. These figures are higher than those of Spain and Ireland, the countries with the lowest income in industrial market economies.2/ The per capita GNP of industrial market economies grew only 2.4% during the same period.

Except for Hong Kong, between 1964 and 1973, the average annual growth rate of the gross domestic product (GDP) of Hong Kong, Singapore, South Korea and Taiwan, during the years 1965-73 and 1973-84 is much higher than that of low income, middle income, or high income oil exporting countries and of industrial market economies (see Table 2).

TABLE 1

BASIC INDICATORS

Country or Region	Population Mid-1984 (millions)	Area (Thous. sq. kilometers)	Per Capita GNP 1984 (U.S. $)	Per Capita GNP Avg. Ann. Growth Rate 1965-84 (%)
Low income economies	2,389.5	31,795	260	2.8
Middle income economies	1,187.6	40,927	1,250	3.1
High income oil exporters	18.6	4,311	11,250	3.2
Industrial market economies	733.4	30,935	11,430	2.4
Far East NICs	67.0	136	2,847	--
Korea	40.1	98	2,110	6.6
Taiwan	19.0	36	3,046	7.0
Hong Kong	5.4	1	6,330	6.2
Singapore	2.5	1	7,260	7.8

Source: For Taiwan, Taiwan Statistical Data Book 1985, Council for Economic Planning and Development, Republic of China; for others, World Development Report 1986, The World Bank.

Table 2
GROWTH OF GROSS DOMESTIC PRODUCT

Country or Region	Avg. Ann. Growth Rate (%) 1965-63	1973-84
Low income economies	5.6	5.3
Middle income economies	7.4	4.4
High income oil exporters	9.0	4.5
Industrial market economies	4.7	2.4
Far East NICs		
Korea	10.0	7.2
Taiwan	11.0	7.7
Hong Kong	7.9	9.1
Singapore	13.0	8.2

Source: Table 1.

High Ratio of Foreign Dependency

The second distinctive feature of the economic development of the Asian NICs is the high dependency on international trade. One can use the following two indicators to express this ratio: The first indicator is the export of goods and nonfactory services as a percentage of the GDP. The second is the export of merchandise as a percentage of the GDP, as shown in Table 3. Using the most recent statistics available (1984), the export of goods and non-factor services as a percentage of the GDP was 37% in South Korea, 58% in Taiwan, 107% in Hong Kong and 176% in Singapore. The ratios of these four countries are quite high by any standard.3/ In 1965 that ratio was still very low, particularly for Korea and Taiwan, at 9% and 19% respectively. The fast increase in this ratio during the last two decades implies a rapidly growing openness of the economy.

As for the city-states of Hong Kong and Singapore, a high foreign dependency ratio is quite natural. With each having an area of about 1,000 square kilometers, Hong Kong and Singapore are only harbors and thus entrepot trade is their main economic activity. This was especially true during their early period of development. As a result, nonfactor services such as shipping, transportation and travel accounted for an important share of the GDP. Only when the industrial sector began to expand rapidly did merchandise exports gradually become important. The importance of entrepot trade can be roughly measured from the difference between domestic exports as a percentage of the GDP and total exports as a percentage of the GDP (see Table 3B). The increasing ratio of domestic exports as a percentage of the GDP indicates the growing share of merchandise trade in total exports, i.e., the structural change from a dominant entrepot to an exporter of primary domestic products.

The main factor behind this increasing openness is the quick growth of foreign trade, which can be seen from the statistics in Table 4. The growth of merchandise exports is very rapid during 1965-1973 and 1973-1984 in all four of the Asian NICs. The average annual growth of merchandise exports registered in double digit rates in almost all four countries between 1964 and 1984, with the exception of Singapore, during 1973-1984. Export performance amounted to an annual increase of 31.7% and 25% respectively from

Table 3

A. EXPORTS OF GOODS AND NONFACTOR SERVICES AS PERCENTAGE OF GDP (%)

Country	1965	1984
Korea	9	37
Taiwan	19	58
Hong Kong	71	107
Singapore	123	174

B. MERCHANDISE EXPORTS AS PERCENTAGE OF GDP

Country	1965	1984
Korea	17.1	35.1
Taiwan	16.0	53.2
Hong Kong		
Domestic Exports/GDP	47.8	57.6
Total Exports/GDP	62.1	92.5
Singapore		
Domestic Exports/GDP	10.1	85.0
Total Exports/GDP	31.1	132.0

Source: A: World Development Report 1986, The World Bank.
B: International Finanacial Statistics Yearbook, 1984, IMF.
For figures on Taiwan, Taiwan Statistical Data Book, 1985.

1965-1973. The two oil crises in the 1970s did not have a great impact on the export growth of these NICs. From 1973 to 1984, the annual growth rates of merchandise exports for these countries maintained levels as high as 15.1% in Korea, 14.1% in Taiwan, 12.9% in Hong Kong and 7.1% in Singapore. In contrast, the rate of exports from middle income economies and high income oil exporters expanded only .8% and -7.8% annually during the same period.

TABLE 4
GROWTH OF MERCHANDISE TRADE

Country/Region	Amount 1984 (US $mil)	Avg. Ann. Growth Rate* 1965-73 %	1973-84 %
	A. EXPORTS		
Low income economies	48,319	1.7	5.4
Mid. income economies	355,439	6.3	0.8
High inc. oil export.	88,380	10.9	-7.8
Indust. market econ.	1,999,846	9.5	4.2
Far East NICs	112,076	--	--
Korea	29,248	31.7	15.1
Taiwan	30,456	25.0	14.1
Hong Kong	28,317	11.7	12.9
Singapore	24,055	11.0	7.1
	B. IMPORTS		
Low income economies	64,903	-1.2	5.0
Mid. income economies	346,948	8.4	4.4
High inc. oil export.	59,328	10.2	16.3
Indust. market econ.	1,292,192	10.1	3.2
Far East NICs	109,700	--	--
Korea	30,609	22.4	9.7
Taiwan	21,959	22.0	7.5
Hong Kong	28,567	10.6	9.3
Singapore	28,565	9.8	7.1

*In real terms, calculated from quantum (volume) indices of exports and imports.
Source: See Table 1.

Since these four Asian NICs are all very poor in natural resources, the rapid rate of growth in their expansion of exports must be supported by fast increases in the import of raw materials and capital goods. As a consequence, imports by these countries also expanded very quickly (see Table 4B).

Structural Change in Trade and Production

The third distinctive feature is the remarkable change in the structure of trade and production since 1965. The data in Table 5 show the commodity structure of exports and imports classifed under five groups: 1) fuels, minerals and metals, 2) other primary commodities, 3) textiles and clothing, 4) machinery and transport equipment, and 5) other manufactured items. Combining groups 1 and 2 as "primary products," and the remaining three categories as "manufacturing products," it can be seen that Korea and Taiwan have undergone a drastic change in the structure of the goods that they export; having moved, in 1965, from being a dominant exporter of primary products to becoming a dominant exporter of manufactured products. In Singapore, in 1965, the big share in other primary commodities, and, in 1983, in fuels, minerals and metals was mainly due to the earlier entrepot trade of rubber and to the later one of petroleum refinery products.4/

Among manufactured products, the big jump in the share of "machinery and transport equipment" trade from 1965 to 1983--from 6% to 22% in Hong Kong, 10% to 31% in Singapore, 3% to 32% in Korea and 13% to 26% in Taiwan--is particularly significant. This implies that the Asian NICs moved from the export of intensive products such as textiles and clothing to exports of technological and capital intensive products such as machinery and transport equipment. When the structure of merchandise exports in low income and middle income economies is compared with that of the Asian NICs, it can be seen in low and middle income economies that primary exports still accounted for 50% or more of their total exports in 1983. Among manufactured products, the share of machinery and transport equipment was relatively small.

Because of the close relationship between trade and growth, the rapid increase and structural change of exports will cause a change in the structure of production. If one divides the GDP into three sectors, namely agriculture, industry and services, one can see the clear trend of a decrease in the relative share of agriculture and an increase in the relative share of both industry and services. Hong Kong is an exception to this pattern. In the 1970s, it gradually developed as a financial center in East Asia; thus the service sector represents its most important activity in 1984 (see Table 6).

TABLE 5

STRUCTURE OF MERCHANDISE EXPORTS (units in %)

	KOREA		TAIWAN		HONG KONG		SINGAPORE	
Groups of Merchandise	1965	1983	1968	1983	1965	1983	1965	1983
Fuels, minerals and metals	15	3	1	2	2	2	21	31
Other primary commodities	25	6	35	8	11	6	44	13
Textiles and clothing	27	25	23	19	43	33	6	4
Machinery and transport equip.	3	32	13	26	6	22	10	31
Other manufactures	29	34	29	44	37	36	18	22
1-2 Primary products	40	9	36	10	13	8	65	44
3-5 Manufacturing products	59	91	65	89	86	91	34	57

	LOW INCOME ECONOMIES		MID. INCOME ECONOMIES		INDUST. MKT. ECONOMIES	
Groups of Merchandise	1965	1983*	1965	1983	1965	1983
Fuels, minerals and metals	12	20	36	31	9	12
Other primary commodities	65	30	48	23	21	14
Textiles and clothing	15	18	4	9	7	4
Machinery and transport equip.	1	5	2	14	31	38
Other manufactures	8	28	10	23	32	32
1-2 Primary products	77	50	84	54	30	26
3-5 Manufacturing products	24	51	16	46	70	74

*For 1982

Source: For Taiwan, Monthly Statistics of Exports and Imports, The Republic of China, Department of Statistics, Ministry of Finance, ROC, November 1984. For others, World Development Report, 1986, The World Bank.

TABLE 6

RELATIVE SHARE OF PRODUCTION

		Distribution of GDP (%)							
		Agriculture		Industry		Manufacturing		Services	
	1984 GDP								
Country	(US$ Mil)	1965	1984	1965	1984	1965	1984	1965	1984
Korea	83,220	38	14	25	40	18	28	37	47
Taiwan	57,207	24	6	34	51	24	42	42	43
Hong Kong	30,620	2	1	40	22	24	22	58	78
Singapore	18,220	3	1	24	39	15	25	73	60

Source: For Taiwan, Quarterly National Economic Trends Taiwan Area, The Republic of China, no. 33. For other Countries, World Development Report 1986, The World Bank.

STRATEGIC FACTORS OF RAPID DEVELOPMENT

Recently, studies on the economic development of the Asian NICs have become quite popular. Although the authors of these studies may have differing opinions, it appears that there is no great controversy among them over the strategic factors of the rapid development of the NICs. This section summarizes some of the commonly held views on the key factors in rapid development.

Outward-Looking Industrialization Strategy

It is generally agreed that adoption of an outward-looking industrialization strategy has been the decisive factor for the rapid development of the Asian NICs. Although import-substitution strategies were adopted in Korea, Singapore and Taiwan, these countries simultaneously embraced a variety of measures and incentives to promote an export industry. The reason for this is very simple: with a relatively small, low income population, import substitution is limited by the growth of the domestic market size. However, export promotion enables access to a much larger international market; hence a country can take advantage of factor endowment without being subject to the demand constraint for specialization.

Since all the Asian NICs have a common factor endowment characteristic, namely, they are poor in natural resources and rich in labor supply, it is to their advantage to develop an industry which imports raw and intermediate materials and capital equipment and employs the country's rich labor supply to process these for export. Simple technology and labor intensive products, such as textiles and clothing, are appropriate to these criteria. These products also satisfy the demands of the domestic market by meeting the requirements of the import substitution industry. In fact, in 1965 textiles and clothing were the most important export commodities of Hong Kong, Korea and Taiwan. However, the various protectionist measures existing in the industrialized countries and the increasing competition from other developing countries in the textile and clothing industry have reduced the comparative advantage of the four Asian NICs. Their share of total exports decreased between 1965 and 1983 (see Table 5).

Meanwhile, the export of machinery and transport equipment and other manufactured goods increased, and the share of these goods in total exports rose. It is evident that an outward-looking industrialization strategy was the main reason for the rapid growth of these exports. The drastic change in the structure of merchandise exports indicates that the four Asian NICs can successfully adjust their exports according to changing comparative advantages.

Freer Trade Policy

Among the four Asian NICs, Korea, Singapore and Taiwan have all used various tariff and nontariff measures as important instruments of an import substitution policy, particularly during early periods of development. In contrast, Hong Kong has been a typical example of laissez-faire economy, where government intervention in economic activities is limited. However, probably due to the adoption of an outward-looking industrialization strategy, there is increasing pressure on these countries to adopt more liberal trade policies in the process of their rapid development.

After joining Malaysia in 1963, Singapore's hope for a common market led it to introduce quantitative import restrictions for the first time.5/ When Singapore became independent in 1965, two major changes were made in its trade policy which were decisive for later development. One was the replacement of all but 88 commodity quotas by tariffs. These were further reduced to 26 in 1969. The other was the increasing reliance on protective duties as the instrument of import substitution industrialization. These levels of protection, however, were low compared to the levels in other countries.6/ In addition, government policy shifted from stressing import substitution to emphasizing export promotion in the early 1970s. Thus, tariffs were gradually eliminated. Since 1981, Singapore's import duties have generally been kept at a maximum *ad valorem* rate of 5%.

Although Korea and Taiwan have employed a very complex regime of industry protection in various stages of their industrialization, there is ample evidence of gradual trade liberalization. Since tariff exemptions and tax rebates are popular schemes with which to promote exports, the adoption of an export promotion policy partially encourages the implementation of a free trade policy.

Nontariff measures are often introduced to control imports and to promote import substitution. The number of items which are permitted to be imported and the percentage of the total goods imported can be used to measure the rate of import liberalization. Taiwan seriously started liberalizing its imports in 1970, while Korea only began doing so in 1975. This can be seen from the increasing rate of import liberalization (see Table 7). While the rate of import liberalization may be too rough a measure of the real degree of import liberalization, it is at least an indicator of the evolvement of a more liberal trade policy.

Foreign Capital

Since domestic savings in underdeveloped countries may be short of total capital required for development, the utilization of foreign capital can be very important in facilitating and speeding up economic development.

In the case of Taiwan, it can be seen from Table 8 that foreign capital inflows and transfers (comprised chiefly of U.S. aid before it terminated in 1965) constituted about 40% of the sources of funds from gross capital formation in the years 1952-1955 and 1956-1960. After 1961, however, the inflow declined sharply and transfer of foreign capital aid from the United States rapidly decreased as it neared its cut-off date in 1965. Therefore, domestic savings not only successfully filled the gap left by the loss of foreign aid, but it also continued the formation of domestic capital at an increasing rate. After 1976, Taiwan became a capital exporting country.

For Hong Kong, from 1961 to 1965, foreign capital inflows accounted for as much as 60% of the gross domestic capital formation. From then on the proportion of domestic

TABLE 7
THE EVOLUTION OF RATE OF IMPORT LIBERALIZATION
OF TAIWAN AND KOREA

Taiwan Year	Taiwan RIL (%)	Korea Year	Korea RIL (%)
1953	55.2	1968	67.7
1956	48.1	1969	55.5
1960	53.7	1970	54.0
1966	52.3	1971	54.5
1968,12	57.9	1972	51.0
1970,7	57.1	1973	51.1
1972,7	82.1	1974	51.0
1974,2	97.7	1975	49.5
1975,1	97.5	1976	50.5
1976,6	97.2	1977	51.0
1978,7	97.6	1978	53.9
1979,12	97.6	1979	67.6
1980,12	97.4	1980	68.6
1981,12	96.8	1981	74.7
1982,12	96.5	1982	76.6
1983,12	96.5	1983	80.4
1984,6	97.2	1984	84.8
1984,12	97.1	--	--

RIL: Rate of Import Liberalization (permis. import items/total items)
Source: Young (1984); Tsiang and Chen (1984); Nam (1981).

capital formation financed by foreign capital declined rapidly. After 1966 Hong Kong was self-sufficient in the domestic supply of capital and thereafter became a net exporter of capital. This is perhaps due less to the relative decline of the supply of foreign capital to Hong Kong than to the fact that the political uncertainty of its future presumably inhibits long-term commitment of investment in capital intensive industries and thus dampens the demand for investable funds in Hong Kong.

In the case of Korea, and particularly Singapore, the reliance upon foreign capital has been remarkably high, though the share of gross domestic capital formation financed by foreign capital inflows has gradually declined.

Except for Singapore, direct foreign investment was not very important as a component of the total gross capital formation in these four Asian NICs. However, there is reason to believe that in the transfer of production and

TABLE 8

SOURCES OF FUNDS FOR GROSS DOMESTIC CAPITAL FORMATION*

Country	Period	Gross Domestic Capital Formation	Gross Domestic Savings	Foreign Capital Inflow		
				Total	Foreign Direct Investment	Statistical Discrepancies
Taiwan	1952-55	100.0	59.3	40.7	1.2	---
	1956-60	100.0	60.0	40.0	1.4	---
	1961-65	100.0	85.1	14.9	4.1	---
	1966-70	100.0	95.0	5.0	7.5	---
	1971-75	100.0	97.4	2.6	5.9	---
	1976-80	100.0	106.0	-6.0	2.9	---
Korea	1953-55	100.0	51.7	48.3	---	---
	1956-60	100.0	19.5	77.8	---	2.7
	1961-65	100.0	41.3	59.5	---	-0.8
	1966-70	100.0	59.1	38.8	---	2.1
	1971-75	100.0	70.9	31.4	2.3**	-2.3
	1976-77	100.0	91.0	5.9	1.1	3.1
Hong Kong	1961-65	100.0	39.9	60.1	---	---
	1966-79	100.0	113.6	-13.6	---	---
	1971-75	100.0	113.8	-13.8	---	---
	1976-78	100.0	120.2	-20.2	---	---
Singapore	1961-65	100.0	19.5	80.5	---	---
	1966-70	100.0	61.7	38.3	10.1***	---
	1971-75	100.0	62.1	37.9	22.9	---
	1976-80	100.0	79.8	20.2	26.2	---

* As Average Percentage of Gross Domestic Capital Formation

** For 1972-75 only

*** For 1968-70 only

Source: Taiwan Statistical Data Book, 1980; R. I. Wu, C. F. Lien-Wang, T. C. Chow and Li, American Investments and Their Effects on Our Country; The Institute of American Culture, Academia Sinica, Taipei, 1980; National Income in Korea 1978, pp. 272-3; and Balance of Payments Yearbook, 1980, IMF; Estimates of Gross Domestic Product 1961-75, Census and Statistics Department, H.K. 1977; and the 1980-81 Budget: Estimates of Gross Domestic Product 1966-78, Census & Statistics Department, Hong Kong 1977; and the Yearbook of Statistics, Singapore, and Balance of Payment: Yearbook 1984, Supplement on Balance.

management technology, it still might have played a significant role. In fact, foreign investments tend to concentrate mainly on the electronic, chemical and petroleum industries, which are more technology intensive. Foreign-operated plants, as well as plants operated jointly by domestic and foreign capital, are apt to adopt more up-to-date methods of production and management, and to produce newer types of products. 7/ Their techniques then spread to other domestic firms through the transfers of trained personnel and technical assistance to local suppliers. Furthermore, a country's direct foreign investment usually brings with it guaranteed foreign markets for its own products, and thus helps to expand the exports of the host countries and increase their foreign exchange earnings.8/

ECONOMIC DEVELOPMENT AND ADJUSTMENT IN THE 1980s

Since the economies of Hong Kong, Korea, Singapore and Taiwan are all highly trade-oriented, their economic growth is closely linked with the growth of the world economy, and in particular, with that of the industrialized countries. This can be proven by the fast economic growth of the industrial countries, whose average annual rate of increase was 4.9% from 1960 through 1973, and the consequent high growth rate in exports from these four Asian NICs during the same period.

The first oil crisis in 1973 seriously affected the world economy. High rates of inflation and unemployment spread all over the world. Under the excuse of saving jobs, various trade barriers in the industrial countries were imposed and those in place were increased. GDP growth in the industrial countries decreased from 4.7% annually during 1965-1973 to 2.8% annually in the years between 1973-1980 and further to 2.2% during 1980-85. Export growth in developing countries also decreased from 5% during 1965-1973 to only 4.1% in the years between 1980-1985.9/

Export growth of the Asian NICs declined even though it was still much higher than the world average. In the 1980s, exports of the four Asian NICs apparently first will depend mainly on the growth rate of industrial economies and second on the degree of protectionism.

These two factors, however, have a close relationship to each other. If economic growth in the industrial countries is prosperous, political pressure from protectionists will be mitigated. If it is not prosperous, protectionist pressure will increase. As a consequence, slow growth in the industrial countries is a likely trigger for a significant increase in protectionism directed against developing countries. Because of the slow growth in the industrial countries from 1980 to 1985 (averaging only 2.2% per annum) there has been a strong threat of increased protectionism. The following statement from the 1985 Annual Report of the U.S. President's Council of Economic Advisors provides a vivid description of this recent trend in protectionism:

> The world is moving away from, rather than toward, comprehensive free trade. In major industrialized countries, for example, the proportion of total manufacturing subject to nontariff restrictions rose to about 30% in 1983, up from 20% just three years earlier. Although tariffs among industrialized countries have been reduced substantially since World War Two, tariffs also remain high in some sectors (textiles, footwear, steel, wood products, and shipbuilding, for example) among developing countries. In non-manufacturing, international trade is subject to even more severe restrictions and market distortions, especially in agriculture and services.

Therefore, the economic growth of the Asian NICs slowed down in 1985.

The World Bank describes two scenarios for the world economy from 1985 to 1995.10/ The high case offers industrial economies a path of sustained and steady expansion, with GDP growth at 4.3% a year, while the low case limits the GDP growth to an average of 2.5% a year--nearly the same as between 1973 and 1979. In the low case, slow growth in developing countries would only average 4.7% a year. In the high case, the prospects for developing countries would greatly improve. Their GDP would grow at about 5.5% a year, almost as fast as the average in the 1960s.11/ The growth of these four Asian NICs from 1985 to 1995 will undoubtedly be affected by the different scenarios.

Today it is not yet clear which scenario will come true. With the total GDP only 6.5% of that of the European Economic Community (EEC) in 1982, the four Asian NICs have no great voice in decisions regarding the direction of international trade policy. The capacity to adapt and adjust their domestic economy to the direction of trade policy in the industrial countries and the challenges from other developing countries are probably even more important to the development of these countries in the 1980s. In fact, their development in the 1980s will depend on how well they handle the pressure that they are subjected to from the widespread protectionism aimed at their exports from the industrial countries and the increasing competition from labor intensive countries.

In the early 1970s Korean exports of labor intensive products (textiles and apparel in particular) met with increasing resistance in the developed countries.12/ Thus, it was believed that the possibility of continued export expansion, essential in financing the growing imports required for sustained economic growth, had a limited future. As a result, the government of Korea began to emphasize the development of both heavy and chemical industries. In 1973, the Heavy and Chemical Industry Development Committee was established to provide support for the largely government-sponsored investment project.13/

Although the drive towards heavy and chemical industrialization in the 1970s succeeded in raising the share of heavy and chemical products of Korea's exports as well as increasing the growth rate of these industries, it was not very effective in developing internationally viable industrial sectors. The overall growth of exports was retarded in the process.14/

In Taiwan the development of heavy and chemical industries also was promoted and became central to the whole industrial structure. The sudden increase in oil prices, after 1973, raised doubts about the feasibility of this policy due to the high dependency on oil imports that followed. As a result, several investment projects in the petro-chemical industry were changed. Instead, the promotion of skill and knowledge intensive industries or strategic industries, became the favored industries of government support. In fact, the basic idea is similar to that of Korea. Investment, however, in skill and technology industries requires more capital and involves high risks. The prospects of a labor intensive industry are limited. As a result, the share of the heavy and chemical industry in Taiwan has increased rapidly.

The government of Singapore adopted an even stronger policy in order to encourage skill intensive industries and eliminate labor intensive industries. In 1979, the National Wage Council recommended a policy to increase wages at a higher rate than the usual one for the three years between 1979 and 1981; this was called the "economic restructuring policy."15/ The basic idea behind this policy was that a higher wage would encourage investors to choose labor saving technology and thus would increase labor productivity and international competitiveness. It is interesting to note that the rate of growth of aggregate labor productivity in Singapore was lower than that of South Korea and Taiwan from 1973 to 1979, and higher than both of theirs from 1980 to 1982.16/ However, economic growth in Singapore was recorded at an unprecedented low level of -1.8 in 1985.

Even Hong Kong, in 1977, after considering a rapidly changing external environment such as world business fluctuation, rising protectionist practices, and growing challenges from other advanced developing countries (notably South Korea, Taiwan and Singapore), set up a 16-man Advisory Committee on Diversification, under the chairmanship of the Financial Secretary, to study the prospects for diversifying its economy. In 1979 a report was published that was criticized for suggesting little more than what had already been publicly debated. Many critics objected to the recommendation of increasing government intervention and assistance on the grounds that efficient allocation exists under the free enterprise system. However, faced with protectionism such as quantitative restrictions, as well as the competition of labor intensive products from other developing countries, a feasible way to combat this situation is to shift towards higher value-added manufactures. Thus, the government's more active role in assisting manpower training, research and development, social infrastructure, etc., will probably be inevitable.17/

CONCLUSION

The adoption of an outward looking development strategy for the Asian NICs has achieved a better growth performance than that of other developing countries during the past three decades. However, this result was not obtained without cost. Their economies now experience a very high ratio of foreign dependency and are vulnerable to fluctuation in the world economy, especially in the industrial countries. The recent trend of increasing protectionism in the industrial countries, especially for labor intensive products, has influenced a trade expansion in the NICs and subsequently, their economic growth. Moreover, the continuing rise in per capita income will inevitably increase wage levels and change their comparative advantage. Thus, exports from other developing countries have gradually become their strong competitor in the international market. How the Asian NICs face these problems and how quickly they adjust their domestic economic structure will be vital to their prospects for development in the 1980s.

NOTES

1. For the list showing low income and middle income developing countries, see World Development Report 1986, (Washington, D.C.: The World Bank).

2. Spain and Ireland had a per capita GNP of U.S. $4,440 and U.S. $4,970 respectively; see World Development Report 1986.

3. For example, in 1984, it is only 9% for low income economies, 25% for middle income economies and 18% for industrial market economies; see World Development Report 1986, Table 5, pp. 188-189.

4. For example, rubber accounted for 22.2% of total exports in 1965, pertroleum products accounted for 33.7% of total exports in 1983; see International Monetary Fund, International Financial Statistic Yearbook, 1984.

5. See Augustine H. H. Tan, "Changing Patterns of Singapore's Foreign Trade and Investment Since 1960," in Singapore: Twenty-five Years of Development, Poh Seng You and Chong Yah Lim, eds. (Singapore, 1984).

6. Ibid., p. 44. Nominal rates of protection for import-competing industries averaged only 7% in 1967. The corresponding effective rate of protection was about 17%.

7. C. S. Tsiang and R. I. Wu, "Foreign Trade and Investment as Boosters for Take-off: The Experience of the Four Asian Newly Industrialized Countries," in Economic Development in the Newly Industrializing Asian Countries, ed. Walter Galenson (Madison: The University of Wisconsin Press, 1985), pp. 301-332.

8. Rong-I Wu, et al., Impact of U.S. Investment on Taiwan Economy, (Taipei: Institute of American Culture, Academia Sinica, 1980)(in Chinese).

9. See World Development Report, 1986, p. 44.

10. Ibid., Chapter 3.

11. Ibid.

12. By 1963 the United States had set up restrictions against imports of cotton textile goods from 17 countries. By 1971 imports of some 37 countries were limited. Other developed nations followed suit, effectively limiting cotton textile exports. Nevertheless, there was an explosion in the import of garments made of man-made fibers from developing countries to the developed countries between 1962 and 1973. A compound annual growth rate of almost 30% expanded the value of apparel imports from $240 million in 1962 to $3,800 million in 1973. Expansion was centered in Hong Kong, South Korea and Taiwan, and exports from these countries accounted for 75% of the 1973 total. In 1971 the

United States began to react to the surge in imports of garments manufactured from man-made fibers and by 1973 negotiations resulted in a new agreement, namely, the Multi-Fiber Arrangement (MFA). Consequently, during the 1970s, textile imports grew by 2.9% annually. See Louis Turner and Neil McMullen, eds., "North America and the NICs," The Newly Industrializing Countries: Trade and Adjustment (London: George Allen and Unwin, 1982), pp. 148-149.

13. See Chong Hyun Nam, "Trade and Industrial Policies, and the Structure of Protection in Korea," in Wontack Hong and Lawrence Krause, eds., Trade and Growth of the Advanced Developing Countries in the Pacific Basin (Seoul: Korea Development Institute, 1981), p. 191.

14. Soogil Young, "Trade Reform in Korea: Background and Prospect," paper presented at the 1984 Joint Conference on Industrial Policies of ROC and ROK, Taipei, 28 December 1984. (Mimeographed.)

15. Chong-Yah Lim, Economic Restructuring in Singapore, (Singapore: Federal Publications, 1984).

16. See Tsao Yuan, "Productivity Trends in Singapore," in You and Lim (1984).

17. Lin and Ho, "Export-Oriented Growth and Industrial Diversification in Hong Kong," in Hong and Krause (1981).

REFERENCES

Ballance, R., Sanzari, J., and Singer, H. The International Economy and Industrial Development: Trade and Investment in the Third World. Sussex: Wheatsheaf, 1982.

Fields, Gary S. "Employment, Income Distribution and Economic Growth in Seven Small Open Economies." Economic Journal 94 (1984):74-83.

Galenson, Walter, ed. Economic Growth and Structural Change in Taiwan, the Postwar Experience of the Republic of China. Ithaca: Cornell University Press, 1979.

Hong, Wontack and Krause, Lawrence B., eds. Trade and Growth of the Advanced Developing Countries in the Pacific Basin. Seoul: Korea Development Institute, 1981.

Kuan, John C. European Economic Community and Asia. Taipei: The Asia and World Institute, 1982.

Kuo, Shirley W. Y. The Taiwan Economy in Transition. Boulder: Westview Press.

Leveson, Irving, and Wheeler, Jimmy W., eds. Western Economies in Transition: Structural Change and Adjustment Policies in Industrial Countries. Boulder: Westview Press, 1980.

Lim, Chong-Yah. Economic Restructuring in Singapore. Singapore: Federal Publications, 1984.

Little, Ian; Scitovsky, Tibor; and Scott, Maurice. Industry Trade in Some Developing Countries. London: Oxford University Press, 1970.

Praet, Peter. "Structural Developments and Euro-Asian Economic Cooperation." Paper presented at the Conference on the Pacific Challenge and Euro-Asian Relations, Taipei, 4-5 December 1984. (Mimeographed).

Sun, Keh-Nan. Tariff Protection and Structural Change in Taiwan. Economic papers no. 8. Taipei: Chung Hua Institution for Economic Research, 1982.

Tsiang, S. C. and Chen, Wen Lang. "Developments Toward Trade Liberalization in Taiwan, Republic of China." Paper presented at the 1984 Joint Conference on Industrial Policies of ROC and ROK, Taipei, 28 December 1984. (Mimeographed.)

Tsiang, S. C. and Wu, R. I. "Foreign Trade and Investment as Boosters for Take-off: The Experience of the Four Asian Newly Industrializing Countries," in Walter Galenson, ed. Economic Development in the Newly Industrializing Asian Countries. Madison: The University of Wisconsin Press, 1985. Pp. 301-332.

Turner, Louis and McMullen, Neil, eds. The Newly Industrializing Countries: Trade and Adjustment. London: George Allen and Unwin, 1982.

World Development Report 1986. Washington, D.C.: The World Bank.

Wu, Rong-I and Hsu, Hwa-jen. "Study on the Strategy on Industrialization in Taiwan." Economic Studies 25 (1984):1-22.

Wu, Rong-I. "EEC and Northeast Asia: Trade and Adjustment." In Jiun Han Tsao and Cheng-Wen Tsai, eds. Northeast Asian and European Relations: New Dimensions and Strategies. Taipei: The Asia and World Institute, 1984. Pp. 216-229.

Wu, Rong-I, et al. Impact of U.S. Investment on Taiwan Economy. Taipei: Institute of American Culture, Academia Sinica, 1980. (In Chinese.)

You, Poh Seng, and Lim, Chong Yah, eds. Singapore: Twenty-five Years of Development. Singapore, 1984.

Young, Soogil. "Trade Reform in Korea: Background and Prospect." Paper presented at the 1984 Joint Conference on Industrial Policies of ROC and ROK, Taipei, 28 December 1984, (Mimeographed.)

PART THREE

Economic Relations Between the Pacific Rim and the Western World

10

Economic Relations Between the European Community and East Asia: Protectionism or Cooperation?

Jacques Pelkmans

The trilateral relations between the United States, Japan and the European Community have greatly intensified during the last two decades. Visible manifestations of the membership of Japan in the Organization of Economic Cooperation and Development (OECD), include its integration into world markets, its closer association with the political values of what was then called Atlanticism, its gradually increasing willingness to take on some of the transaction costs of leadership in managing the public good of relatively free trade, and its influential, though strictly peaceful, role in East and Southeast Asia. Other countries in the "Western Pacific" do not seem to fit a similar picture. Some of them have been heavily dependent on the United States only in an economic and military sense (Taiwan, South Korea, the Philippines), while their relations with the European Community have remained much less important. Others--having once been European colonies--have given primacy to political independence, no matter how symbolically, and in the case of ASEAN have attached great value to intra-regional security. A few have developed a curious mixture of post-colonial ties and self-reliance while embarking on export-led development. Some of these countries are now *de facto* developed countries. Some are still poor, with populations ranging from two million to 160 million. Some possess abundant raw materials and fuel resources, others have next to none. The single common characteristic relevant to the European Community that Japan and other non-socialist East Asian countries share is a common *dynamism* expressed in the high-growth rates of national income and exports, particularly of manufactured goods.

Needless to say, dynamism is something to be satisfied with. Is not the rapid growth of ASEAN countries and the

Asian Newly Industrialized Countries (NICs) precisely the fulfillment of the dream of development economics? Is not the remarkable catching-up of Japan something gratifying, both economically and politically? Is not the proven capacity to export manufactured goods competitively in world markets a welcome sign of a deepening global division of labor, freeing relatively less productive resources in the community from the constraints of low, if not falling, wages and even lower profits? Is not the economic dynamism, generated by mixed but definitely capitalist economies a proof of the resilience of the market-oriented and relatively free organization of society, even in the face of a colossal duopoly of communism? For all their diversity, can it seriously be argued that the key common property of East Asian countries is a _problem_, imposing hard choices on us and them?

The answers to these questions are affirmative. Nevertheless, this chapter will argue that a problem exists. What is surprising about the export dynamism of East Asian countries, and, to a lesser extent, the exports of the European Community to that region, is that it has evolved seemingly unabashed _despite_ ongoing or newly emerging protectionism. The Community's economic relations with East Asia are typified by _a curious mixture of protectionism and cooperation_. The policy problem, identified and dealt with briefly in this chapter, is how to improve this mixture in the short run and eradicate this protectionism in the long run to the mutual satisfaction of both sides. The discussion will focus on Japan and ASEAN.

THE NATURE OF THE PROBLEM

The problem has economic, institutional and political aspects. The _economic problem_ is whether and when protectionism in EC-East Asian relations can be justified? And, if so, what is the least costly form of protectionism for which objective and over what period? If protectionism is not justified, how quickly should it be removed without unduly jacking up the adjustment costs?

A long tradition in economic analysis strongly rejects protectionism. No form of protection can yield higher world production than free trade; neither will it be advantageous for the country installing it, apart from optimum tariffs for monopsonists. Economists interested in _explaining_ protection tend to invoke redistributional arguments combined with some infusion of political economy or "public choice" theory. Would there be any reason to question the validity of these solidly established propositions in the case of EC trade relations with Japan and ASEAN? Possibly, for the following reasons.

First, among the assumptions underlying the free trade theorems are the absence of scale economies and free entry to (and exit from) the product market. Accusations about Japan's "laser-beam" approach in the export of consumer electronic products, for instance, could perhaps upset the textbook notion of market-induced specialization patterns in the context of a global division of labor. Scale economies in such products can be so large that world oligopolies emerge. If all oligopolists are believed to not only come from one country but also to collude in foreign markets, at least tacitly, a _de facto_ world monopoly could arise. It would seem that if scale economies were static, given and known, very special assumptions would be employed to produce such an outcome. Otherwise, new entrants from ASEAN [and Asian NICs as well] are bound to threaten the achieved market dominance. This is the pattern in steelmaking and it may also become the pattern in car components and assembly. The well-known shifting of comparative advantages over time, from countries relatively well endowed with physical and human capital to those with more low-skilled labor, would also eventually take place in these instances. However, if scale economies are not static and not given, but depend on the experience gained in production (say, a positive function of the cumulative total of production) two determinants become critical: _time and entry barriers_.

If, in any given period, a producer in country "A" can find market outlets twice as fast as a producer in country "B," other things being equal, adaptations of process technology will serve to enhance scale economies more rapidly in "A." The firm in "B" will become less and less (price) competitive. A technical way of putting this is that they move with different speeds up the "learning curve," creating temporary absolute cost advantages for "A." This raises the question of why the first producer can find outlets that apparently the second producer cannot find. One suggestion could be that particular barriers prevent the second producer from entering the "A" market, but not the other way around. What is disturbing for the traditional free trade approach is that one-sided protection in this case renders the producer in "A" unambiguously _more_ competitive than the one in "B." This result is contrary to the normal allocative results in trade theory.

Furthermore, not only can there be barriers to national markets, a problem of access, the question is complicated by barriers-to-entry to product markets. Product development can serve as a barrier to entry. Combined with large economies of scale, the total investments will make it extremely costly to enter the market and equally costly to get out. In case products are complex, requiring components characterized by large-scale economies, exit costs may expand because, first of all, component producers see their outlets disappear, which would make these products (say, in "B") less competitive, and secondly, the human and technological capital may have to be largely written off. In product markets where firms compete by permanent innovation in scale-driven products, adjustment costs might therefore be extremely high and global market dominance might arise. Nevertheless, even if these arguments are correct, they apply only to a limited group of scale research and development products in the EC-Japanese product trade.

A second argument against protection in economic theory is based on efficient allocations. However, empirical tests have shown that the allocation benefits in free(er) trade are, though positive, very small. Virtually all economists recognize that protection damages technical efficiency, that is, cost minimization in the long run. In trade theory this recognition is still being debated, but in policy-oriented papers a fear of deterioration in technical efficiency is frequently the predominant argument against protection and in favor of exposure to world markets. In the case of Japan however, protection seems, if anything, to have <u>improved</u> technical efficiency in many industrial products, so that exports could be expanded rapidly. In the case of ASEAN, some members are not protectionist (Brunei, Singapore) and some are, but the latter seem to have found a structure of protection that does not unduly harm export-led development. In the European Community protection aims to protect jobs or redistribute incomes, and it tends to have the effect of slowing down adjustments considerably, that is, it restores technical efficiency only slugglishly, if at all.

The decisive economic arguments is removing EC protectionism vis-a-vis East Asian countries are <u>positive adjustment</u>, restoring resilience and helping to raise economic growth. These arguments are not the same as the ones for removing protection in ASEAN countries, namely "<u>graduation</u>" <u>in the General Agreement on Tariffs and Trade</u> (GAAT) obligations without disrupting the process of economic development. Nor are they identical to the argument to remove protection in "depressed industries" in Japan, that is, providing secure market access for NICs. Nor are they similar to the argument for removing protection in growth industries in Japan, that is, exposing the internal Japanese market to the same risks in the early phases of the product life cycle as in the EC, and thereby preempting protection from working as a vehicle for global market dominance.

The least costly form of protection in comparative-disadvantage products consists of making it temporary under international surveillance with clear guidelines, with a restructuring program based on such guidelines, and with automatic decreases in the stringency of protection. An economic reason to justify such temporary protection could be adjustment costs that are too high, given the (expected) speed of market penetration in the presence of large unemployment. The least costly form of protection in hi-tech markets is controversial. Not only is there room for argument for subsidies, proto-type contracts, etc. and possibly even trade protection in the so-called "pre-competitive" stages of research and development, it is exceedingly hard to derive hard and fast rules for proper hi-tech protection when innovation and the actual launching on the market are at issue. The armor is opaque and might also include ingenious forms of industrial collaboration, exempted by competition policy. Still, cooperation should aim to minimize such protection as much as possible.

The institutional problem is that multilateral economic cooperation has not been sufficiently effective in preventing or solving trade conflicts between the European Community and East Asia. Therefore, bilateral diplomacy takes over, but with fewer strings of international economic law attached. This approach represents a setback of economic multilateralism that has served the world economy so well. For the Japanese it confirms their reservations about legal instruments in general, while serving the interests of the powerful economic bureaucracy by making international economic obligations "malleable." For both Japanese and ASEAN exporters, bilateral approaches present opportunities to construct arrangements maximizing their profits (or at least avoiding serious damage to them) while gradually achieving an informal status of a traditional supplier with the implicit guarantee of sufficient market access. For the European Community, bilateralism is a second-best solution in the attempt to fuse adherence to the international trade order with occasional eruptions of domestic politics that may threaten the political coalition in power or particular blocks in the Parliament. The Community's problem is aggravated by the fact that its trade policy is formally conducted at the EC level, and, with a few exceptions only, related to imports from Japan. A substantial part of the bilateralism is still pursued at the Member State level.

Solving this institutional problem is difficult and unfortunately should not be expected to happen overnight. While ASEAN countries, for example, have every interest in a strong GATT to secure their access to EC and Japanese markets, the mere existence of a weak GATT compels them to conclude bilateral deals like the "Byzantine" Multi-Fibre Agreement (and its comet-tail-like array of bilateral arrangements) and narrow one-product deals. A specific example is Article 19 of the GATT and the exceptions for agriculture and subtle non-tariff barriers. This short term rational behavior is bound to erode the effectiveness of the GATT still further, in the long run. History, public administration organization and the economy create no incentives for Japan to take the present GATT very seriously. It perceives the GATT more as a rock-bottom minimum for international consensus building which is a permanent process, seeking an equilibrium of positions through negotiations. Although the process may be lengthy and painful, it yields a profound mutual appreciation for the "true limits" of maneuvering. Through Japanese eyes, that appreciation is a sufficiently solid basis for mutual agreement. What for Americans, and to a lesser extent Europeans, with their traditions of legality and litigation, represents the international trade order itself, is for the Japanese at best the expression of a one-time explicit consensus. Nor can they draw any other lesson from the history of their membership of GATT: they have been confronted with an endless series of formally correct derogations from GATT rules, specifically applied against them, supplemented later by a myriad of special bilateral deals, making a mockery of the solemn adherence to GATT by other contracting parties.

The European Community struggles with the double problem of internal disagreements on trade policy and on GATT reform, while being incapable of assuming worldwide leadership to strengthen GATT rules. The diplomatic investments, the concessions or "sweeteners," whether in financial, economic, political or military terms, as side-payments, and an exemplary consistency required in respectable policy behavior add up to transaction costs that are too high. A confederation such as the European Community is too ineffective to first identify a joint position, and then generate leadership to get its position codified into worldwide rules.1/

Since the United States has also given up its leadership role in trade, a diffuse circuit of diplomacy is emerging that is meant to "build confidence" but does nothing to secure or improve actual market access. This lack of diplomatic leadership is apparent in the OECD ministerial meetings, economic summits, the GATT Council of Ambassadors or Ministers, the Group of 18 (top civil servants) and the quadrilateral meetings. Such a situation encourages renewed surges of bilateral "cooperation," as the vehicle for actual trade policy.

The political problem is that most of the EC countries involved have never perceived their relationship with East Asia in other than commercial terms. The EC's politico-military ties were and are with the United States. Although the latter still is true, EC-East Asia relations are no longer developed in a political vacuum. With ASEAN, this is a very recent phenomenon. With Japan, it has slowly emerged through its membership in the OECD and, later, in the annual economic summits. Also, the bilateral cooperation between the European Community and Japan has become more and more enmeshed in conventional foreign policy issues. Of course, it is not necessarily true that political friendship obviates commercial conflict as the history of transatlantic trade policy has shown. Yet, the obverse of this point should not be lost when reflecting on EC-East Asia economic relations: permanent commercial strife is hard to keep fully separate from "high politics" which only encourages inward-looking and isolationist currents. The long-run consequences are hard to predict, but neither should they be stubbornly ignored.

CURRENT PROTECTIONISM

The dynamic evolution of trade between the European Community and East Asia has occurred despite a good deal of protectionism from all sides. This section provides a non-exhaustive survey of EC and Japanese protectionism. ASEAN protection is not treated due to its disparate and at present relatively unproblematic nature. The ASEAN countries slowly seem to be moving towards free trade, that is, by not touching upon national trade policy vis-a-vis third countries.

The EC's protectionism can be analyzed under four headings: EC formal protection, EC informal protection, formal national derogations of the so-called "common rules for imports," and informal national protection.

The formal protection of the European Community virtually exclusively consists of tariff protection, which is generally rather low (the weighted average being less than 7% in the post-Tokyo Round). Tariffs on textiles, clothing in particular, are frequently in the 10-20% range which is important for ASEAN, and even Japan. Until 1986, tariffs on consumer electronics, decisive for Japanese market access, ranged from 4.8% (home computers) and 4.9% (cameras), to 8% (video-tape recorders) and to 14% (radios, tuners, TV sets, car radio-cassette players). In December 1985, however, the European Community decided to reshuffle its tariffs for some consumer electronics after failure to reach agreement with the Japanese over compensation in the framework of Article 28, GATT. The European Community formally "...found it desirable to replace the present voluntary export restraints on television image and sound recorders and reproducers, which are due to expire on 31 December 1985, with an appropriate tariff measure,"2/ meaning that video-tape recorders would henceforth carry a 14% tariff, compensated by a fall to zero for certain radios, electronic calculators and sound tape recorders. This unique reshuffling clearly is the result of heavy lobbying by the hard-pressed EC consumer electronics industry, which has adjusted to those items now carrying zero import duties, but insists on getting its share of the buoyant video-tape recorder market, dominated by imports from Japan. Personal cars carry an import duty of 10%, and that of most car components is 5.4%. The only explicit example of infant industry protection in the European Community is the temporary 19% duty on imported compact discs, which will eventually decrease again to its original 9.5%. It remains to be seen whether the consumer electronics industry will attempt to get this infant protection extended now that the compact disc player clearly no longer is an "infant" product.

At the formal EC level no other instruments exist. There are no subsidies, no EC public procurement, and only a rather limited stock of European technical standards without an EC-wide testing policy. The curious mixture of the Multi-Fibre Agreement (MFA) will be discussed below.

At the informal EC level, the European Commission has strengthened its position by negotiating, in February 1983, informal "voluntary export restraints" with Japan on products ranging from fork-lift trucks and cars to video tape recorders. Penetration levels of these products were already considerably high, with Japanese video-tape recorders taking some 80% of total EC demand. Restraints on video-tape recorders from Japan were stepped up in 1985, creating a lower import volume, but, given a lower demand, this is not expected to alter the market share. The Commission has occasionally negotiated voluntary restraints for other products, such as manioc, in the Thai case, which was renewed early in 1986, but it is still quite rare with respect to ASEAN. Again, the exception is the MFA. In addition, the European Community employs the instrument of statistical monitoring, an accelerated and targeted statistical procedure, to inform policymakers. It is a roundabout way to shift discussion (and hopefully decision making) on "sensitive imports" to the Community level rather than the Member State level. In this sense it is part of the "institutional problem," conveying a warning signal to the NICs, including ASEAN at times, and Japan. The monitoring can be narrowed down to one Member State, France (the leader by far, but followed by Greece, Italy and Ireland). However, it also exists at the common level.3/

At the level of Member States, both formal and informal trade policies exist. The Commission employs "salami-tactics" by regularly slicing off a portion of the remaining staunchly defended national competences. Thus, a key element in the so-called "common rules for import" is a long list of Community-agreed national derogations, most of which are formally considered to be of temporary character. Politically however, they may well be a lot less temporary. In the 1985 list, no less than 137 products (defined at the four-digit NIMEXE statistics level) were given. Ignoring all textile and clothing products since only some of them are outside the MFA arrangements, 92 products remain. Of these some categories comprise large import sectors with many six digit NIMEXE products. Many of these national restrictions have been only formally placed under the aegis of the EC, although their renewal will give rise to some discussion. Japan is by far the most frequently mentioned target. Italy maintained a small quota allowing a little over 2000 cars to be imported from Japan, which was increased to 3300 in 1986; in addition, it applies volume restriction vis-a-vis Japan in photographic and film products, a number of special chemicals, some rubber products, virtually all ceramic products, many steel products, a few electrical and non-electrical machinery items, motor-bikes and virtually all toys. France utilizes a "zone II" concept, applied to a group of exporting countries of incredible diversity including Japan and the ASEAN countries of Thailand, Indonesia and the Philippines, for products such as footwear, ceramic products, cutlery, electrical machinery items (mainly consumer electronics), optical and measurement instruments, watches and toys. But all Member States have at least a few volume restrictions outside the MFA. Benelux for example, limits imports of cutlery, a few ceramic articles, nuts and bolts, some footwear and a few fertilizers from Japan.

The Multi-Fiber Agreement is, however, the greatest bone of contention, causing permanent irritation between the European Community and the ASEAN countries, even though the latter ones are not hit as hard as Taiwan, Hong Kong or South Korea. The MFA was formally concluded by the Commission and operates at the Community level. However, for many products EC quotas are broken down into separate national quotas. So, for the exporting country, the power of the MFA is felt mostly at the Member State level. The nature of the MFA, with its bilateral quota arrangements, safeguard clauses, escape clauses, and special surveillance for goods having different degrees of sensitivity, makes it inevitable that irregular new volume measures are taken by the European Community. Though still important for ASEAN, this sector is less crucial than before because it has substantially diversified its commodity export structure. In 1983, 30% of ASEAN's textile and clothing exports went to the European Community. Growth may well be hampered by the MFA since ASEAN's manufacturing exports to the European Community increased 37% between 1980 and 1983, but textiles and clothing only increased 24%.

Finally, Member States apply informal methods to put a brake on imports, especially on those from Japan. The case of personal cars is infamous: voluntary export restraints to the French market up to a ceiling of 3% of the market share, up to 11% of the United Kingdom market, probably up to 25% of the BENELUX market, and up to 10% of the German market (although conflicting reports exist on this restriction). Italy has a formal quota close to 0%, and Ireland is allowed to apply special provisions from the Treaty of Accession. This adds up to a formidable restriction by the European Community. There also have been other highly informal pressures on Japan: an export cartel in Tokyo, for example, takes care of restraints of numerically controlled machines (primitive robots) shipped to the French market.

Furthermore, at the national level other instruments can be employed under the formal and sometimes effective surveillance of the Commission. In many cases, the sectors protected in one way or another at the outer frontier of the Community, or the Member States, also receive subsidies and/or discriminatory public procurement. In rare cases, tests of standards or regulations are applied in a way to make Japanese access difficult. EC Steel subsidies had grown to a ridiculous magnitude before their reduction in the mid-1980s. In cars, shipbuilding, textiles and clothing, large totals can also be found, although much lower than in steel. The subsidies are not specifically targeted to counter Japanese market penetration, but they obviously make penetration more difficult. Subsidies and public procurement play an increasing role in hi-tech industries as well.

In Japanese protectionism, if the word "dialogue" is at all appropriate, the dialogue between Japan and the European Community on access to the Japanese market has long been one between two convinced camps. Allegations of a closed market have been countered by claims about the "failure to try harder." Since the early 1980s, Japanese semi-official institutions and the government itself have admitted to Japan's protectionism. Similarly, calls to try harder have resulted in a much more precise knowledge of all the hidden obstacles EC exporters or direct investors encounter. The Japanese government was confronted with a long list of requests from the European Community in November 1982, and a revised one in April 1984. The Japanese have taken up a considerable number of these requests for further study, further negotiation or for concrete action. It was of paramount importance that the United States with even greater insistence concurred in pressing Japan to take concrete action. The American action was probably a "positive" function of its bilateral deficit with Japan which is three times as large as that of the European Community. No less than seven "packages" to facilitate access have been announced by Japan since early 1982. There is no doubt that the Japanese will improve access and reduce the costs and delays of "trying harder." The question is: how much? Many of the measures have little operational significance or only will work in the long run.

At the same time, it should be admitted that the problem of access to the Japanese market is in a state of flux which makes it even harder to enumerate and assess the economic impact of the protectionism existing in 1986. For instance, in 1985 the Japanese government announced a three-year "action program" on a number of non-tariff barriers as well as on rather trivial reductions of 1800 tariffs, mostly on products where Japan is in a strong export position. The following account represents an attempt to register facts amidst a flow of smaller and larger legal and administrative changes and new announcements. Some of the "fact-finding" may be overturned by new facts, some may be colored by Western traditions. There is also deliberate attention to practices inhibiting European exporters, which frequently have different concerns than American or ASEAN exporters, who have filed their own complaints.

First, there are a few general problems, arising from the tradition of Japan's isolation. Japanese society oscillates between an implicit mistrust for foreign products and customs, and an occasional preference for them as being "exotic." At times it seems as if products made abroad are considered alien. The problem does not lie in their newness, since the Japanese have a great appetite for variation and new gadgets. Penetrating a market which is permeated by bureaucratic and social preferences and which systematically encourages perceptions about the alien character of foreign products is very difficult. Ordinary assumptions used when penetrating other markets in the world do not easily apply: mass production is usually out of the question in the years of initial penetration; prices will remain high; damaging delays may be frequent; and uncertainty will prevent the formation of goodwill.

Second, the lack of information and precision in laws and regulations is a serious handicap for foreigners in two ways. 1) It acts as a high barrier for getting in and becoming established. For example, the relevant information available to foreign firms increases with their having the appropriate and recognized contracts; however, foreign lawyers of an exporting multinational company have great difficulty coming to Japan for legal counseling because they cannot open offices or employ Japanese colleagues. 2) Without transparency and precision, the rule of law is partially replaced by the rule of bureaucracy. Low-ranking civil servants have great discretionary powers so that "The Law" can vary according to location resulting in problems of access to justice and attempts to check the legality of bureaucratic treatment. In these circumstances, discrimination can be endemic without any formal rule, without any proof and without possibility of litigation. To some extent, both problems can be viewed as transitional. At present they are still compounded by a lack of Japanese-speaking business experts and technicians and a lack of English translations of specific regulations, standards, tests, etc. On the latter point, organizations such as JETRO (Japan External Trade Organization) are active in providing English translations and guides. In addition, European business in Japan has recently become better organized through the establishment of a European Business Council in 1983 and a Steering Committee dating back to 1972.

A list of specific manifestations of implicit or explicit protectionism is provided in Table 1, which speaks for itself. Noteworthy is the contrast between EC and U.S. strategies in bilateral negotiations with Japan. The United States vigorously applies what is called a "MOSS approach" (market orientated sector specific). The European Community has to find internal compromises on relevant demands to Japan, thus making a long, diffuse request list with details on relatively minor items, which is ill-conceived for purposes of negotiations. Another point of interest is that Japan's protectionism is so malleable that concessions to the United States may, but need not, lead to improved access for many EC or ASEAN comparative advantage products.

The list conveys the impression that a true opening up of the Japanese market is bound to require a series of profound changes both in laws, regulations and administrative guidance, and radically different policies from the traditional ways of dealing. _It will be very hard to achieve all or most of this by means of bilateral negotiation_. Domestic commercial and political constituencies, such as the powerful block of small shop-owners, will surely prevent this process from becoming very sweeping. In addition, a number of instruments are not very "Japanese" at all though they have been on the EC request list for years. Fiscal charges are an example: even inside the highly integrated European Community, the problems of discriminatory excises on alcoholic beverages in different Member States have only been partially overcome through case law by the European Court of Justice. The Commission has great difficulty in further harmonizing rates, the failure of which hampers intra-EC trade. One of the greatest problems is bound to remain the question of legal certainty versus bureaucratic discretion. An overhaul of Japanese traditions in market regulation is required before a genuine impact can be expected.

The author has inserted impressionistic judgments in column three of Table 1: degree of protection. Given the fact that there is no serious chance to ever expect rigorous measurements of the instruments listed, there seems to be no alternative.

Finally, the question can be raised, is Table 1 capable of explaining the relatively low import share for manufactured products in Japan? The share of manufactured GNP imports in 1960 was 2.4% and in 1981 it was 2.5%, as compared with 5.7% for the European Community (1960: 3.3%) and 5.0% for the United States (1960: 2%). As a share of total Japanese imports, including raw materials and fuel, which

TABLE 1
SPECIFIC FORMS OF PROTECTIONISM IN JAPAN

Form	Nature	Degree of Protection	On EC List of Requests*	Japanese Response Before the End of 1985
1. Tariffs				
a. General		Low		
b. Specific Exceptions: Food Products	Ad valorem duties between 10-35%; high specific duties	Considerable	60 product categories; duty reduction	Some in 1983; little thereafter
Industrial Products	Fairly low duties, except leather, some clothing items and machinery	(See left)	+ 70 product categories; no duties or lower duties	Some in 1983; nothing on shoes, leather or machine tools
2. Quotas	Few, but very restrictive; Quota volumes are not always published	Very high in these few cases	Leather and food products; silk	
3. Import Licenses	Considerable bureaucratic discretion no conformity with GATT Code in practice, only in the 1979 law; uncertainty; lack of transparency; repetitive procedures; ministerial licenses may not suffice	Considerable; sometimes almost prohibitive		
4. Fiscal Charges	Excises can have discriminatory effects	Considerable in alcohol, etc.	Yes	No, except quality wines marginally
5. Customs	Too many and revealing documents costly inspection; discretion; occasional information leaks	Variable, but discouraging		
6. Standards, Tests	Lack of harmonization with ISO or IAC standards or tests; cumbersome procedures with heavy administrative burdens; frequent retesting; no recognition of GLPs** or EC tests information leaks are normal	High; occasionally prhoibitive	Pharmaceutical products; electrical appliances; cars; boilers; food additives; veterinary checks; phytosanitary controls on procedures; avoidance of repitition;	Partial and conditional acceptance of some points; studies for others; a few maoderate simplifications; occasional participation of EC firms, JIS and

7. Distribution	Complex and opaque system protected by unpenalized market dominance; protection of specific small shops; restrictive policy for new sites of supermarkets; no supervision by Fair Trade Commission	High; occasionally prohibitive	Yes		An investigation by the Fair Trade Commission
8. Counterfeiting	Grossly insufficient protection of luxury branded goods, trademarks, labels, designs, forms, names; misleading labeling	Yes, of particular importance; EC quality food and clothing products	Nothing yet		
9. Patents, foreign	Not well protected; patent filing and enforcement are underdeveloped	Some			
10. Subsidies					
To depressed industries	Some, with capacity reduction conditions;	Moderate (unknown for more and more industries)			
To advanced industries	Considerable, in the pre-competitive stages				
11. Competition Policies	Weakened over time; highly manipulated; high concentration through opaque cross-participation, joint-ventures and long-run private procurement; in protection can go very far	Complete in new, products (see #12); high in traditional products (see #7)			
12. Industrial Policy (with #10 anf #11)	P.m., in general not import-oriented at all except for some energy-guzzling industries	Considerable			

*The revised list of April 1984
**GLP = good laboratory practices (recommended by OECD)
***JIS = Japanese Industrial Standards award; JAS = Japanese Agricultural Standards award
Sources: EC list, April 1984; EBC 1984; Unice, 1985, Ugonis, 1984; Anjaria, et al., 1982; Interviews by the author; Van den Panhuijzen, 1985; Ballon, 1980; BDI, 1982; Christelow, 1985/86; EC, 1985-b

Japan does not possess, the 1982 figure was 23% (29.3% in 1970), compared with the European Community and the United States which were in the 40%-50% range. According to business circles, it is exceedingly rare for EC produced goods to acquire a market share as high as to 8-10% in Japan, yet Japan has achieved much higher shares in particular product markets in the European Community and the United States. Given this comparison and the fact that neither South Korea nor ASEAN has a strong foothold in Japan, one is tempted to view Table 1 as the overriding cause. Knowing that takeovers by foreign firms are next to impossible in Japan and joint ventures are difficult, this is even more likely to be correct.

Nevertheless, the literature contains an attempt to test the validity of the "low-import-of-manufacturers-propensity" complaint that has driven the European Community to initiate a procedure under Article 23 of GATT. Based on an empirical version of the Heckscher-Ohlin-Samuelson theory of trade, Saxonhouse employs a test, the conclusion of which is quoted below:

> When the differing quantity and the quality of Japanese labour, capital and natural resource endowments, and distance from trading partners are properly given their full allowance, the Japanese share of manufacturers in total imports is comparable to European and American experiences.
>
> The above results, which question the differential direct impact of Japanese government policies on Japanese trade and industrial structure, should not be understood as dismissing the role of government policy in Japanese industrial evolution and postwar growth. Rather, the above analysis should be seen as a decomposition between sectoral and macroeconomic explanations of rapid Japanese structural evolution. The differential influence of sectoral policies is dismissed in favour of a macroeconomic explanation of Japanese performance.4/

One empirical issue is that all of the underlying data are taken from the period <u>before</u> 1973. However, it is only since the early 1970s that Japan has begun to develop trade surplusses. The question arises whether the "normalized" import/export patterns detected by Saxonhouse's calculations in the early 1970s would also explain the low-import/high-export pattern of the 1980s, particularly because the fundamental determinants (factor endowments, distance, lack of natural resources) have not greatly changed.

A second problem is that the most conspicuous property of Japan's manufacturing trade, the very low degree of intra-industry trade as compared to other OECD countries, cannot be dealt with in a Heckscher-Ohlin-Samuelson (HOS) model. Intra-industry trade is the two-way trade of similar products. An HOS approach imposes specializations between products with different factor contexts, which lends itself to applications between emerging NICs and OECD countries. Among the major OECD countries, differences in factor endowments are small and do not normally lead to conspicuous differences in the product structure of trade, apart from raw materials and fuel. While concentration on scale-driven exports may still explain the industrial export structure of Japan to some extent, it does not explain the very low level of imports nor the low shares in virtually all industrial product markets in Japan. Although all OECD countries, and particularly the Federal Republic of Germany which has a comparable lack of natural resources, experienced in 1974 a sudden drop in the manufactures' share in total imports, only Japan remained at that share and stayed even lower recently. The other countries have enjoyed a great increase in intra-industry trade. However, apparently Japan cannot develop intra-industry trade or come close to a comparable level with the OECD countries.

This paper is not the proper place to discuss the methodology of the Saxonhouse approach or his macroeconomic explanation of Japanese performance. Christelow, in any event, found radically different results using a comparison of sectoral "revealed comparative advantage" indicators with sectoral import propensities for 1983, juxtaposing Japan, the European Community and the United States.5/ Christelow found

> ...strikingly lower import propensities for Japan than for the United States and the European Community in virtually all product groups. This is true...also in cases where similar comparative advantages would lead one to expect similar propensities... (and for) products for which Japan has a comparative disadvantage, while the United States and the European Community have a comparative advantage.6/

Her conclusion is that this is caused by restrictive intangible barriers in Japan.

CURRENT COOPERATION

Multilateral cooperation and EC-East Asian economic relations: Fitting the EC-Japan and EC-ASEAN economic cases of relations into an appropriate and effective multilateral framework has proved difficult. The former case is a particularly unhappy and unending story.7/ The present emphasis on bilateral deficits (both US-Japan and EC-Japan) in a multilateral economic system represents a fundamental departure from the principles of the latter. Traditionally, the European Community runs a substantial trade surplus with Switzerland and an even larger deficit with the United States. Due to the very high dollar rate of exchange, EC trade with the United States showed a surplus from 1983-1986. Such fluctuations have always been considered normal elements in a system that creates a rough overall balance, disregarding economic shocks. In trade, Japan and the European Community have been protectionist towards each other both before Japanese bilateral surplusses with the European Community arose and also during the history of the surplusses. The GATT Rounds and other concessions have driven industrial tariffs to low levels. Although other barriers remain on the EC side, these barriers still allow considerable market access in all but a few cases. Many formal quotas disappeared in the 1960s, and yet the EC Member States found ways to negotiate voluntary restraints, beginning with the Long Term Cotton Textiles Agreement in 1962, when Japan was still highly competitive in these products. Meanwhile, industrial imports have been managed equally effectively by Japan, without quotas.

In international finance, the IMF has not played an effective role in liberalizing Japanese capital and money markets or in internationalizing the yen. The OECD Code for Capital Liberalization has not been effective either, since Japan has filed long lists of exceptions. Hence, the multilateral system has helped reduce barriers in a period when EC-Japan trade amounted to no more than a trickle, but it has not directly served to tackle the key issues of the last twelve years: the European Community's volume protection, the question of access to Japan's market and the internationalization of the yen.

Indirectly, the GATT framework has been moderately useful, at best. First, the Tokyo Round brought a number of codes, some of which could reduce the capacity of Japanese protection in standards, customs valuation, licensing, and government procurement. Expectations should not be set too high on this. It is widely known that the Procurement Code has not worked anywhere. Why should Japan be an exception? The high-pressured MOSS approach has led the Americans, and the Europeans in their wake, to insist on liberal purchasing policies of NTT, the Japanese telecom monopoly. Now that NTT has become private, it remains to be seen what the actual outcome will be. Import licensing in Japan does not take place according to GATT practice. The standards issue is much too pervasive to be usefully approached by the modest Standards Code. Except for the Customs Valuation Code, all these codes allow for much discretion, and implementation surveillance is weak. On the EC side, the Anti-Dumping Code is likely to have improved market acess for Japan and ASEAN since the discretion and arbitrariness in anti-dumping cases has been greatly reduced, especially for market economies where the so-called "normal value" is usually traceable. On the other side, the Community has begun to employ more systematically an anti-dumping policy to counter the "laser-beam" approach of Japanese exports.

Second, the European Community has filed a complaint under Article 23 of the GATT, requesting "consultations" with Japan based on a request list in view of perceived or threatened "nullification or impairment of the benefits accruing to the European Community as a result of successive GATT negotiations." When the European Community did not receive a satisfactory response from Japan, it asked (under Article 23, paragraph 2) for the establishment of a working party to examine the matter. The grievance of the European Community was summed up in the phrase: "...the general GATT objective of 'reciprocal and mutually advantageous arrangements' has not been achieved.... The European Community considers that the objective of Article 23 is to restore the balance of interests of the Contracting Parties." There is no doubt that, apart from the elusive and overly sweeping legal aspects of the complaint, this drastic approach has yielded a better negotiation position for the European Community. After further concessions by Japan, the European Community has, for the time being, shelved the Article 23 complaint, although the issue can be reopened at will at any time. Nevertheless, one should realize that such overall "attacks" on the entire socio-economic system of a GATT Contracting Party cannot become the framework of fruitful methods for multilateral cooperation.

Third, it is sometimes claimed that the MFA, although second best and in conflict with GATT rules, is actually beneficial to ASEAN because it would provide them with more security of market access, higher prices and some export growth. A removal of the MFA would cause a flurry of completely uncontrolled bilateral quotas, if not unilateral quotas. The author acknowledges that there is a grain of truth in these allegations. Nonetheless, it remains true that the GATT system has failed to maintain "order," to the detriment of ASEAN and other NICs, mainly because of the impracticality of Article 19, while the MFA has no restructuring conditions, no automatic decreases in protection and no terminal objective to return to GATT. In its actual performance and re-negotiation exercises, blatant blackmailing to "obtain" safeguard clauses and exceptions to what is already outside the GATT framework is standard practice, also for the European Community. One possibly useful function of GATT would be rewriting Article 19 and thus preempting a continuation of the MFA.

Finally, the annual Economic Summits of the Seven-Plus (the "Plus" is the president of the EC Commission) have certainly influenced the Japanese position. On several occasions Japan has attempted to avoid the role of "culprit" in such a well-published world forum by making conciliatory trade policy gestures.8/ However, the Summits have also been significant in firmly establishing a framework of trilateralism at the highest level, with informal discussions on security and power politics, even though Japan is not a NATO member. The effect has been to create an atmosphere in which trade conflicts with one partner (especially the one that the other six wanted to introduce into Western high politics) had to be treated with political caution. Moreover, Economic Summits have no implementation and reporting mechanisms so that, once again, the follow-up had to be bilateral.

EC-Japan Cooperation

An intensive, near-permanent bilateral commercial diplomacy has developed between Japan and the European Community. In fact, little or no difference can be detected between the longstanding Atlantic commercial diplomacy and informal modes of trade conflict management and the Japan-EC pattern of trade cooperation. Of course, the term "cooperation" has an ambiguous meaning because it extends beyond joint rule-making and common agreements to include institutionalized dealing with acrimonious trade policy conflicts, like the Poitiers incident for Japanese video-tape recorders in late 1982.

The European Community and Japan have permanent representations with each other at the ambassadorial level in

Tokyo and Brussels. In addition, the following four modes of commercial cooperation have emerged:

First, bi-annual high-level consultations are held at the Directors-General level, usually the Director General I of External Relations and the Director General III of Industry for the EC Commission. These consultations have now existed for twelve years and are considered indispensable in avoiding the erruption of a trade war.

Second, since 1983 a substantial portion of the European Community's industrial imports from Japan has been "managed" or "organized." An imprecise "moderation agreement" was concluded for products such as cars, fork-lifts, pick-up trucks, TV sets, stereos, quartz watches, numerically controlled machine tools and motorcycles. In addition, a precise voluntary export restraint for video-tape recorders was agreed upon, with the understanding that there would be an alignment in the prices, comparable to the European Community competitors. Finally, a ceiling was set for the imports of large size TV tubes. This moderation agreement, accompanied by special "monitoring" on the EC side, is governed by quarterly meetings at the senior official level of MITI and DGs I and III (usually directors). In short, the "organization of trade" is implemented with a rigor that is in conflict with "voluntary" and "informal" restraints.

Third, in May 1984 a Ministerial Roundtable was held in Brussels with EC Commissioners and Japanese ministers, including the Economic Planning Agency attached to the Prime Minister's Office. Irregular contacts at this political level had taken place before, but this roundtable represented a clear attempt to infuse diplomacy with a political will for cooperation, and a search for ways of cooperation outside the painful trade issues. European Political Cooperation network contacts seem to have benefited from the roundtable approach. A second roundtable was held in Tokyo in October 1985.

Fourth, one result of the roundtable was the establishment of a joint Trade Expansion Committee which held its first meeting in February 1985 and since then has met regularly. It can be seen as a response to several problems at the same time. The task of the TEC is to solve very concrete problem areas expeditiously--in less than a year--and not just those in priority areas. The point is to show tangible results, however small, in order to alter the climate of disbelief in the European Community about the opening up of the Japanese market. The intent is to fend off protectionist pressures and also to bypass the extreme vagueness of Article 23 in GATT procedures. (Article 23 is not specific; this approach is.) Finally, the TEC is a way for the Commission to shorten the hopelessly long and detailed request list by cutting corners on small items at a low level, while handling priority issues at a high level.

In the wake of the Tokyo Summit of May 1986, Prime Minister Nakasone and Commission President Delors appointed personal representatives, Deputy Minister for Foreign Affairs Reichi Tejima and Director-General Leslie Fielding) for "informal" monitoring of the bilateral questions. Whether this added channel of cooperation will alter anything is doubtful. In the first half of 1986, the monitoring duo was immediately given a major task when Japanese exports were deflected from the United States to the European Community in view of the relatively moderate increase of the yen/ECU exchange rate (compared to a drastic rise of the yen/dollar rate).

Bilateral consultations also occur before and "around" the biannual meetings of the Quadrilateral Group (European Community, United States, Japan, and Canada) on trade policy. This highly informal sort of round table at ministerial or deputy levels fits into the framework of the Economic Summits.

Finally, a number of structural programs exphasize the attempt to give the cooperation a more positive meaning. Besides the stepping up of trade promotion efforts by Member States, the EC Commission has developed a modest but effective Export Promotion Program with active participation by Japanese industry and semi-official institutions. An executive training program, with intensive language courses and business trainerships, that brings young European business people to Japan for 18 months is included. Also available is a management program at the senior level, for 3 months only, and a series of other activities such as mixed participation conferences, trade missions and direct-connection electronic tendering.

Much of this is valuable. It is worthwhile to try harder and let the Japanese help. But all of this painstaking diplomatic and practical activity does not do away with the simple fact that the key issue of protectionism on both sides has only been marginally tackled. A hesitant beginning has been made of the consultations with Japan on macro-economic matters. The European Community Commission drew up a document for the Council on these questions in April 1986 advocating the opening up of financial service markets in Japan, the development of short-term financial markets and better consultation on the yen/ECU exchange rate.9/

EC-ASEAN cooperation

Despite substantial growth in absolute volume, in relative terms, EC-ASEAN trade steadily declined over the 1970s and early 1980s. In 1983, The EC share in total ASEAN exports fell from 14.5% in 1970 to 10.5%. In total ASEAN imports, the EC share to the region declined from 18.9% in 1970 to 12.2% in 1983. Viewed from the EC end, small increases can be observed. A disaggregated analysis makes it clear that, virtually without exception, EC market shares fell inside ASEAN, apparently due to the waning competitiveness of EC industry.10/ This lacklustre performance has led to greater demands for economic cooperation in light of the dynamism of ASEAN and the large EC market size.

Both in multilateral and bilateral frameworks the EC-ASEAN relationship is one of moderate happiness and calm. With the exception of Thailand, the colonial experiences of the ASEAN countries, were followed in the 1960s and early 1970s by the gradual decrease in the intensity of economic and political ties. The recent "rediscovery" of ASEAN by the European Community is both political and economic. The threat of Vietnam and the impending weight of China have given rise to serious security concerns over Kampuchea, Vietnam, and Communist subversions that touch upon political cooperation within the Community. Commercially, ASEAN proved to be even more dynamic in the 1970s than Japan, and came to be seen as a potential market for EC exports. For ASEAN the commercial domination of Japan in the region is regarded with apprehension, although it ought to be added that Japan is also greatly admired in its economic dealings and management. For ASEAN a strong EC presence in the region offers possibilities for diversification in exports and imports and for increases in direct investments.

In 1980 the European Community and ASEAN concluded a non-preferential Cooperation Agreement running until October 1985. In November 1984, in Dublin, a continuation of the cooperation was agreed upon with little change in form. Though not very spectacular, the Agreement grants Most-Favored-Nation treatment to ASEAN countries; it contains very modest and vague promises for economic cooperation and development; and it establishes a joint Cooperation Committee. The five ministerial meetings held thus far were attended by foreign ministers. Only in Dublin was it proposed for the first time that the ministers of economic affairs should meet informally to discuss trade matters in greater depth. The first such informal meeting was held in Bangkok in October 1985.

Matters of economic and development cooperation with ASEAN at the EC level (unlike those at the individual Member State level) are still insignificant when compared to trade issues. The points of friction are relatively few: ASEAN exports to the European Community in 1983 were 10.5% of all ASEAN exports, while imports from the European Community were 12.2%; the Community's exports to ASEAN in 1983 were less than 3% of all EC exports. Access of ASEAN to EC markets is perhaps more problematic, than the other way around, despite very high ASEAN tariffs. The following points can be mentioned.

A few more detailed points should be made within the larger EC-ASEAN framework. The Multi-Fibre Agreement was not restrictive for ASEAN in its early stages (1973-77), but has become more so since then. Typically, sensitive items in MFA III EC bilateral agreements with ASEAN countries cannot grow more than 2% to 5% annually, plus the growth of EC consumption. The uninviting atmosphere around the European Community's MFA implementation is so discouraging to ASEAN that a full exploitation of its comparative advantage is not possible. For instance, clothing exports to the European Community from ASEAN actually fell from 1982 to 1983. In comparison with the USA and Japan, the European Community is nevertheless very open to ASEAN textiles and clothing: some 30% of these exports go to the European Community, another 16% to the USA and a meager 4.5% to Japan, although the latter geographically is located much closer and is, by far, the larger trading partner of ASEAN.

The Generalized System of Preferences (GSP), as implemented by the European Community, is a relatively liberal one in the world for industrial products. Yet, only in 1979 did ASEAN obtain recognition of the principle of the cumulative origin of imports. The effect was to transfer quotas among ASEAN members. In other items where the European Community's GSP is problematic, ASEAN competes with the interests of LOME (Lome Convention) countries, which take priority. In 1982, 38% of ASEAN manufacturers' exports to the European Community were covered by GSP.

One final point, the export of commodities to the European Community is crucial to ASEAN, accounting for over half of all ASEAN-EC exports. Unlike the United States, for instance, the European Community is moderately sympathetic to the strong ASEAN backing of UNCTAD's (United Nations Conference on Trade and Development) Common Fund and the Integrated Program for Commodities. The Dublin Declaration of 1984 confirms this, backs the Tin, Cocoa and the Tropical Timber Agreements, and at the same time shows a willingness to negotiate a new International Rubber Agreement. It also provides for a mere "empty" statement on the International Sugar Agreement. Given the EC's promise to LOME countries for a guaranteed sugar import quota originated by them, despite the high EC sugar price and despite the surplus, it is painful to observe. The Common Agricultural Policy (CAP) played a negative role in putting a break on manioc exports from Thailand to the European Community. Manioc (taken from the root of the cassava), like soybeans, takes a low tariff and no variable levy, even though its high starch content makes it a good substitute for feedstock grains. The very rapid increases in EC imports were considered as undermining the intra-EC supply of (costly) grains for feedstock, thus adding to other CAP problems. Ironically, also the United States pressed the European Community to impose moderation on Thai manioc exports because of an old informal deal between the European Community and the United States. That deal guaranteed that the latter's export of soybeans would not suffer from variable levies, and was threatened by the sharp competition from manioc imports. A voluntary export restraint and some EC aid to convert crop land resulted in a fall of manioc exports to the European Community of 35% (some 400 million ECU). That decline was borne by Thailand alone. The Thai plea for keeping at least this level of remaining imports was only accepted by the European Community when Thailand broke ASEAN unity in resisting the protectionist bilateral MFA agreements with the European Community in early 1982 and declared its willingness to sign. It is no wonder that these EC tactics caused resentment. In 1986 the restraints were renewed.

A potential source of future cooperation in commodities is the oil trade. The ASEAN countries of Indonesia, Brunei, and Malaysia are major oil producers, but so far they have exported no oil to the European Community.

On economic and development cooperation one can be brief. At the EC level, spending is modest; total EC aid, including project financing, all food aids, regional projects and trade promotion has averaged approximately 45 million ECU a year since 1980, with a low of 26 million ECU in 1984. Flows from individual EC Member States to individual ASEAN Member States frequently are larger. Counting the European Community and Member States together, the Community is the largest donor to ASEAN. At the enterprise level, the Commission claims that the European Community is the biggest foreign investor in Singapore and Malaysia, but far behind Japan in Indonesia, for instance. However, as pointed out by Langhammer, the statistical basis for these statements is at best weak and direct investments by EC firms may well be declining, in fact.11/ The success story of ASEAN electrical machinery exports to the European Community represents a good example of trade-inducing direct investments, contributing to a better world division of labor without serious protectionist reactions. Not surprisingly, there is a feeling that the cooperation potential remains underdeveloped. A hesitant scientific and technological cooperation potential has begun, but it remains largely underdeveloped. Similar to Japan, a European Business Council in ASEAN has been founded, which reports directly to the Joint Cooperation Committee. Relative to ASEAN dynamism and opportunities, the Committee is not yet very convincing. As Kirby sums up the mood, the European Community's "...cooperation is cordially desired but by people who have changed, with much wider horizons and capabilities not inferior to the Europeans."12/ Langhammer, who has serious reservations both about the potential and the economic rationale of EC-ASEAN cooperation in its present form, offers an even more skeptical and critical view.13/

TWO PROPOSALS FOR COMMUNITY POLICY

Two sets of proposals for a Community policy for improving the EC trade relations with East Asia, especially between ASEAN and Japan, will be offered. One is about safeguards, and the MFA is the biggest present bone of contention in this respect; the other is about a more rational Japan policy.

About Safeguards and the MFA

The European Community should have learned long ago that refusal to anticipate changes in the world division of labor will magnify the adjustment costs at a later stage, especially since the European Community is the world's largest trader. This lesson has now been driven home rather painfully as shown by absolute and comparative economic performance in the European Community itself as well as in third markets. Long-standing protectionism and near-certainty about political responses favorable to laggard, vested interests cause the costs of sheltering to mount for the economy at large. This is also true for the Asian NICs and ASEAN that serve as the present and future "third" markets for the European Community.

It is therefore in the interest of both groups that Article 19 of GATT be rewritten and that the MFA be phased out immediately. The rewrite of Article 19 should be based on all of the following considerations:14/

*Market disruption" and "serious injury" must not be defined in ways that permit "safeguards" against import competition driven by the comparative advantages of the Asian NICs and ASEAN. The speed of market penetration and adjustment can (temporarily) be disruptive, and that is all there is to it. The safeguard should be made selective as long as the decision is not unilateral but multilateral, the surveillance is multilateral, the period is short, and ample import growth is still permitted. Repetition should not be possible without a break of several years in between.

*Every request, such as the rewritten Article 19 of GATT, should automatically lead to public hearings. GATT should receive funds to enable it to invite neutral experts to testify at these hearings. The outcome of any request must be decided within a maximum of three months. A summary of each hearing must be published by GATT.

*A GATT Surveillance Authority should implement the new article.

*In the transition period, any 'illegal' safeguard has to be removed; hence, a program for the dismantling of the MFA is required, and other instances of 'rollback' need to be agreed upon.

The phasing out of MFA, coupled to the Article 19-rewrite should be based on the following elements:

*It should be phased out in five years.

*During a first phase of one-and-a-half or two years, European Community Member State quotas must disappear and the poorest countries (by UN definition) must be fully excluded from any volume restriction.

*A second phase should address the more sensitive products. A five-year restructuring plan should be defined with a mixture of decreasing EC trade protection and Member State subsidies. The relevant quotas should be increased by 10% a year during the restructuring, but abolished thereafter. Market disruptions and serious injury should be referred to the GATT surveillance authority.

*The most sensitive products may be eligible for subsidies thereafter, but with explicit consideration of the high EC tariffs and without volume protection (except as agreed to under GATT). During the five-year transition period, quotas should be increased by 5% the first three years and 10% for the other two years. The surge mechanism and other restrictive features ought to be removed during the first three years.

*The Textiles Surveillance Body must disappear before the end of the transition period as its task will become superfluous.

For the ASEAN countries and other NICs this set-up would remove many of the man-made uncertainties surrounding their industrialization strategy. The Community might seriously consider a return to GATT rules as a big non-negotiable "concession" if the Asian NICs and ASEAN would not make any concessions either. Although this stance ignores the heavy costs that the MFA imposes on the Community itself, it is nonetheless possible to ask for a "concession" befitting the evolution towards a mature and deepened global division of labor. The rewrite of GATT, Article 19, together with the termination of the MFA, could be connected to a long-term agreement of "graduation" in GATT. Hong Kong, Singapore and Taiwan have now reached per capita income levels comparable to Greece, Spain, Ireland and Portugal. Undoubtedly, an evolving world division of labor cannot forever be based only on obligations from OECD countries. On the one hand, a graduation of the number of ambitions of the GATT obligations is (at least diplomatically) an unreasonable request as long as the developed countries refuse access by measures, <u>contrary</u> to GATT rules. On the other hand, if the latter removes volume protection and returns to genuine multilateral decision-making, it would be equally unreasonable of the Asian NIC's and ASEAN not to lower the many tariffs that are above the 50% and even the 100% level, in order to improve market access for the comparative advantage products from countries, such as those in the European Community. Unlike the silent diplomacy that is now suggested by Geneva, "graduation" is just as much a prerequisite for optimal world trade as a removal of EC volume protection. In the specific case of ASEAN, this could be combined with a liberalization of their intra-ASEAN trade, perhaps in the form of a free trade area.

A MORE RATIONAL JAPAN POLICY

The Japan policy of the Community hitherto has largely failed to open up the Japanese market, while having emphasized a defensive, somewhat ad hoc protectionism with negative effects on the EC internal market. This is odd. A rational policy would attempt to employ <u>more effective</u> instruments with the aim of forcing market access in Japan. In any event it would <u>prevent</u> <u>costly</u> <u>protectionism</u> and a disruption of intra-Community trade which is the basis of the Community's industrial competitiveness.

Apart from genuine emergencies, trade policy should be employed solely as a <u>diplomatic</u> weapon to sustain a multilateral trade order. Allowing the sudden massive importation of video-tape recorders through a tiny inland customs office in Poitiers, as France did in the fall of 1982, may be viewed as setting up a "diplomatic deterrence," and it seriously risked the loss of goodwill that trade cooperation requires. The problems with the "Poitiers detour" were that 1) it was too ostentatious; 2) it was used to force the Commission and the EC Council into a joint but <u>defensive</u> Japan policy, seeking volume protection; 3) it damaged the EC internal market. The exploitation of commercial diplomacy for achieving reciprocity of concessions and their implementation is not wrong, but the absence of reciprocity of concessions is especially painful when very large swings in exchange rates occur. The sudden drastic increase of Japanese industrial exports to the Community in the first half of 1986--approximately 50% more than in the first half of 1985, despite the 15% appreciation of the yen vis-a-vis the ECU--clearly represents a desperate attempt by the Japanese to minimize their losses from the higher priced yen. In the United States, Japanese imports were bound to suffer, given the 40% appreciation of the yen vis-a-vis the dollar, no matter how much of a profit margin the Japanese were prepared to sacrifice for the sake of maintaining their share of the market. However, in the European Community lower profit margins might minimize reductions in Japanese market shares, while still keeping overall profits positive. Such a strategy would be out of the question for the European

Community in Japan and this is telling. Unfortunately, some form of "deterrence" appears to remain necessary for the Community.

One may also argue that the reciprocity of concessions and its implementation underlies the GATT Rounds and GATT philosophy, under the imperative constraint of multilateralism. It is precisely in the field of non-tariff barriers that multilateralism has suffered greatly under the GATT. The GATT Codes agreed upon in 1979 have different groups of signatories and little to no serious surveillance. So, it is unclear what exactly is meant by reciprocity of previous concessions, unlike the tariff case, where GATT, Article 23, is clear in intent though perhaps not in the calculation of compensation.

The European Community should rationalize its Japan policy on the basis of the following considerations:

*Interrupting intra-EC industrial trade for the purpose of protection in relation to Japan is tantamount to the tail wagging the dog. Article 115 of the EEC must be resorted to only in very extreme cases; at present no such case exists. The EC internal market should assume absolute priority.

*The Community should get rid of its protection vis-a-vis Japan as soon as possible. It hurts the EC economy while hardly having any impact on Japan. Above all, it weakens the EC firms in third markets.

*During a transition period for the removal of this protection, the Commission must take into account "cumulative protection" in these sectors, i.e., voluntary restraints, tariffs, subsidies, Member States government procurement and the degree of actual competition (such as cartellization or regulation), before deciding the appropriate speed of liberalization. The rule of thumb should be: the more cumulative the protection, the more rapidly volume protection should be removed.

*At the same time, a "hi-tech code" should be proposed to GATT Contracting Parties, preferably together with the United States; the reasons for this have already been given. The key objective of that code is that GATT should have a hand in devising "infant protection." The connection between pre-competitive subsidization and exemption from competition law, on the one hand, and trade protection, on the other, should be recognized, with its possibly drastic consequences in early stages of the product cycle. This may also lead to further improvements in an anti-dumping policy for such products.

*The European Community ought to set up a Community-wide standards and tests policy, to be used as a trade policy weapon until or unless GATT defines a clear and satisfactory policy and institutes multilateral surveillance on the meaning of reciprocity under the Standards Code. Such a policy could constitute a logical complement to the present improvements on the EC-wide harmonization strategy in technical regulations and standards15/ while undoubtedly inducing the Japanese to give up dragging their feet on a long list of protectionist peculiarities in standards and testing.16/ For example, Japan recently switched from "Special Approval" for imported electrical appliances to an "Application for Japan Endorsed IEC Standards," after a long postponed recognition of (most) EEC standards in this category. Nothing seems to have changed, however, since retesting still takes place in Japan, although the European Community does not act in the same manner. In addition, there are other very discouraging details regarding interpretation, utility, etc. In this case, the European Community should require retesting of Japanese electrical appliances until reciprocity is achieved, or the GATT Code is further clarified. This policy would form a powerful aid in restoring industrial competitiveness in the European Community by making the most of its internal market--an effective and sound strategy vis-a-vis Japan--while using commercial policy not to defend or pamper vested interests but merely as a promptly reversible instrument of diplomacy to achieve a further opening up of the Japanese market. Better coordination with the United States could increase the effectiveness of this diplomatic instrument.

*The Community should seriously reflect on the relative importance of competing with Japanese industry in the European Community and the world market, on the one hand, and in Japan, on the other. Although the latter is not without interest, it is the former that is really crucial. The competitiveness of European industry should be or become such that the former problem is overcome, rendering the latter both less difficult and less important. This priority is clearly not adhered to in the European Community.

*Rapid development and opening up of the Japanese financial system will make the yen more "international" and make durable undervaluation less likely. The European Community should collaborate closely with the United States on this point.

All in all, the Community's recent insistence that Japan would have to assume "a quantified target with a timetable for a significant increase in its imports of manufactured goods and processed agricultural products" is neither an effective nor an economically useful approach.17/ It should be replaced by the policy set out above, in the economic and political interests of the European Community and Japan.

NOTES

1. J. Pelkmans, "The Bickering Bigemony: GATT as an Instrument in Atlantic Trade Policy," in Europe, America and the World Economy, ed L. Tsoukalis (Oxford: Basil Blackwell, 1986).

2. See Council Regulation EEC/3679/85 of 20 December 1985, in Official Journal of the EC, L 251 of 28 December 1985.

3. On this monitoring or "surveillance," see, for instance, J. Pelkmans, "Community's Trade Policy Towads Developing Countries," in EEC and the Third World, Vol. 6, eds. C. Stevens and J. Verloren van Themaat (London: 1986).

4. G. Saxonhouse, "The Micro- and Macroeconomics of Foreign Sales to Japan," in Trade Policy in the 1980s, ed. W. Cline (Cambridge: MIT Press, 1983), pp. 293-295.

5. As first employed in Balassa, 1965.

6. D. Christelow, "Japan's Intangible Barriers to Trade in Manufacturers," Federal Reserve Bank of New York Quarterly Review 10 (Winter 1985/86):16.

7. See, for instance, G. Curzon and V. Curzon, "The GATT," in International Economic Relations of the Western World, 1959-1971, vol. 1: Politics and Trade, ed. A. Shonfield (London: Oxford University Press, 1976).

8. J. Pelkmans, "Collective Management and Economic Cooperation," in Economic Summits and Western Deceision-

Making, ed. C. Merlini (London: Croom-Helm, for the European Institute of Public Administration, 1984).

9. EC Commission, "Monetary and Financial Relations with Japan," in Documents, Agence Europe, 1401/2 (April 1986).

10. R. Langhammer and U. Hiemenz, "Declining Competitiveness of EC Suppliers in ASEAN Markets: Singular Case or Symptom?" Journal of Common Market Studies 24 (December 1985). Also, R. Langhammer, "ASEAN-EC Economic Relations on a Side-Track: Can Supernatural Institutions Act as Locomotives?" Euro-Asia Business Review (1986).

11. Idem, "ASEAN Economic Relations."

12. S. Kirby, "A New Deal is Required," paper presented to a CEPS Discussion Group: ASEAN and the Asia-Pacific, Actual and Potential Interests for the EC, Brussels, 5 July 1984, p. 21.

13. Langhammer, "ASEAN-EC Economic Relations;" also, R. Langhammer, "The Economic Rationale of Trade Policy Cooperation Between ASEAN and the EC: Has Cooperation Benefited ASEAN?" ASEAN Economic Bulletin 2 (November 1985).

14. See Pelkmans, 1985; and B. Scott et al., "Has the Cavalry Arrived?" a report on trade liberalization and economic recovery for the Trade Policy Research Center, London, 1984.

15. See Official Journal of the EC, 4 June 1985 and the relevant section in the White Paper on the Internal Market, COM(85)310, 14 June 1985.

16. See also the appendix in Christelow, "Japan's Intangible Barriers," for U.S.-Japan problems of a similar kind.

17. EC, "Council Conclusions on EC-Japan Relations," Agence Europe, 12 March 1986, p. 9.

REFERENCES

Anjaria, S.; Igbal, Z.; Kirmani, N.; and Perez, L. Development in International Trade Policy. Washington, D.C.: IMF, 1982.

Ballon, R. "Does Japan's Closed Society Mean Closed Import Market?" Aussenwirtschaft 35 (September 1980).

Bundesverband der Deutschen Industrie. Administrative Import--Beschrankungen in Japan (Koln)(March 1982).

Christelow, D. "Japan's Intangible Barriers to Trade in Manufacturers." Federal Reserve Bank of New York Quarterly Review 10 (Winter 1985/86).

Curzon, G., and Curzon, V. "The GATT." In International Economic Relations of the Western World, 1959-1971. Vol. 1: Politics and trade. Edited by A. Shonfield. London: Oxford University Press, 1976.

European Business Council in Japan. Doing Business in Japan: A European View. (Tokyo)(October 1984).

European Community. Official Journal of the EC. Council Regulation EEC 1440/80, concerning the conclusion of the Cooperation Agreement between the EC and ASEAN.

--------. Revised List of Requests to the Japanese Authorities by the EC. Brussels, April 1984.

--------. Joint Declaration of the Fifth EC/ASEAN Ministerial Meeting. Dublin/Brussels, 16 November 1984.

--------. Official Journal of the EC. Updating of the 1985 NIMEXE code of Annex 1 to Council Regulation EEC 288/82; List of products subject to national quantitative restriction C 38 of 11 February 1985.

--------. Commission communication to Council, COM(85)574. Analysis of the Relations between the Community and Japan, 15 October 1985.

Harris, S., and Bridges, B. European Interests in ASEAN. No. 19: Chatham House Papers. London: Routledge & Kegan Paul, 1983 .

Kirby, S. "A New Deal is Required. "Paper presented to a CEPS discussion group on ASEAN and the Asia-Pacific: Actual and Potential Interests for the EC, Brussels, 5 July 1984.

Langhammer, R. "The Economic Rationale of Trade Policy Cooperation Between ASEAN and the EC: Has Cooperation Benefited ASEAN?" ASEAN Economic Bulletin 2 (November 1985).

--------. "ASEAN-EC Economic Relations on a Side-Track: Can Supranational Institutions Act as Locomotives?" Euro-Asia Business Review (1986).

Langhammer, R., and Hiemenz, U. "Declining Competitiveness of EC Suppliers in ASEAN Markets: Singular Case or Symptom?" Journal of Common Market Studies 24 (December 1985).

Panhuyzen, W. van den. "Japan's Industrial Policy: From Promotion to Protection." Tijdschrift voor Economie en Management 30 (1985).

Pelkmans, J. "Collective Management and Economic Cooperation." In Economic Summits and Western Decision-Making. Edited by C. Merlini. London: Croom-Helm, for the European Institute of Public Administration, 1984.

Pelkmans, J. "The Bickering Bigemony: GATT as an Instrument in Atlantic Trade Policy." In Europe, America and the World Economy. Edited by L. Tsoukalis. Oxford: Basil Blackwell, 1986.

--------. "Community's Trade Policy Towards Developing Countries." In EEC and the Third World Vol. VI. Edited by C. Stevens and J. Verloren van Themaat. London, 1986.

Saxonhouse, G. "The Micro- and Macroeconomics of Foreign Sales to Japan." In Trade policy in the 1980's. Edited by W. Cline. Cambridge: MIT Press, 1983.

Scott, B., et al. Has the Cavalry Arrived? A Report on Trade Liberalization and Economic Recovery. London: Trade Policy Research Centre, 1984.

Ugonis, M. "L'Evolution des Relations Entre la CEE et le Japon." Revue de Marche Commun No. 274 (February 1984).

UNICE. Main Obstacles to Imports from Japan. (Working paper)(Brussels)(February 1985).

11

Japan's Trade and Investment Relations with the European Economic Community

Pieter van Veen, F. H. Saelens and Th. van Bergen

Since the early 1970s, Japan's exports to the European Economic Community (EEC) have risen much faster than its imports from that region. The bilateral trade account, still more or less in balance during the early 1970s, subsequently turned into a surplus for Japan, reaching US $10 billion in 1984. That change was mainly brought about by the successful proliferation of Japan's high-technology industries. Exports from such industries act as an engine of growth for Japan, and they are concentrated on the markets of developed countries, mainly the United States and the EEC. Imports predominantly originate from natural resources producing countries, including OPEC. In combination these two conditions, i.e., Japan's export-led growth and its dependence upon external sources of supply for materials and fuels, have led to its now well-known bilateral trade surpluses and deficits.

From an economic viewpoint nothing is wrong with bilateral trade surpluses or deficits. What matters is the overall current account of a country. Nor is there anything wrong with shifting comparative advantages. On the contrary, shifting trade patterns generally reflect increasing worldwide efficiency and productivity. Economics teaches us that countries should specialize according to their comparative advantages. Free trade will lead them to specialize in the production of those goods which are most efficient. Technological and managerial innovations will continuously change these patterns. For the sake of "the wealth of nations" industrial patterns should be adjusted to these changes and not hampered by diplomatic pressure or straightforward protectionism. However, adjustment is a costly matter for certain groups in society. The overall economic result of adjusting to shifting comparative advantages may be beneficial, but the resulting advantages will be unequally distributed over producers, consumers, labor, capital, etc. The losers may be able to exert sufficient political pressure to have governments apply restrictive trade policies.

This is exactly what happened towards the end of the 1970s and during the economic stagnation of the early 1980s. The United States and the EEC put into effect protective policies, mostly by "convincing" Japan and Newly Industrialized Countries (NICs) of the benefits of voluntary export restraints (VERs). Fear of further increases in protectionism in the 1980s may be a driving force for Japanese companies to move production from Japan to the European and U.S. markets as they already had to some extent during the 1970s.

Protectionism is not the only stimulus for Japanese direct investment in the EEC. In the 1970s, Japanese establishments in the EEC were mainly trade promoting in nature. By the mid-1980s there were several hundred Japanese establishments in Europe, most of which were quite small and engaged in commerce and financial services.

It is interesting to observe that, whereas the EEC and the United States are reluctant to adjust to shifting international trade patterns, they seem to be quite interested in Japanese direct investment, and especially investment in the manufacturing sector. Publicly funded campaigns to attract Japanese production to EEC countries are quite common. This, of course, has much to do with the desire to create employment and to import Japanese management and production technology.

This chapter will deal with EEC-Japanese economic relations in some detail. The main emphasis will be on Japan's external performance rather than the EEC's direct investment and exports to Japan. The introduction is followed by a section which describes the evolution of the bilateral relationship and the positions of the Japanese and West-European governments. These positions are explained in terms of Japan's more coherent policymaking, in contrast to the fragmented policies of a divided Europe. Japan's international "penetration" seems to be guided by long-term "visions." Unfortunately, the European reaction to this planned development shows little cohesion.

The second section will examine how Japan serves the European market through exports or through local production. Based on results derived by a wider study carried out by one of the authors at the University of Manchester Institute of Science and Technology in the United Kingdom, it is concluded that exports are the dominant mode. It is unlikely that, for the foreseeable future, Europe will be subject to large-scale penetration by Japanese multinationals.1/

The third section will look at the bilateral relation from a wider, macro-economic point of view. Japan's relative labor costs are compared with those of the EEC, and it is shown that, until 1980, Japan maintained her labor costs at a low level vis-a-vis competing countries. Since 1980, however, the EEC has done better than Japan. It is also argued that Japanese direct investment will hardly make any substantial contribution to the unemployment problem of EEC countries.

EURO-JAPANESE COMMERCIAL POLICIES

After World War II the European nations and Japan both faced the same task, that is, reconstruction of their economies. During the 1950s their efforts towards economic recovery were monitored and supported by the United States. After regaining its sovereignty in 1952, Japan became a member of the International Monetary Fund (IMF) and the World Bank, and in 1956, of the United Nations. Already in 1951 Japan applied for membership in the GATT. Because of its dependence on imports, Japan needed wider export outlets. Remembering Japan's prewar trade practices, a number of West European nations strongly opposed Japan's membership, but its international integration appeared to be unavoidable. So, after lengthy negotiations Japan became a member of GATT in August 1955, and consequently has been a member of this body for thirty years.

Japan perceived the creation of the EEC in 1957 with mixed feelings. On the one hand it feared increased protectionism as a result of the common external tariff. On the other hand, an integrated and prosperous European market could be beneficial to Japan. Although Japan obtained GATT membership in 1955, it could not reap the full benefits right from the start. A number of the fourteen countries, including Great Britain, France, Belgium and the Netherlands, invoked Article 35 of the Agreement, thereby withholding Most Favored Nation (MFN) treatment from Japan.

In July 1960 Germany signed a trade agreement with Japan granting defacto MFN treatment, and two weeks later the Benelux countries agreed on disinvoking Article 35 in exchange for a bilateral safeguard clause. When Great Britain applied for EEC membership the first time in 1961, Japan saw an opportunity to further open up the European market via Great Britain, which was already her most important European export market. After reaching a deadlock with France and failing in negotiations with Italy in November 1961, the Japanese focused their diplomatic offensive on Great Britain and concentrated their efforts on a Treaty of Commerce and Navigation (TCN) with the United Kingdom which was signed on November 14, 1962. In this treaty the United Kingdom also rescinded Article 35 of the GATT by which it had withheld Most Favored Nation status from Japan. The price Japan had to pay for this was a renewable bilateral safeguard clause combined with a negative list of sensitive products on which Japan would maintain voluntary export restraints.

The Anglo-Japanese negotiations over the TNC also had positive effects on Japan's trade relations with France. In January, 1962, France and Japan signed an annual trade protocol relaxing 125 French quotas. This was followed by a French-Japanese Trade Agreement, signed in May 1963, which covered a period of six years. The French government negotiated a safeguard clause to be automatically renewed unless both partners agreed to its expiration. In exchange, the French authorities reduced the number of quotas applicable to Japanese imports and relaxed remaining ones. In May, 1963, negotiations with the Italian government also resulted in a reduction of Japanese import restrictions. Germany and the Benelux had already signed Trade Agreements with Japan in 1960.

By the end of May 1963 Japan had reached its goal, that is, all EEC-members maintained trade relations with Japan on the basis of the MFN principle. Nevertheless, Great Britain, France and the Benelux countries retained the right to restrict those Japanese imports which would seriously damage or threaten domestic industries.

Parallel to these bilateral talks, the EEC Commission also started discussions on trade with Japan as a prelude to a common commercial policy. In the Commission's opinion, every bilateral trade agreement with Japan should contain safeguard clauses such as in the British TNC. These bilateral clauses could then be combined later to a common safeguard clause. However, the Japanese opposed this approach. They already had agreements with Germany and Italy without such restrictions. Also, they considered the idea of a common negative list of "sensitive products" to be unacceptable as this would boil down to the most restrictive list in force, the Italian one. Hence, Japan refused an invitation by the Commission to start informal trade negotiations in February 1964. The Commission received little backing from the member states for this approach. The latter suggested that the process of transforming bilateral trade restrictions into common EEC-wide restrictions vis-a-vis Japan should occur more gradually.

A few years later, during the Kennedy Round of tariff negotiations (completed in 1967), Japan asked to reopen the negotiations. Again the EEC member countries refused to give a mandate to the Commission. The latter pressed for a combined approach as the only way to open up the Japanese market for European products. However, the Commission's efforts were in vain. The positions and interests of the countries in favor of more trade liberalization, Great Britain, Germany and the Benelux, were opposed to those of more protectionistic nations such as France and Italy.

In 1970, the Commission became responsible for a common trade policy according to Article 113 of the Treaty of Rome. It immediately started exploratory talks for a trade agreement with Japan. The EEC pressed for liberalization on the basis of reciprocity, elimination of Japanese administrative non tariff barriers (NTBs) and a common safeguard clause. In view of growing U.S. protectionism, which was expected to massively divert Japanese exports to the EEC, the Council of Ministers authorized the Commission to start negotiating with Japan on July 20, 1970. The matter of a common safeguard clause fell outside the scope of the mandate, but the Commission's request for wider powers was rejected. Despite growing protectionism by the EEC, the trade negotiations failed. As before, bilateral negotiations remained in force resulting in separate voluntary export restraints (VERs) for such products as steel and ball bearings.

The enlargement of the EEC on January 1, 1973, gave new life to the Commission's plans for a common trade agreement with Japan. The Commission no longer stressed the need for a common safeguard clause, but emphasized the need to remove Japan's NTBs. Agreement was reached on regular, semi-annual High Level Consultations on trade between the EEC and Japan. However, the Commission's powers to negotiate remained limited by the mandate it received from the member countries. Bilateral VERs and sectoral agreements still conflicted with the Commission's desire for a common policy. This, of course, weakened the Commission's position vis-a-vis Japan. At the High Level Consultation meeting in February 1974 the Commission again proposed a trade agreement with a common safeguard clause. Japan simply refused. One positive element in EEC-Japan official relations was the opening of an EEC office in Tokyo in October, 1975, which gave the EEC a more official image in Japan.

At the end of 1976 a major crisis occurred between the EEC and Japan which Japanese authorities had not anticipated. A mission of Keidanren, the Japanese Federation of Economic Organizations, met with strong anti-Japanese protectionistic feelings while touring in Europe. The members of the mission felt that the trade problem had now turned into a major political issue. In November, 1976, Japan promised to exempt EEC car exports to Japan from the strict emission regulations for three years and to increase the price of exported ball bearings. In response to an "ultimatum" to show results before the meeting of the Council of Ministers on November 29, 1976, Japan cut a number of tariffs, simplified certain import procedures and increased a few import quotas. This relaxed the tension between the EEC and Japan, but only for a short while. Otherwise the Japanese followed a policy of "conflict control." If there were sectoral problems, they would discuss them and, if necessary, "ease the pain" with a VER.

Another crisis occurred early in 1980, mainly as a consequence of the second oil price shock. Both Japan and the EEC countries feared a deterioration of their trade balances. The Commission again tried to reach an EEC-wide freeze on Japanese exports of such sensitive products as cars and consumer electronics. Again various member countries, especially France and Italy, refused to give such a mandate. The plan for a "common freeze" was quickly abandoned.

This chapter only touches on the essence of the Euro-Japanese trade talks. Excellent in-depth analyses of this problem area are readily available.2/ In conclusion, there have been few real changes in the nature of the problem over the last thirty years. On the one side, Japan remains a nation with a high degree of concensus between policymakers in trade affairs and business. Policymakers are alert and able to react rapidly and adequately to changes in the international scene. On the other side, the countries "united" in the European Common Market remain reluctant to transfer mandatory powers to the Commission, and this has resulted in fragmented EEC trade policies. As long as bilateral terms were more attractive, there was little pressure on Japan to accept EEC-wide terms.

However, during the last few years some progress has been made. On February 12, 1983, the Commission reached an EEC-wide agreement with Japan on yearly renewable ceilings on Japanese exports of certain electronic products. It has taken a long time, but the first signs of a common commercial policy towards Japan are starting to emerge.

JAPAN AND THE EUROPEAN MARKET: EXPORTS VERSUS DIRECT INVESTMENTS

The most remarkable characteristic of the Japanese economy has been its impressive and unsurpassed growth relative to Western industrialized countries. For example, in the mid-1950s Japan's GNP was less than half of the United Kingdom's GNP, but by the mid-1980s it was more than double. Growth was not evenly distributed across the economy. Agricultural employment especially declined, releasing labor resources for the higher productivity of manufacturing where growth was most conspicious. Over the period 1952-1972, real annual growth in the manufacturing sector averaged 14.4% against 9.1% for the economy as a whole. However, after the turmoil of the 1974 oil crisis real overall growth settled on a stable pattern of about 4% per annum.

Within manufacturing, growth rates across industries were more or less equal across various industries up to the mid-1950s, but thereafter industries such as textiles and food, characterized by high labor but low intensity in research and development, rapidly declined in importance. Instead, the emphasis shifted to two other broad industrial categories. Firstly, Japan developed materials-processing and relatively capital- and energy-intensive industries such as chemicals and iron and steel. Since the oil crisis, however, Japan, being poorly endowed with natural and energy resources, has found it difficult to maintain its competitive position in these sectors and little growth has been recorded in the past few years. The second broad sector to develop, and one which has well maintained its momentum throughout the economic difficulties of the last decade, consists of various machinery industries. The machinery sector is technology-intensive in nature, permitting substantial value to be added per person employed.

Industrial Structure and Trade

Japan's growth and the transformation of its industrial structure are reflected in the evolution of its trade. On the export side, Japan's participation in world-trade has grown considerably, from 3% of free-world exports in 1958 to 8.5% in the 1980s.3/ Japanese exports are increasingly dominated by machinery industries which accounted for about two-thirds of all exports during the early 1980s, as opposed to slightly over 40% during the late 1960s. Geographically, the distribution of exports has, during the past decade, remained quite stable. The exception is the emergence, since the oil crisis, of the Middle East as a significant market for Japanese goods. However, the United States and South East Asia jointly still account for 50% of Japanese exports.

On the <u>import</u> side, Japan's share of the free-world total grew from 3% in 1958 to 7.5% in the early 1980s. The import structure in Japan remains heavily biased towards materials and fuels. In fact, imports of manufactured products show a long-term decline and now account for only 20% of total imports. In absolute terms, Japan's imports of manufactured goods are about the same as those of Switzerland, a country with one tenth Japan's GNP. Japan's scarce natural resources make it more dependent on external supplies than any other large industrial nation. The present industrial transformation will undoubtedly reduce its vulnerability, but as in the past, the adequate supply of raw materials will retain top strategic priority. Hence, the Middle East, Indonesia, Australia and the United States will be significant exporters to Japan for the foreseeable future.

Finally, a comparison of the regional distribution of imports and exports reveals Japan's most serious external economic problem, that is, the trade imbalances it is compelled to run at the regional or national level. Given the unequal distribution of natural resources throughout the world, these imbalances are a fundamental feature of the Japanese economy, though the continuing transformation of industry may bring some relief.

<u>Foreign Direct Investment: An Overall View</u>

There are two official sources of information on foreign direct investment (FDI) for Japan. The first source consists of data published by the Bank of Japan (BOJ) as part of the balance of payments. These data show actual outflows but provide no detail. The second source consists of statistics collected by the Ministry of Finance (MOF) and published by them or the Ministry of Industry and International Trade (MITI). However, these data refer to notifications and/or authorizations of FDI, not actual outflows. As a significant ratio of projects is subsequently cancelled, the MOF-data are not an accurate reflection of actual investment. In contrast, the figures do not include reinvested profits or capital raised overseas.

This has led some commentators to conclude that, on balance, the MOF data are reasonable proxies for actual investment.4/ For comparative purposes these figures are still inflated as they include debt investment which is neither a U.S. nor an IMF practice.

The importance of outward FDI to Japan's economy has steadily increased in absolute terms, and the most recent figures even suggest an acceleration, as shown in Table 1.

TABLE 1

JAPAN'S FOREIGN DIRECT INVESTMENT FLOWS

Year*	BOJ Data**	MOF Data***	MOF Cum.
1965	77	159	949
1966	107	227	4,476
1967	123	275	1,451
1968	220	557	2,008
1969	206	665	2,673
1970	335	904	3,577
1971	360	858	4,435
1972	723	2,338	6,773
1973	1,904	3,494	10,267
1974	2,012	2,396	12,663
1975	1,763	3,280	15,943
1976	1,991	3,462	19,405
1977	1,645	2,806	22,211
1978	2,371	4,598	26,809
1979	2,898	4,995	31,804
1980	2,385	4,693	36,497
1981	4,894	8,931	45,428
1982	4,540	7,703	53,131

*Calendar year for Bank of Japan Data; Fiscal Year (April 1 - March 31) for Ministry of Finance Data.

**Direct investments as recorded on the asset side of the long-term capital account of the balance of payments as published by the Bank of Japan. Direct investments are the net investments by Japanese companies in their overseas branches and subsidiaries, including long-term loans.

***Foreign direct investment as published by MOF. Before December 1980 such investment includes acquisition of securities and obligative rights (loans) of foreign companies in which Japanese capital investment accounts for 25% or more, establishment/expansion of branch offices and acquisition of real estate. In accordance with the revised Foreign Exchange Law, from December 1980 all foreign corporations in which Japanese capital investment accounts for 10% or more is included while acquisition of real estate is dropped.

Sources: The Bank of Japan, Balance of Payments Monthly January 1984, Tokyo, February 1984, p. 53; Ministry of Finance, Direct Overseas Investment Registered During Fiscal 1982, Tokyo, 1982, p. 2; Ministry of Foreign Affairs, Statistical Survey of Japan's Economy, Tokyo (various editions).

TABLE 2
FDI RELATIVE TO SELECTED ECONOMIC VARIABLES

Year	FDI Flows (US $ Mil.)	% of GNP	% of Fixed Assets[1]	% of Exports
1972	2,338	0.7	3.0	7.9
1973	3,494	0.8	3.0	9.0
1974	2,395	0.5	2.0	4.2
1975	3,280	0.7	3.1	5.9
1976	3,462	0.6	2.9	5.0
1977	2,806	0.4	2.0	3.4
1978	4,596	0.4	2.1	4.7
1979	4,995	0.5	2.3	4.7
1980	4,693	0.4	1.9	3.4
1981	8,906	0.8	5.4	5.9
1982	7,703	0.7	4.7[2]	5.6

1. As percentage of domestic private investment in fixed assets.
2. Authors' estimate.

Source: Ministry of International Trade and Industry, The Overseas Activities of our Country's Companies, Edition 10/11, Tokyo 1983, p. 71 (in Japanese).

However, despite the recent surge in FDI activity, the ratio of FDI flows to GNP was not higher in 1982 than it was in the early 1970s, as Table 2 shows. Similarly, a comparison with export volumes reveals current ratios to be historically unexceptional. The ratio of FDI flows to private domestic investment in fixed assets shows an upturn in the early 1980s, but this is partly due to the business-cycle related weakness of private investment during that period. On balance, the data show that Japan's FDI flows are running at a steady, if low, level. During the last decade there have been few if any drastic developments, at least in the aggregate flows here considered.

The analysis above was conducted in terms of domestic economic variables and sheds little light on Japan's propensity to invest abroad relative to other major industrial countries. In Table 3 Japan's FDI is compared to that of the United States, the United Kingdom and Japan's favorite yardstick, West Germany. The data show that Japan and West Germany exhibit a number of similarities in FDI. Part A of Table 3 suggests that these countries' FDIs have developed in a very similar fashion during the last decade. Part B shows that their cumulative FDI is small in comparison to that of the world's two largest investors, the United States and the United Kingdom. Finally, Part C demonstrates that both countries have a similar and strong preference for exports compared to FDI, relative to the United States and the United Kingdom.

Within this context, Japanese outward FDI has traditionally focused on bypassing imperfections in raw material markets, supporting export activities and relocating labor- and capital-intensive production stages for which Japan had lost its comparative advantage. Investment in technology-intensive sectors has mainly been a response to trade restrictions.

During the past decade there have been few changes of any significance in this pattern. If anything, trade supporting investment has increased, particularly in developed countries. In contrast, manufacturing FDI to these nations continues to flow in at an unexciting pace. Japan remains the preferred location from which to serve the world's markets, especially for technology-intensive industries.

Japanese FDI in Western Europe

Japanese FDI in Europe is largely intended to support trading activities, particularly exporting. As Table 4 shows, as of 1982 cumulative FDI in manufacturing is only 22% of total FDI. Conversely, combined FDI in banking/ insurance, commerce and services has consistently accounted for more than 70% of the total, a trend which continued unabated throughout the period 1978-1982. As one official Japanese source states, a major component of Japanese industry's response to the global recession has been "the keen desire of Japanese firms to increase export sales, and the number of their employees assigned to overseas marketing duties has consistently increased".5/ Within manufacturing, FDI has particularly grown in the electrical machinery and transport equipment sectors. Investment in the former sector is concentrated in consumer electronics and semiconductors, in the latter sector in the automobile and motorcycle industries.

TABLE 3

JAPAN'S FDI POSITION RELATIVE TO OTHER MAJOR INDUSTRIAL COUNTRIES

A. Comparative Size and Growth of FDI

Investing Country	Cumulative FDI in US $ Billion			Average Annual Growth in %	
	1970	1978	1981	1970-1978	1978-1981
Japan	4	27	44	27	14
United States	78	168	227	10	11
West Germany	7	29	37	23	8
United Kingdom	20	35	79	19	31
Total	109	259	387	17	14

B. Relative Position in World FDI (Cumulative, in %)

Investor	1970[1]	1981[2]
Japan	2.5	5.1
United States	52.0	47.1
West Germany	4.5	7.7
United Kingdom	13.0	16.5
Others	28.0	23.6
World Total	100.0	100

C. Cumulative FDI Relative to GNP and Exports for 1981[3]

Investor	% of GNP	% of Exports
Japan	3.9	29.0
United States	7.7	97.0
West Germany	5.4	21.0
United Kingdom	18.5	65.6[4]

1. Rounded to nearest half percent.
2. Note the discrepancy between the absolute size of Japan's FDI in Part A and its share in Part B. This is due to the use of MOF data in the former and BOJ data in the latter part.
3. MOF data for Japan.
4. 1980.

Source: A. Keizai Koho Center, Japan 1983--An International Comparison, Tokyo, 1983. B. Ministry of International Trade and Industry, The Overseas Activities of our Country's Companies, Edition 9, Tokyo, 1981, p. 22. C. Ministry of International Trade and Industry, The Overseas Activities of our Country's Companies, Edition 10/11, Tokyo, 1983, p. 73.

TABLE 4
JAPAN'S CUMULATIVE FDI IN EUROPE BY INDUSTRY
(in U.S. millions)

Industry	1978	1982	Difference 1982-1978	FDI at the Margin (%)*	Avg. Growth 1978-1982 per annum (%)	Composition (%) 1978	Composition (%) 1982
Manufacturing							
Foodstuffs	38	44	6	15.8	3.7	1.5	0.8
Textiles	110	156	46	41.8	9.1	4.2	2.9
Lumber & Pulp	0	0	0	--	--	0.0	0.0
Chemicals	81	158	77	95.1	18.2	3.1	2.9
Iron & Nonferro	85	171	86	101.2	19.1	3.2	3.2
Indust. Machinery	80	145	65	81.3	16.0	3.1	2.7
Elec. Machinery	51	226	175	343.1	45.1	1.9	4.2
Transport Mach.	11	115	104	945.5	79.8	0.4	2.1
Other	66	166	100	251.6	25.9	2.5	3.1
Subtotal			660	126.7	22.7	19.9	22.0
Agriculture/Forestry	0	0	0	--	--	0.0	0.0
Fisheries & Marine	2	2	0	0.0	0.0	0.1	0.0
Mining	79	79	0	0.0	0.0	3.0	1.5
Construction	11	40	29	263.6	38.1	0.4	0.7
Commerce	515	1,455	940	182.5	29.6	19.7	27.1
Banking/Ins.	568	1,288	720	126.8	22.7	21.7	24.0
Services		1,110	278	33.4	7.5	31.8	20.7
Real Estate	26	38	12	46.2	10.0	1.0	0.7
Branches	63	171	108	171.4	28.4	2.4	3.2
Total**	2,618	5,366	2,750	105.0	19.7	100.0	100.0

*Difference of cumulative FDI as of 1987 and 1978 divided by 1978 cumulative FDI.
**Excluding the US$ 780 million Abu Dhabi Marine Area Investment made from the UK in 1972.
Source: Ministry of Finance, Direct overseas Investment (1978 & 1982 editions).

CASE STUDY: THE AUTOMOBILE INDUSTRY

The large increase in FDI (see Table 4) in the transport equipment sector during the period 1978-1982 is mainly due to two Nissan investments. In January 1980, Massey-Ferguson in Spain sold its 36.8% share in Motor Iberica, Spain's leading but financially troubled tractor and agricultural machinery producer, to Nissan, Japan's second largest car manufacturer, for a cash sum of U.S. $40 million. The reported motives for the investment were a combination of entry into a highly restricted market, distribution channels in South America and easy access to EEC markets after Spain joins.

By 1984 Nissan had acquired 70% of Motor Iberica's shares and it is likely to further increase this. Motor Iberica is now being transformed into the parent's European base for commercial vehicles. In 1983 production of one Japanese model was started, followed by a second one in 1984, with a combined capacity of 30,000 vehicles. The investment has been accompanied by drastic rationalization measures, including severe employment cutbacks. By early 1984 increases in productivity had allowed Motor Iberica to take 50% of the relevant Spanish market, and the government asked the firm to ease back in order to protect Santana SA, a Spanish affiliate of British Leyland.

Simultaneous to the Spanish deal Nissan negotiated a joint venture with Alfa Romeo for the production of, initially, 50,000-60,000 passenger cars. Half the production is intended for the Italian market which otherwise remains virtually closed to imports of Japanese cars (See Table 5). The investment evoked considerable opposition in Italy, particularly from Fiat. Finally, the government authorized the investment as part of a wider plan to rehabilitate the struggling car industry. The venture, named ARNA, built a plant near Naples with employment for some 1,500 persons after becoming fully operational in 1984.

TABLE 5
CONTROLS ON IMPORTS OF JAPANESE PASSENGER CARS
IN WESTERN EUROPE (1981)

Country	Type of Control	Japanese Share
Spain	High tariffs, quotas	0.1%
Italy	Pre-EEC quota	0.1%
France	Market share limit (3%)	2.6%
Portugal	High tariffs, quotas, Domestic contest	12.5%
West Germany	Export restraint agreement	9.7%
United Kingdom	Market share limit (11%)	11.0%
Benelux	Export restraint agreement	24.5%

Source: McArdle J. Associates, The Japanese Automobile Challenge, London 1982 (from excerpts in the Financial Times, October 6, 1982).

Following these two ventures Nissan continued to develop its European strategy by taking over its Dutch importer and by establishing a U.S. $40 million parts distribution center in the Netherlands. Other Nissan units in Europe include several sales subsidiaries and small knock-down kit assembly units in protected markets such as Portugal and Ireland and a licensee in Greece. In February 1984, Nissan also announced its long-awaited decision to manufacture passenger cars in the United Kingdom. The proposed plant, a strongly watered-down version of the original plan, will assemble some 24,000 Japanese-made car kits per year from 1986 onwards. In a second phase the plant will be expanded to produce about 100,000 cars per year by 1991, with 80% local content. The initial investment by Nissan amounts to $50 million and will provide direct employment to 500 persons. A substantial proportion of the plant's output will be exported.

The investment has been accompanied by considerable controversy. It took Nissan three years to arrive at a decision, a fact closely related to the opposition the investment engendered within the firm. The British government has given staunch support and indeed solicited the investment, but resistance came from a variety of pressure groups including French and Italian authorities, local competitors and Japanese trade unions. Not surprisingly, employment issues loomed large in the discussions.

Nissan's major domestic competitor and Japan's largest car manufacturer, Toyota, has so far not made any major investment, though during 1980-1981 it was reported to be conducting in-depth feasibility studies on possible production in Spain, in the event that the Spanish government proposed cooperation with the problem-ridden SEAT company. The parties concerned finally settled for a non-equity arrangement which allows Toyota to assemble some 15,000 cars using SEAT's considerable excess capacity.

Recently Toyota also acquired a 16.5% share in the financially troubled U.K. Lotus Car Company with which it already maintained a technology-exchange program. Other Toyota ventures are limited to small assembly operations in Portugal and Ireland. These ventures are likely to be abandoned when import restrictions are lifted in compliance with EEC regulations.

Other Japanese car manufacturers have also limited their investments in Europe or opted for alternative arrangements. Honda concluded a license agreement with British Leyland to manufacture the Triumph Acclaim, a medium-sized saloon car. This cooperation has now been extended to a new model, code-named XX. Both projects have sparked off a controversy over the definition of local content, and France threatened to regard the Triumph Acclaim as a Japanese car despite its certification by the EEC authorities. The British government is known to favor a larger Honda commitment through an equity stake in British Leyland. Peugeot of France favors a similar tie-up with the Mitsubishi Motor Company which already maintains strong links with the Chrysler Corporation in the United States. Another Japanese manufacturer who invested in European car production is the Suzuki Motor Company, one of the smaller Japanese producers and a specialist in sub-subcompact cars. Suzuki will start joint production of 1,000 CC cars with Santana SA of Spain. The companies envisage assembly of some 10,000 units a year. The agreement was consolidated through the purchase by Suzuki of 5% of Santana's equity capital.

In conclusion, Japanese FDI in the European automobile industry, as summarized in Table 6, exhibits the following characteristics:

1. Japan is the world's largest producer of motor vehicles. As of the mid-1980s it served global markets predominantly through exports in preference to local production.

2. For Europe, based on 1983 imports and FDI projections for the mid-1980s, the ratio of local production to imports (in units) is approximately 12%.

3. FDI has mainly been a response to import barriers. Host countries typically provide a large local market with actual or potential access to the EEC, and relatively cheap labor.

4. Access to other protected markets is often conditional on joint ventures with local, mostly ailing, producers whose protection domestically has accorded them little comfort in export markets.

5. Manufacturing entries by Japanese producers often generate considerable opposition from local firms, fearing the competitive edge of Japanese multinationals which seems based on superior production and marketing skills rather than on innovative products. By implication, Japanese strategies focus on the same market segments as those served by local producers.

6. Countries such as France and Italy have on occasion hindered the flow of goods produced by local Japanese subsidiaries even though such products carried the EEC label of

origin. Consequently, future Japanese manufacturing FDI may show a preference for hosts which combine a large market with sufficient political clout to enforce access to other markets.

7. FDI in car manufacturing is impeded by the fact that current annual imports of Japanese cars, though running at a level of about 800,000 units, are spread over nine manufacturers and 45 models, only two of which achieve sales in excess of 90,000 units. Hence, the opportunities for operating at minimum optimal scales of production are limited. This also helps to explain why Honda and Toyota have invested in the production of passenger cars in the United States but not (yet) in Europe. The United States imports currently twice as many Japanese cars than Europe.

As exemplified by the preceding case study, Japanese FDI in European transport machinery is primarily a response to such market imperfections as tariffs and import quotas. Not all manufacturing FDI is of this nature. Further analysis would show that it is relatively more conspicuous in those sectors where Japan's locational advantages as a source of supply are weak or deteriorating, such as industries which derived their original strength from favorable access to capital and labor, but of rather low technical complexity. In the more research and development intensive industries, exports remain the preferred method of access to the European market. Nevertheless, such observations should not be allowed to detract attention from the key issue, namely that Japanese FDI in Europe is small.

TABLE 6

JAPANESE FDI IN EUROPEAN CAR MANUFACTURING

Investor	Subsidiary/ Affiliate	Country	Ownership	Product	Output	Start of Production
Nissan	Motor Iberica	Spain	Majority	Light Com. Vehicles	30,000	1983/1984
Nissan	ARNA	Italy	Co-owned	Small-Med. Cars	60,000	1983/1984
Nissan		UK	Wholly-owned	Med. sized Cars	24,000	1986
Toyota	Lotus	UK	Minority	Sports Cars	--	1983
Suzuki	Santana	Spain	Minority	Sub-subcompact	10,000	1983

SOME MACRO-ECONOMIC OBSERVATIONS

A major characteristic of Japan's economic development over the past decades has been the ability to develop and make the most of its comparative advantages, shifting over time respectively from labor-intensive to capital-intensive to knowledge-intensive production in its exporting industries. This success was partly due to the "planned" character of the Japanese economy: the cooperation between government, in particular MITI, and business. An interesting question is whether Japan's performance was partly due to such favorable factors as low labor costs, low inflation rates, an under-valued yen, etc. Generally speaking a country will be more successful in exploiting its comparative advantages, the better its overall international competitive position. The evolution of its labor costs and its effective exchange rate are important ingredients of that position.

The cost of labor is a major determinant of a country's competitive strength in the world market. What matters is not the absolute level of compensation per employee expressed in the national currency, but rather the cost of labor per unit of output relative to that of competing countries (with all costs measured in a common currency). To compute such a measure we need, for each relevant country, information on the level of compensation, productivity growth and evolution of effective exchange rates. Table 7 summarizes indices developed by the EEC for labor costs in Japan, the EEC and the United States. The figures in column 5 indicate that, measured over an extended period, Japan managed rather well in controlling its relative labor cost. In 1980 this cost was 18% below the 1975 level (index 1975 = 100). In 1980 the EEC's relative labor cost was 14.1% above the level of 1975. Hence, over this period Japan improved her competitive position vis-a-vis Europe. The growth of Japan's bilateral trade surplus from U.S. $2.3 to $10.3 billion is a reflection of this trend. However, during the last four years the respective labor costs have evolved quite differently. Column 5 shows a substantial decrease of the EEC's relative labor costs since 1980, by approximately 27%, whereas Japan's relative labor costs increased by 8%. The EEC countries have clearly improved their competitive strength over the last five years. Column 6 shows that this improvement for the EEC, and the deterioration for Japan, was mainly caused by an effective depreciation of the ECU and an effective appreciation of the yen. The bilateral EEC-Japan trade balance and relative labor costs are depicted in Figure 1.

TABLE 7

UNIT LABOR COSTS IN MANUFACTURING INDUSTRY

(Index 1975 = 100)

Country/ Region	Year	(1) Compensation per employee (Nat. Currency)	(2) Productivity (Output per Employee)	(3) Labor Cost Per output unit (Nat. Currency*)	(4) Relative unit Labor Costs (Nat. Currency*)	(5) Relative unit Labor Costs (Com. Currency)	(6) Effective Exchange Rate
EEC	1960	21.8	52.6	41.4	82.1	80.3	97.8
	1970	50.8	85.7	59.3	91.5	88.2	96.5
	1980	174.4	121.9	143.1	111.0	114.1	102.9
	1984**	242.4	138.0	175.9	114.7	87.2	76.4
Japan	1960	12.7	28.8	44.1	84.5	76.4	90.4
	1970	44.0	79.7	55.2	81.5	75.2	92.3
	1980	139.2	148.0	94.1	65.0	82.0	126.1
	1984**	169.9	172.8	98.4	55.4	90.3	162.9
USA	1960	43.2	65.1	66.4	148.9	172.1	115.5
	1970	67.3	84.7	79.5	132.1	156.9	118.8
	1980	155.0	108.9	142.3	104.6	97.1	92.8
	1984**	208.7	125.7	166.2	100.2	130.3	130.1

* Unit labor costs in national currency by reference to the weighted average for 19 main competing countries.

** Provisional forecasts.

Source: European Economy, March 1984, Number 19, Tables 3, 6, 8, 14 and 15.

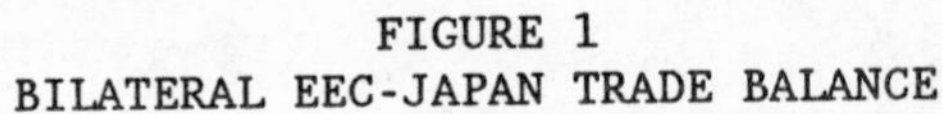

FIGURE 1
BILATERAL EEC-JAPAN TRADE BALANCE

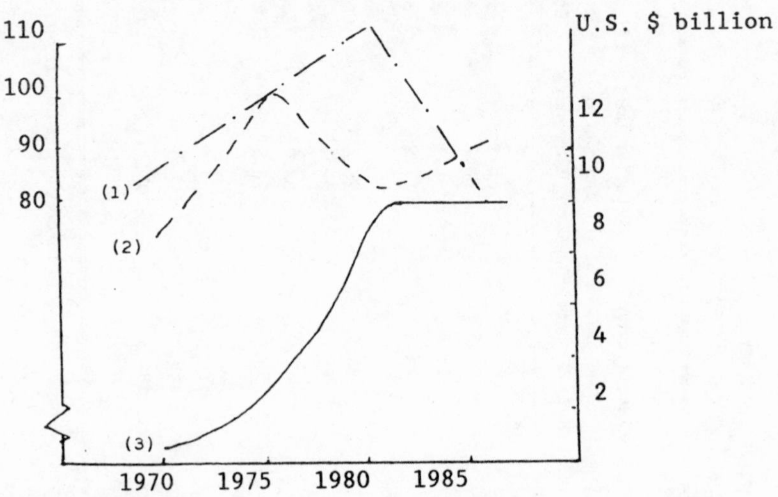

1) Relative unit labor cost in common currency for EEC on left axis (1975 = 100).
2) Same for Japan.
3) EEC-Japan trade deficit in US $ billion on right axis.

The EEC countries also improved their labor costs vis-a-vis the United States. Since 1980 U.S. relative labor costs have increased by approximately 33%, mainly caused by the strong appreciation of the U.S. dollar. Therefore, since 1980 the EEC has improved its position relative both to Japan and the United States. Trade figures for this period are fully in line with these EEC data. The trade deficit vis-a-vis Japan has remained stable since 1980, at a level of about U.S. $10 billion: The trade deficit which the EEC incurred in 1980 with regard to the United States may well turn into a surplus during the current year.

The conclusion is that during the 1970s Japan maintained her competitive position relative to Europe and the United States. Labor costs, an important indicator for that position, developed favorably for Japan. Exporting industries, backed by relatively slow developing labor costs, made the best of their comparative advantage. Since 1980 this has changed. The EEC successfully slowed down the rise in its labor costs, thereby improving its position vis-a-vis its main competitors, Japan and the United States.

This development also put a brake on the rapid penetration by Japan of EEC markets. The stable EEC-Japan trade deficit of about U.S. $10 billion may well reflect the "structural" bilateral trade position of these partners in the larger world economy.

Japan's direct investment in the EEC since 1980 has clearly been stimulated by these developments, especially by direct investment in the manufacturing sector. As explained above, Japan's direct investment in Europe until recently occurred mainly in commerce and services. Direct investment in manufacturing may further increase if Japan's labor costs relative to Europe's continue to deteriorate. Other important determinants of the expansion of Japanese production in the EEC will be growth of certain European markets, and more importantly, the threat of increasing protectionism.

As already indicated in this chapter, Japan's direct investment in the EEC is relatively small. As of March, 1984, only 12% of the global stock of such investment was located in Europe. In this respect North America, Asia and Latin America are far more important for Japan than Europe. Conversely, from a European viewpoint, the importance of Japanese establishments in Europe is limited, especially in terms of employment. Former research done by the authors indicates that Japanese subsidiaries in the EEC do not employ more than 60,000 people.6/ Table 8 relates this figure to total employment and unemployment in EEC countries.

These figures clearly show that Japan's direct investment does not make a substantial contribution to the EEC's employment problem. Even multiplying by, say, a factor of 10 would not produce a significant effect. There is, on the one hand, some additional indirect employment. On the other hand, the establishment of Japanese companies may destroy existing employment in competing European firms.

TABLE 8
EMPLOYMENT IN THE EEC
AND IN JAPANESE SUBSIDIARIES IN 1982
(in millions)

Total employment EEC	165
Total unemloyment EEC	11
Employment in Japanese subsidiaries in the EEC	0.06

Source: Economische Aspecten van de Japanse Directe Investeringen in het Buiutenland, Tilburg University, June 1984.

CONCLUSION

Both the EEC and the United States have huge trade deficits vis-a-vis Japan. Europe's deficit over 1984 was, however, only about one-third of the U.S.-Japan deficit (see Table 9). Over the last few years there are signs of growing equilibrium in EEC-Japan trade relations. This may be due to increasing Japanese relative labor costs and a growing mutual understanding in matters of trade policy.

Japanese FDI in Europe is small, particularly in manufacturing, and is mainly geared towards sustaining Japanese exports. There are a few indications of comprehensive strategies developed to serve European markets from local plants. For the foreseeable future, Europe is likely to be supplied by exports from Japan, or from Japanese plants located in various less-developed countries or even the United States. Europe, as perceived by Japanese investors, may well present a market which is significant in terms of size, but also one which, for purposes of local production, is fragmented, beset by social problems, and offering few growth prospects.

FDI in manufacturing is most conspicuous in sectors of relatively low research and development intensity, mostly in industries in which Japan is losing her comparative advantage. In contrast, manufacturing FDI in industries of higher research and development intensity occurs less frequently and is typically a response to trade barriers. Aggressive FDI intended to exploit some unique technology or other organizational asset seems rather exceptional. Japanese FDI in the EEC is not only small in an absolute sense, but also relative to FDI originating from other nations. In the United Kingdom, Japanese FDI over the period 1976-1980 accounted for only 1.9% of all net inward investment. In West Germany, Japanese FDI accounted for about 2.5% of the country's net FDI stock as of end 1980. In France, Japanese FDI during the period 1976-1980 accounted for approximately 1.5% of total FDI flows, and figures of a similar magnitude will be found for other European nations. In line with these low figures, employment created by Japanese FDI in the EEC is, as Table 8 shows, almost negligiable. In comparison, American investment in the EEC is altogether of a different magnitude, particularly in manufacturing. In the United Kingdom there are more than 1,500 U.S. subsidiaries against less than 30 Japanese factories as of the mid-1980s.

TABLE 9
JAPAN'S MERCHANDISE TRADE WITH USA AND EEC (1971-1984)
(U.S. $ million, customs clearance basis)

Year	Total Japanese Merchandise Trade			with USA			with EEC[1]		
	Exports	Imports	Balance	Exports	Imports	Balance	Exports	Imports	Balance
1971	24,019	19,712	4,307	7,495	4,978	2,517	1,635[2]	1,138[2]	497[2]
1972	28,591	23,471	5,120	8,848	5,852	2,996	2,203[2]	1,395[2]	808[2]
1973	36,930	38,314	-1,384	9,449	9,270	179	4,400[3]	3,177[3]	1,223[3]
1974	55,536	62,110	-6,574	12,799	12,682	117	5,968[3]	3,982[3]	1,986[3]
1975	55,753	57,863	-2,110	11,149	11,608	-459	5,675[3]	3,371[3]	2,304[3]
1976	67,225	64,799	2,426	15,690	11,809	3,881	7,234[3]	3,623[3]	3,611[3]
1977	80,495	70,809	9,686	19,717	12,396	7,321	8,736[3]	4,195[3]	4,541[3]
1978	97,543	79,343	18,200	24,915	14,790	10,125	11,105[3]	6,072[3]	5,033[3]
1979	103,032	110,672	-7,640	26,403	20,431	5,972	12,685[3]	7,581[3]	5,104[3]
1980	129,807	140,528	-10,721	31,367	24,408	6,959	16,650[3]	7,842[3]	8,808[3]
1981	152,030	143,290	8,740	38,609	25,297	13,312	18,894	8,552	10,342
1982	138,831	131,931	6,900	36,330	24,179	12,151	17,064	7,560	9,504
1983	146,927	126,393	20,543	42,829	42,647	18,182	18,523	8,120	10,403
1984	170,130	136,450	33,680	60,000	26,900	33,600	19,400	9,300	10,100

1. Ten countries.
2. Six countries.
3. Nine Countries.

Sources: Keizai Koho Center, Japan 1984--An International Comparison, Tokyo, 1984; and NRC-Handelsblad, d.d. 15 January 1985.

Hence Europe, as potential host to manufacturing investment, does not seem to occupy a prominent place in the priorities of Japanese producers. Indeed, a variety of sources, including interviews with Japanese government officials and academics, maintain that Japanese FDI will, for the foreseeable future, flow mostly towards LDCs and the United States, with Europe taking a distant third place. Europeans are considered to be arrogant and self-indulgent, and Europe to be in a state of economic, political and social decline.7/

While the Japanese may perceive Europe as a fragmented and stagnant continent, it nevertheless remains an important market for Japanese goods, accounting for some 15% of its exports. Moreover, if Japan continues to restructure its industry towards more knowledge-intensive products, its dependence upon the European markets is likely to increase, not decrease. However, investment in the future, as in the past, will mainly be intended to safeguard export markets.

POSTSCRIPT

The research-work for this chapter covers the period up until January 1985. Trade problems between the EC and Japan did not become any smaller in number nor have they become unmanageable since then. Although there are strong protectionist tendencies in the EC and in the United States vis-a-vis Japan, the main problem for the Japanese exporters at this moment is to be found in the steep fall of the Yen/U.S.$ exchange rate, from a level of 244 in 1984 to close to 160 (July 1986). The Yen also increased in value against the European currencies, but only by approximately 10% in the same period (see tables 10 and 11). These exchange rate movements can, and probably will, lead to a diversion of Japanese exports from the United States to the EC. The United States and the EC favor a more expensive Yen because it should lead to a reduction of Japan's exports and an increase in its imports. The opposite effect is also possible. If the Japanese domestic economy, as an effect of the exchange-rate development would "shrink," this will heighten export pressure and restrain imports.8/ During the first 6 months of 1986, Japanese exports to the EC rose to U.S. $14,31 billion from a level of U.S. $9 billion in the first half of 1985. Even if the effect of the lower dollar is taken into account, recalculated in ECU, this results in a 27% rise. This leaves the EC with a six-month record trade deficit of U.S. $7.53 billion. The full impact, though, of the exchange rate changes will be delayed for about a year because of the so-called J-curve effect. A permanent higher value of the Yen against the U.S. dollar and European currencies can also be a catalyst for change. Japanese companies will have to review their management strategies and shift away from export dependent activities. They could make efforts to promote an international division of labor by expanding overseas production. After the oil-crises in the mid- and late-1970s, the Japanese economy showed a great capability to adjust to the higher energy- prices. The recent exchange rate developments presented the Japanese with a new challenge. The outcome of this new "struggle" will be of great importance to Japan's trade and investment relations with the EEC.

TABLE 10
VALUE OF THE ECU
(1 ECU = Units of National Currency)

Year	YEN	US $
1982	243.5	0.981
1983	211.4	0.890
1984	187.0	0.789
1985	180.5	0.762
1986 Jan	178.4	0.891
Feb	171.0	0.928
March	170.4	0.954

Source: European Economy, Commission of the EC, Supplement A, no. 4, April 1986.

TABLE 11
YEN/US EXCHANGE RATE

FY 1982	249.66
1983	236.39
1984	244.19
1985	221.09
1986 Jan/March	187.88

Source: Economic Eye 7 (2 June 1986) Keizai Koho Center, Japan.

NOTES

1. F. H. Saelens, Japanese Direct Investment in Western Europe, (University of Manchester, Institute of Science and Technology, 1984). (Unpublished PhD Thesis).

2. M. Hanabusa, Trade problems between Japan and Western Europe, (London, 1979). M. Noelke, EEC Protectionism: Present practice and future trends (European Research Associates, Brussels, 1983). A. Rothacher, Economic Diplomacy Between the European Community and Japan 1959-1981, (London, 1983). E. Wilkinson, E., Japan versus Europe: A History of Misunderstanding, (London: Penguin Books, 1983).

3. Keizai Koho Center, Japan 1984 - An International Comparison, (Tokyo, 1984). p. 36.

4. T. Ozawa, Multinationalism, Japanese Style, (Princeton, N.J.: Princeton University Press, 1979,) p. 237.

5. Ministry of International Trade and Industry, White Paper on the International Trade 1982 (Tokyo)(October 1982):50.

6. Saelens, Japanese Direct Investment, p. 110.

7. UNCTAD, "Trade as per cent of apparant consumption in the EEC, USA, Canada and Japan," Handbook of International Trade and Development Statistics (1983), p. 153.

8. K. Mizutani, "The Rise of the Yen: Causes and Effects," Economic Eye 7 (Keizai Koho Center)(June 1986): 16.

REFERENCES

Commission of the European Communities. "Unit Labor Costs in Manufacturing Industry and in the Whole Economy." European Economy 19 (March 1984).

--------. "The Foreign Trade of the Community, the United States of America and Japan" European Economy 16 (July 1983).

Pelkmans, J. "De georganiseerde handel tussen de Europese Gemeenschappen en Japan." Economisch-Statistische Berichten, 22 June 1983.

Gerritse, G. and Vosse, J.P. "Economische Aspecten van de Japanese Directe Investeringen in het Buitenland." Tilburg University, 1984. (Unpublished research paper.)

12

Japan's Trade and Investment Relations with the United States

Imanuel Wexler

"Japan," a knowledgeable American businessman observed recently, "is neither the perfect model of the future nor the perfect villain of the present."1/ Such a statement is highly instructive, because it provides a telling commentary on the ambivalence that for some time has typified American attitudes toward the economic accomplishments of Japan. It is an ambivalence arising out of a mixture of grudging respect, puzzlement, suspicion, resentment, real or imagined fears, frustration, and, perhaps most importantly, conflicting domestic economic interests. Moreover, it is an ambivalence, not confined entirely to the United States. Indeed, the so-called "Japanese phenomenon" has prompted diverse and varied reactions from private sectors and official circles in almost every other country in the Organization for Economic Cooperation and Development (OECD).

Throughout the late 1960s, the 1970s and early 1980s, the economic stature of Japan has occupied a central place in negotiations in the General Agreement on Tariffs and Trade (GATT), OECD discussions, EEC discussions, and economic summit meetings. This is quite understandable. In the 1970s, Japan consistently outstripped the major OECD countries in GNP growth, averaging an annual growth rate of over 5%. Moreover, between 1970 and 1985, Japan's share of world exports rose from 6.9% to 10.2%, and its share of world manufactured exports increased from 11.2% to 18.8%. As seen in Table 1, Japan was the only one of five major industrial countries to experience a significant increase in both of these shares. During the decades of the 1960s and the 1970s and through 1985, Japan out-performed the major OECD economies with respect to average annual increases in industrial productivity.2/ As of the beginning of 1984, Japan had the lowest inflation rate among all OECD countries and lower unemployment than in any OECD country except for Switzerland, Iceland and Luxembourg.3/ In short, Japan's position as the second ranking economy in the free world, is not a concern unique to Americans.

Nor can the impressive economic performance of Japan during the past three decades be attributed exclusively to its relationship with the United States. Although that country indeed had played an important role in facilitating the postwar economic recovery of Japan, an explanation of its economic advances rests on a variety of factors, both internal and external. Some of these factors admittedly were shaped by the American presence and policies during the occupation period (1945-1951) and by the Korean War boom that followed.4/ Most of them, however, have been the product of the Japanese economic environment, socio-political structure and attitudes, and socio-economic behavior patterns.

It is not necessary to probe into all the supposed ingredients of Japan's global economic successes, in the present context, except to suggest that both myths and realities have contributed to the widely held notions about the performance and challenge of the Japanese.5/ Nevertheless, it would be useful to examine briefly some of the major factors that can be said to have influenced the course of the economic development of Japan during the past 30 years. Indeed, it is only against the background of such an examination that Japanese trade and investment relations with the United States can be meaningfully considered and analyzed.

TABLE 1
SHARE OF WORLD EXPORTS AND MANUFACTURED EXPORTS OF SELECTED INDUSTRIAL COUNTRIES, 1970 AND 1985
(In Percentages)

Country	Share of World Exports 1970	Share of World Exports 1985	Share of Mfg'd Exports* 1970	Share of Mfg'd Exports* 1985
U.S.	15.4	12.3	18.4	17.7
France	6.4	5.9	8.3	8.0
W. Germany	12.1	10.6	19.0	17.6
U.K.	7.0	5.8	10.1	7.6
Japan	6.9	10.2	11.2	18.8

*Excluding exports to the United States.
Source: U.S. Department of Commerce, International Trade Administration, Current International Position of the United States, Washington, D.C., June 1986.

JAPAN'S POSTWAR DEVELOPMENT: SOME CONTRIBUTING FACTORS

One must remember that during the 1930s Japan became one of the major trading nations in the world even though it emerged from World War II with what could be described fairly as a shattered and underdeveloped economy.6/ Japan's recovery from the widespread physical damage and economic dislocations was slow, painful, and heavily dependent on American financial assistance. From 1945 to 1951, U.S. economic aid to Japan amounted to U.S. $2 billion, financing about 57% of its imports during that period.7/ An additional U.S. $4 billion in military expenditures on procurement, following the outbreak of the Korean War, helped to balance a cumulative dollar deficit which in 1955 stood at U.S. $6.2 billion. Military procurement expenditures alone reached a cumulative total of U.S. $7.2 billion by 1964.8/

There can be no question that U.S. economic aid and, even more importantly, U.S. military demand (especially during the 1950s) played a significant role in Japan's economic recovery by providing a stimulus to increased production and the funds that financed industrial re-equipment and modernization. Equally significant, for the future course of events, was the American political decision, reached in 1947-1948, to shift the emphasis of Allied Occupation policies from imposing socio-political reforms to facilitating economic recovery; and the institution, in 1949, of a full-blown Japanese recovery program that closely paralleled the European Recovery Program (the Marshall Plan).9/ Although Occupation policies failed to achieve a sound revival of Japan's industry by the eve of the Korean War, the very shift in policy had the practical effect of enabling Japanese bureaucratic and political elites to remain in power, thus ending earlier attempts to break up and diversify ownership of industry. It also led to the establishment, in 1949, of Japan's Ministry of International Trade and Industry (MITI)--an institution which was destined to play a leading role in the years ahead.

In the final analysis, however, it was not American, but rather Japanese policy decisions and actions that early on laid the foundation for the postwar economic development of Japan. Given the extremely frail state of its economy after the war, the ever-present dependence on imported foodstuffs, energy and raw materials, the desire to attain economic parity with the West, and the domestic consensus that the latter required the development of a strong industrial base, the Japanese authorities adopted for the next twenty years or so, a policy mix that can be described as a protectionist trade policy combined with a comprehensive industrial policy. It can be argued, in fact, that throughout the 1950s and 1960s (and to some extent in the early 1970s), Japan's trade policy was based on a classic case of the "infant-industry" argument. Instead of adhering to a free-trade doctrine in the late 1940s and thus resigning itself to specialization in labor-intensive light manufacturing, Japan chose to promote the establishment and growth of industries which required intensive use of capital and technology. This highly restrictive trade policy--defended during the 1950s and part of the 1960s on grounds of the balance-of-payments disequilibrium--offered protection, behind which such industries could develop and become internationally competitive. Meanwhile, industrial policy has served to formulate and seek consensus on national goals, to provide "administrative guidance" to the private sector, to allocate resources, and to channel direct and indirect assistance to targeted industries.

The essential point here is that one of the major factors contributing to the postwar economic successes of Japan has been the sustained pursuit of national policies designed to: 1) initially protect "infant industries"; 2) conceive and formulate long-range national goals; and 3) allocate resources to strategically important sectors and industries. The effectiveness of these policies largely is due to the ability of government, business, and labor to reach a consensus on national goals and on the policy measures necessary for their attainment--an ability rooted in the nature of government-business and business-labor relationships in Japanese society.

A second important factor that explains Japan's economic effectiveness is a very astute perception about the nature of comparative advantage. Specifically, Japanese policymakers have accurately perceived comparative advantage as a <u>dynamic</u> process, subject to changing domestic and international economic circumstances. Accordingly, they have not hesitated to withdraw both their protection and resources from declining sectors and industries and to shift their priorities and resources to more promising ones. The most notable example of such adjustments in policy has been the gradual shift away from the textile sector into such high-growth lines as steel, autos, electronics, etc. It is also noteworthy that in the wake of the oil crises in the 1970s, Japan was able to effect considerable adjustments in such industries as shipbuilding, aluminum smelting, open-hearth steel, synthetic fibers, and chemical fertilizers, resulting, in some cases, in a deliberate reduction of domestic capacity. Since 1980, the general thrust of industrial policy has been to shift emphasis from efforts to improve existing technology to the development of new technologies. Yet, the main point remains: Japan has shown a willingness and ability to tailor different policies to different industries at different times.

Still a third factor influencing Japan's postwar economic performance has been the high degree of integration and complementarity between industrial policies and macroeconomic monetary and fiscal policies. Such complementarity was especially notable during the 1960s, when MITI's powers and influence were at their greatest. Through foreign exchange regulations, control over foreign investment and acquisition of technology, and a variety of other measures, industrial policy allocated and guided resources into targeted industries. At the same time, monetary/fiscal policies served to create an overall climate conducive to the attainment of the national economic goals: a tax system favoring domestic savings, tax credits and accelerated depreciation allowances favoring investment and research and development expenditures, persistent maintenance of low interest rates, and concessionary financing--all dovetailing nicely into other policy measures.

A fourth factor influencing its economic accomplishments is Japan's early access to foreign technology. In the course of its postwar economic development, it could be said that it occupied a strategic position in the so-called "product cycle." Japan was among the first and most vigorous of the follower countries to seek and acquire sophisticated technologies developed elsewhere, especially from the United States. Moreover, Japan's active pursuit of foreign technologies often has been matched not only by its ability to adapt these technological acquisitions to local conditions, but, in many cases, to improve on them. This technological quest has persisted, even in recent years. Though it outranked the United States in the number of new industrial patents registered for 1981, Japan was still a net importer of technology.10/

To summarize: Japan's early choice of a particular industrial/trade policy mix, its perceptions about the nature of comparative advantage and ability to adjust to changing circumstances, its effective integration of macroeconomic and microeconomic policies, and its active acquisition and adaptation of foreign technologies have been the major and most visible ingredients of its global economic successes and its emergence as the second ranking national economy in the free world. The same ingredients, of course, have played a role in the evolution of the bilateral economic relations between Japan and the United States. But before turning to this specific subject, two important addendums are in order.

The first concerns the supposed role and influence of MITI, as well as of the Japanese government in general, in regulating and orchestrating private business decisions and behavior. As noted above, MITI enjoyed its greatest powers during the 1960s, and especially during the early years of that decade. Yet even then, and certainly later, it was not always able to impose its own views on Japanese industrialists and force them into particular lines of action.11/ Nor was it always successful in persuading other government ministries to follow a particular policy.12/ Notwithstanding such notions as "Japan, Inc.," government policies, including industrial policy, have not been as powerful in dominating and directing business activities as claimed by many foreigners. In recent years MITI itself has become more of a coordinator rather than a director and regulator of economic activities.

In trade policy, Japan's postwar trade and payments restrictions gave way to a process of trade liberalization during the 1960s. Beginning with an overall tariff schedule revision in 1961, Japan proceeded to liberalize and/or remove quantitative import restrictions on a wide range of items, to free foreign exchange transactions, and to relax (though not eliminate) controls on capital movements. Indeed, by 1964 Japan had achieved a level of trade liberalization which qualified it for full membership in the IMF, GATT, and OECD.13/ Upon joining the OECD Japan lifted further restrictions with respect to foreign fund transfers, and the tariff concessions granted during the Kennedy Round of trade negotiations (1964-1967) brought down the average tariff rate on manufactures from 17.6% to 10.7%.14/ And another unilateral across-the-board cut, implemented in 1973, further lowered it to 8.5%.15/ By 1973, moreover, the number of items subject to residual import quotas had been reduced from 453 (in 1962) to a mere 32.16/ During the Tokyo Round of multilateral trade negotiations many of Japan's concessions took the form of further relaxation of import quotas and major reductions of certain key tariffs.

If a lesson can be drawn from these brief comments, it is this: neither the notion of a harmonious and all-powerful government, freely imposing its will on the behavior of the private sector, nor a picture of Japan surrounded by protectionist walls can stand the test of existing reality. There are, to be sure, areas of economic activities where the government can and continues to play a helping and guiding role, just as there still exist direct and indirect barriers to the entry of foreign goods and capital into the economy of Japan. But a perception of present-day Japan as a political/economic monolith and a bastion of trade protectionism is simply not warranted by the facts. In considering Japan's economic relations with the United States, this lesson must be kept in mind.

SCOPE AND NATURE OF U.S.-JAPANESE TRADE AND INVESTMENT

U.S.-Japanese trade and investment relations may be viewed from several vantage points. There is, in the first place, the statistical picture. The _relative_ importance of the United States and Japan as trading partners is clearly illustrated in Tables 2 and 3. Especially illuminating are the changes, over time, in the U.S. share of Japan's foreign trade, for they indicate the overwhelming predominance of the United States as a market for Japanese exports. The figures also show that the importance of the United States as a source of Japan's imports has declined during the last 15 years or so. Japan's share of U.S. foreign trade, with one or two exceptions throughout the entire period considered, has shown a steady increase. Still, the data serves to confirm the significant position of Japan and of the United States as each other's overseas trading partners.

TABLE 2
U.S. SHARE OF JAPAN'S FOREIGN TRADE
(Percent of Total)

Year	Japan's Exports	Japan's Imports
1950	21.7	43.3
1960	27.2	34.6
1970	30.7	29.4
1980	23.8	14.9
1981	25.4	15.2
1982	27.3	15.9
1983	27.9	17.5
1984	35.4	16.9
1985	40.5	17.1

Source: Data from U.S. Department of Commerce, _Survey of Current Business_, selected years.

TABLE 3
JAPAN'S SHARE OF U.S. FOREIGN TRADE
(Percent of Total)

Year	U.S. Exports	U.S. Imports
1950	4.1	2.1
1960	7.1	7.3
1970	10.8	14.7
1980	9.4	12.4
1981	9.3	14.3
1982	9.9	15.3
1983	11.0	15.7
1984	6.4	13.1
1985	6.1	15.4

Source: Computed from data in U.S. Department of Commerce, Survey of Current Business, selected years.

Equally siqnificant is the absolute statistical relationship. As seen in Table 4, U.S.-Japanese bilateral trade has registered a steady--in fact, phenomenal--increase during the past three decades. The value of U.S. exports to Japan rose from U.S. $418 million, in 1950, to over U.S. $22 billion, in 1985, while the value of Japanese exports to the United States increased from a mere U.S. $182 million to an incredible U.S. $71.2 billion during the same period. But what is particularly striking, when viewing Table 4 in its entirety, is the fact that since 1965 the United States has run a persistent deficit in its bilateral trade with Japan. Although the size of the deficit was significantly reduced between 1972 and 1973, it soon began to rise again. And continued to rise--at times at an accelerated rate--reaching nearly U.S. $44 billion in 1985, and an estimated U.S. $61.3 billion for 1986. Indeed, if there is one "great" issue that can be said to have dominated Japanese U.S. economic relations in recent years, it was--and continues to be--the fast growing trade surplus of Japan with the United States; or, conversely, the growing U.S. trade deficit with Japan.

The aggregate figures, in themselves, do not provide an explanation of this phenomenon. However, they do permit an inference as to a likely underlying cause--namely, the extremely strong competitive position of Japan in export markets. Such an inference may be reasonably made on the basis of the data presented in Table 1 above, as well as the fact that for many years Japan has run a substantial trade surplus with the rest of the world.17/ Still, the major component of Japan's global trade surplus has been its surplus with the United States. Thus, while it may seem plausible as far as it goes, this inference does not go far enough in pinpointing the specific factors influencing the bilateral trade relations between Japan and the United States. A basic question still remains: What lies behind the U.S. trade deficit with Japan?

TABLE 4
U.S.-JAPAN BILATERAL TRADE AND TRADE BALANCE
(in millions of U.S.$)

Year	U.S. Exports to Japan	U.S. Imports from Japan	U.S. Trade Balance
1950	418	182	236
1955	683	432	251
1960	1,452	1,149	303
1964	2,018	1,768	250
1965	2,087	2,414	-327
1970	4,652	5,875	-1,223
1971	4,055	7,261	-3,206
1972	4,963	9,076	-4,113
1973	8,356	9,665	-1,309
1975	9,567	11,257	-1,690
1976	10,195	15,531	-5,336
1977	10,522	18,622	-8,100
1980	20,806	31,217	-10,411
1981	21,796	37,598	-15,802
1982	20,694	37,685	-16,991
1983	21,677	41,307	-19,630
1984	23,240	60,211	-36,971
1985	22,146	71,180	-43,390
1986*	22,300	83,600	-61,300

*Official U.S. estimates.
Source: U.S. Department of Commerce, Survey of Current Business, various years.

In addressing this question, the evidence presented in Table 4, which suggests that this deficit is chronic rather than cyclical in nature, should be kept in mind. During the last two decades, in spite of changing business cycles and fluctuating yen/dollar exchange rates, an uninterrupted string of trade deficits with Japan has been run up by the United States. And while it could be argued that the recent strong dollar and the accelerated economic recovery in the United States may have added to the problem at the margin, these developments in themselves cannot explain the overall trend.

Some early explanations of the growing trade surplus with the United States have attributed this phenomenon to a widening divergence in internal price levels between the two countries in the late 1960s. Specifically, it has been argued, a favorable performance of prices in Japan, coupled with an accelerated inflation in the United States in the late 1960s, resulted in a loss of some of the cost advantage that it had enjoyed during the first half of the decade vis-a-vis Japan and other countries.18/ The problem was aggravated further, according to some observers, by the fact that once the American price level had diverged from the Japanese price level, neither country was willing or able to take the domestic measures necessary to bring its international payments into balance at the then-existing Bretton Woods parity of U.S.$1=Y360.19/ Under the circumstances--and in view of the growing U.S. deficit--the logical alternative would have been an adjustment in the exchange rate. Under the Smithsonian Agreement of December 1971, such an adjustment was eventually carried out, when Japan formally agreed to a 16.8% revaluation of the yen, bringing it to a new parity of U.S.$1=Y308. In any event, explanations attributing the U.S.-Japanese trade imbalance to a divergence of domestic price levels, in a regime of fixed rates of exchange and in a world of floating rates, surely cannot serve a useful purpose. The basic causes of the continuous growth of the U.S. trade deficit with Japan must be sought for elsewhere.20/

On the surface, a very simple and straightforward statistical explanation presents itself: the growing U.S. deficit has been caused by a much more rapid growth of Japanese exports to the United States than of U.S. exports to Japan; or, conversely, U.S. imports from Japan have increased much more rapidly than Japanese imports from the United States. This much is clearly seen in Table 4. What the table does not reveal, however, is the fact that for the past 15 years or so the bulk of Japanese exports to the United States has consisted of manufactured products, of both capital-good and consumer-good varieties, while the United States has exported to Japan mainly agricultural products and industrial raw materials.21/ It can be reasonably argued that the composition of their exports to each other provides the most important clue to the persistent U.S.-Japanese trade imbalance and, particularly, to the growing U.S. deficit. This argument can be stated slightly differently by suggesting that the rapid expansion of Japanese exports to the United States can be explained by a sustained growth of American demand for certain high-quality sophisticated products and the ability of Japanese producers to supply such products at competitive prices.

Thus stated, the argument implies, in turn, that U.S.-Japanese bilateral trade has been actually influenced by the operation of two major sets of forces--"export push" and "import pull."22/ In this context, "export push" factors refer to Japanese actions and tactics that have been the major catalytic agents of that country's export growth. Such factors can be said to include concentration of investment in specific industries; direct and indirect government subsidies; home market protection for targeted industries; the highly competitive and export-oriented attitudes of Japanese business managers; aggressive marketing and sales campaigns; actual or alleged predatory pricing practices, etc. In other words, strictly speaking, the "export push" explanation of Japanese export growth attributes this phenomenon, to Japanese-initiated and implemented action. And it is essentially this particular thesis that customarily has been offered as the explanation of Japan's successful penetration of the American market.

In contrast, "import pull" factors refer to actions or non-actions in foreign countries that invite and facilitate import penetration. Or, to put it in the specific context of U.S.-Japanese trade: the "import pull" force entails considerations of circumstances internal to the United States that have afforded Japanese (as well as other foreign producers) a better opportunity to gain and hold increased market shares in that country. Such circumstances include any changes within the U.S. competitive environment; changes in consumer attitudes and upward structural shift in the demand for Japanese (and other foreign-made) goods; American management philosophies, leading to certain decisions and actions by U.S. firms; changes in the composition and attitudes of the U.S. labor force; domestic monetary/fiscal policies pursued by the U.S. government, etc. Although the impact of the various "import pull" factors that facilitate the expansion of U.S. imports from Japan has naturally varied from case to case and from time to time, these factors share one common feature--namely, they constitute a situational framework in which Japan is cast in the role of responding to a strong or rising foreign demand caused independently of any action Japan itself may have initiated.

Existing evidence suggests that the strong, widespread Japanese competition in the United States as reflected in Japan's bilateral trade surplus may be attributed to both "export push" and "import pull" factors. Indeed, one may view these two sets of forces as the blades of a pair of scissors, interacting to influence the evolution of the American market and, hence, the quantity and value of U.S. imports from Japan. The evidence also suggests, however, that the relative importance of "export push" and "import pull" has varied among different industries.23/ And finally, it suggests that Japanese performance, in capturing a share of the American market, has also differed among major product categories.24/

A sample of U.S.-Japanese bilateral trade in selected manufactured products is given in Table 5. A comparison between the growth of Japanese exports to the United States and U.S. exports to Japan during the period covered, serves to confirm the basic argument made above--namely, that Japan's trade surplus with the United States can be essentially explained in terms of the specific products which it exports to the latter. This is an important point, for it argues that a meaningful explanation of the macroeconomic picture, or the aggregate trade imbalance, must necessarily rest on microeconomic considerations. That is, it must rest on an examination of the demand and supply characteristics of specific products (or product categories) traded between the two countries, and the relative performance of American and Japanese industries which produce them. Such an examination, of course, lies beyond the scope of the present paper. It is merely being suggested here as the proper route toward a better understanding of the aggregate statistical record of U.S.-Japanese trade relations.

Turning now to the bilateral investment relations, several observations can be made. First, even though the United States and Japan are each other's largest overseas trading partners, Japan does not constitute a major destination of U.S. foreign investment; nor does it represent the major source of foreign investment in the United States. To be sure, American companies continue to be the major foreign investors in Japan--well ahead of investors from Hong Kong, the United Kingdom, and West Germany. Thus, at the

TABLE 5
U.S.-JAPAN BILATERAL TRADE
IN SELECTED MANUFACTURED PRODUCTS, 1963-1981
(In Millions of $)

Product	1963	1972	1977	1981
Autos and Trucks:				
Japanese exports to U.S.	7	1,411	5,030	11,491
U.S. exports to Japan	9	25	90	63
Iron and Steel Products:				
Japanese exports to U.S.	209	1,018	2,285	3,939
U.S. exports to Japan	8	7	16	39
Machine Tools:				
Japanese exports to U.S.	1	16	111	752
U.S. exports to Japan	25	31	22	55
Telecommunications:				
Japanese exports to U.S.	134	1,111	2,326	3,052
U.S. exports to Japan	6	45	71	160

Source; U.S., I.T.C., Report on Industrial Targeting by Japan and its Effects on U.S. Industries.

end of 1985, the value of U.S. direct foreign investment in Japan stood at U.S. $9.1 billion. Yet this figure represented only 3.9% of the total value of U.S. direct foreign investment at the end of that year. Measured by the net book value of foreign investors' equity and loans to U.S. affiliates, Japanese direct foreign investment in the United States increased from U.S. $259 million, in 1973, to U.S.$19.1 billion by the end of 1985.25/ Still, Japan's share of the total value of direct foreign investment in the United States, in that year, came to 10.4%, lagging far behind the United Kingdom and the Netherlands.

Secondly, Japanese and American direct investments in each other's economy show distinctly different patterns. The bulk of the U.S. direct investment in Japan has been concentrated in manufacturing and petroleum. By the end of 1985, investment in manufacturing and petroleum accounted for 50.5% and 24%, respectively, of the total value of U.S. direct investment in Japan, while wholesale trade and banking/finance accounted for 15% and 6%, respectively. In contrast, Japanese direct investment in the United States has been concentrated largely in the trade sector which accounted for 61% of the total by the end of 1985, with manufacturing and banking accounting for 13.6% and 11.5%

respectively. This suggests a strong link between the development, by Japanese companies, of trade infrastructures and export-related facilities in foreign countries and the overall growth of Japan's exports, especially to the United States.

In recent years, however, there have been significant changes in both the magnitude and pattern of the Japanese investment in the United States. The most notable, perhaps, has been its fast growth. From 1980 to 1985, Japanese direct investment nearly tripled. And, between the year ends of 1984 and 1985 alone, the total value of Japanese owned assets in the United States rose from U.S. $67.6 billion to U.S. $101.8 billion. The bulk of this particular increase was accounted for by stepped-up Japanese purchases of U.S. bonds and stocks (mostly U.S. government bonds) and lending activities of Japanese banks, about which more will be said below. But even Japanese direct investment in the United States is estimated to grow at a rate of 14.2% each year between now and the year 2000.26/

This fast growth has been accompanied by a notable shift toward increased investment in manufacturing--a trend that can be expected to continue, and possibly accelerate, for some time. To a large extent, such a shift may be viewed as a reaction to the growing protectionist sentiments expressed in various American circles (including the Congress of the United States). Japanese producers, fearful of new U.S. trade barriers, have responded to the protectionist clamor by relocating some of their plant capacity to the United States. Moreover, Japanese companies have either bought manufacturing plants from, or formed joint ventures with American firms. In part, however, the shift toward a manufacturing investment can be attributed to the recent rise in the value of the yen against the dollar and other major currencies. The dramatic appreciation of the yen has had a dampening effect on Japan's exports; and those Japanese companies that have found their exports curtailed, have been--and still are--looking for offshore manufacturing sites.27/ For many of them, locating in the United States is, a logical choice.

Whether as a reaction to a perceived American protectionist threat or as a strategic response to a rising yen, Japanese companies have increasingly channelled their investment in the United States toward the manufacturing sector--encompassing a broad range of products and many geographical locations. In the State of Tennessee alone, Japanese companies are currently operating 36 plants which employ some 8,000 people and which represent an investment of U.S. $1.2 billion. Throughout the United States, over 300 Japanese companies operate nearly 500 plants, producing automobiles, metals, electronics, high-tech products, office equipment and other products. More recently, the Japanese have made significant inroads into the domestic construction market as well. And it might also be noted that several states (e.g., Oregon, Washington, California, Georgia, and Indiana) have been actively seeking Japanese investment into their economies.

Another notable aspect of the Japanese investment in the United States has been the spectacular rise in portfolio investment. Japan, of course, has not been the only source of financial capital flowing into the United States in recent years. Nor are Japanese investors alone in continuing to find U.S. securities attractive, despite the recent decline in the value of the dollar. Indeed, the record shows that, far from slowing down, the total flow of foreign capital into the United States actually increased during 1985 and 1986. And the evidence suggests that foreign portfolio managers--despite losses incurred as a result of the decline of the dollar--continue to view the United States through "bullish" eyes. In at least three respects, Japan still presents a special case.

First, the rate at which Japanese investors have increased their purchases of U.S. securities has been truly phenomenal. In the first quarter of 1981, net Japanese purchases of U.S. bonds amounted to about $1 billion; in the first quarter of 1985 they were $5.3 billion; and during the first quarter of 1986 they were estimated at over $12 billion.

Second, Japanese investors show a distinct preference for U.S. bonds, mainly U.S. government bonds. It might be mentioned, in this connection, that the principal Japanese institutions buying U.S. and other foreign securities are 23 life insurance companies and seven trust banks that manage large corporate pension funds. These institutions, especially the life insurance companies, generally take a long-term view and are inclined to hold bonds to maturity. Hence, their calculations in managing their portfolios focus more on the cumulative return over time than on short-term gains or losses due to currency fluctuations and/or stock market movements.

Third, both directly and indirectly, Japanese institutional investors have been encouraged by their government to remain enthusiastic about continuing to invest in the United States. Fearful that a reduced flow of capital might create additional frictions with the United States, the

Japanese government (mainly the Ministry of Finance) has often closed its eyes to certain practices (i.e., understating book value losses on foreign securities) of Japanese banks and insurance companies. More importantly, in March 1986, the limit on assets that life insurance companies could invest in foreiqn securities was raised from 10% (in effect since 1969) to 25%. There is no question that this move was designed to further stimulate Japanese investment in the United States.

How long the massive inflow of foreign capital in general and Japanese investment, in particular, will continue is a question that is easier raised than answered. But, in looking at U.S.-Japanese trade and investment relations to date, the statistical record is quite clear: it shows that the United States and Japan are each other's largest overseas trading partners; that their bilateral trade has been in persistent imbalance for the last 20 years; and that although Japan is not a major destination of U.S. foreign investment, in recent years the United States has become a growing target of direct and portfolio investment by Japan.

MAJOR ISSUES IN U.S.-JAPANESE ECONOMIC RELATIONS

The story of U.S.-Japanese economic relations does not end with the statistical record. Indeed, the changing composition of Japan's exports to the United States, increased competitiveness and, hence, growing market penetration with respect to certain products, and its continued pursuit of various industrial and trade policies have given rise to a number of bilateral issues at different times during the last twenty years. And once raised, such issues have often led to prolonged controversies, outright conflicts, and much acrimony between the two countries. In fact, one may discern a recurring scenario in U.S.-Japanese relations over the years: the U.S. government raises an issue or several issues; the Japanese respond after considerable delay; the United States judges the response inadequate and applies more pressure; and the Japanese finally come up with further concessions. Each round of this process elevates the degree of anger and frustration on both sides, with the result that relatively small issues often reach outlandish proportions.

There is, of course, an element of irony in such a pattern of challenges and responses. In the first place, the controversy and acrimony generated by a particular issue often turn out to have been wasteful and unnecessary in view of subsequent developments. And secondly, the lessons which might have been learned from the process of settling one issue are often forgotten when another issue arises later. A most instructive case, in this connection, was the textile controversy that lasted from 1969 to 1971 and resulted in a voluntary restraint agreement which set a three-year limit on increases in Japanese exports of wool and man-made fiber textiles to the United States. It was an agreement forced on the Japanese by, among other things, an American threat to invoke the "Trading with the Enemy" Act, under which the U.S. President would be empowered to impose import quotas on a wide range of Japanese products. But shortly after it had been signed, the agreement proved to be inconsequential, because between 1970 and 1973, Japanese textiles lost their comparative advantage. By 1973, the former trade adversaries found themselves on the same side in signing the multilateral Multifiber Textile Agreement, aimed at regulating and limiting textile imports from other countries.28/

With the textile issue settled, there followed a period of relative calm in U.S.-Japanese economic (and political) relations, leading some observers to hope that a new and enduring basis of mutual understanding had been reached.29/ But these hopes soon proved to be premature, for by the late 1970s several new conflicts had emerged. For example, between 1975 and 1976 Japanese sales of color TV sets in the United States more than doubled, eliciting strong reactions from American producers and resulting in a finding of "injury" by the U.S. International Trade Commission. In turn, in the spring of 1977, this led to the negotiation and conclusion of an Orderly Market Agreement, restricting such sales. During the late 1970s, moreover, U.S. imports of steel (from Japan as well as from other countries) rose sharply, prompting the American steel industry to complain bitterly about the "influx of low-priced steel" and assign blame to an overexpansion of foreign steel-production capacity and massive subsidizations by foreign governments.30/ In response, the Carter Administration adopted a system of "trigger prices," to be used as a basis for monitoring U.S. steel imports and for initiating accelerated anti-dumping investigations.31/ And, in 1980, the U.S. automobile industry began <u>its</u> appeal for temporary protection from Japanese imports--an appeal whose practical outcome, effective April 1981, was an official U.S.-Japanese agreement on Voluntary Export Restraints (VER), limiting Japanese auto exports to the United States to 1.68 million cars per year (later raised to 1.85 million cars per year).

This twice renewed agreement expired in March of 1985; its net result was a rise in the price of both American and Japanese-made cars sold in the United States.32/

During the second half of the 1970s, the issues and conflicts pertaining to specific U.S. industries were overshadowed by an increasing official preoccupation with the troubling growth in the U.S. aggregate deficit with Japan, which reached a record U.S. $5.3 billion in 1976, and climbed further to U.S. $8.1 billion in 1977. For both countries the bilateral trade imbalance was, in fact, part of their overall trade positions, that is, a global trade deficit for the United States and a global trade surplus for Japan. The U.S. approach to the issue is part of a multilateral growth strategy. Specifically, the United States suggested that if Japan would stimulate its economy more, and further liberalize its imports, it would simultaneously reduce its overall trade surplus and would contribute to worldwide recovery by buying products from other countries. This so-called "locomotive" strategy, originally proposed by the OECD in 1976, was a topic of discussion at the London Economic Summit in May 1977, where gentle pressure was exerted on Japan (and West Germany) by both the United States and Great Britain. But when it became clear that Japan was unwilling to undertake expansionary domestic policies to stimulate economic growth, American pressure became stronger. Details of this particular controversy, which continued throughout 1977 and 1978, need not be discussed here.33/ Suffice it to say that the American demand, in 1978, for an official Japanese commitment to a 7% growth rate (which Japan finally agreed to) was neither justified nor realistic. It merely served to increase the tension between the two countries, and in the end did little to alleviate their bilateral trade imbalance.

Another bilateral issue that was initially raised within a multilateral context should be mentioned here. During the 1977-79 negotiations of the code for government procurement policies, under the Tokyo Round of multilateral trade negotiations, the United States requested that Japan open up the purchases by Nippon Telegraph and Telephone Corporation (NTT) to competitive bidding. The Japanese refused on the ground that most telephone monopolies in the world used the same closed, negotiated contract system as did NTT. In effect, the Japanese government refused to include the matter of NTT purchasing policies in the discussions of the government-procurement code. What followed proved to be one of the most heated and prolonged disputes in U.S.-Japanese relations, a dispute whose satisfactory resolution--despite a number of compromises and Japanese accommodations--is not yet in sight.34/ At issue, of course, is a whole range of matters involving one of the fastest growing, high technology industries--telecommunications. This is an industry which best exemplifies the on-going battle and strong competition between the high technology and capital-intensive industries of these two nations. It is this battle, with all its implications, that underlies the major U.S.-Japanese trade conflicts in recent times.

But while the high technology battle appears to dominate U.S.-Japanese trade relations in the 1980s, another dispute that began in the late 1970's continues to share the limelight. It is a dispute whose economic significance has been overshadowed by its symbolic value: it is, in a word, the long-lasting and continuing dispute over Japanese import quotas on citrus and beef. Ever since the controversy began in 1977, the United States has viewed the Japanese import restrictions on these two agricultural products as symbols of the "closed" Japanese market and has pushed hard for increased Japanese concessions. The Japanese have regarded the U.S. position--and pressures--not only as unreasonable but, at times, as hypocritical.

This particular dispute is noteworthy largely because of the several ironies it contains. In the first place, it serves to illustrate that the protection accorded to citrus and beef farmers by the Japanese government has been no less a function of domestic political considerations than have the continued restrictions imposed by the U.S. government on imports of several agricultural products, including beef and citrus. Secondly, the heated and grave arguments surrounding this issue have masked, or more correctly, ignored the fact that Japan is actually the world's largest importer of agricultural products and that the United States is Japan's foremost supplier of such products.35/ But, at the same time, the American insistence on freer access to beef and citrus has tended to overstate the quantitative significance of these two products either in the total bilateral trade or even in the bilateral agricultural trade of the two countries. Of the $6.2 billion worth of U.S. agricultural exports to Japan in 1983, beef and citrus together accounted for less than $1 billion (or, for about 16%). Within the context of total trade, and especially within the context of the U.S. bilateral deficit, citrus and beef exports amount to very small proportions. The trade potential of these two products, even if the Japanese quotas were to be completely eliminated, is very insignificant and would, in any event, hardly affect the U.S.

bilateral deficit. Still, in 1984, the United States managed to wrestle a new four-year agreement from Japan, providing for annual increases of 6,900 metric tons in the quota for U.S. beef and 11,000 metric tons in the quota for oranges.36/

Several other agreements between the United States and Japan have been reached or renewed during recent years: a renewed three-year agreement with NTT, providing improved access for U.S. suppliers to the Japanese telecommunication market, as well as to NTT-sponsored research and development activities; a commitment by MITI to facilitate increased sales of U.S.-made semiconductors; another MITI action designed to improve Japan's import certification procedures; elimination of restrictions (limitations) on foreign ownership of most companies providing Value Added Network (VAN) services; an agreement between the the Treasury of the United States and that of Japan to further deregulate Japan's domestic interest rates, and improved access to Japan's capital markets for foreign financial institutions. During these years, moreover, the Japanese government has announced several additional "packages" of trade liberalization, containing reductions in both tariff and non-tariff barriers.

What can be concluded from the preceding narrative? Or, more specifically, what can be said about the essential character of U.S.-Japanese economic relations?

The characteristic that emerges clearly since the mid-1960s is that U.S. policy has been governed by a major dual objective: to gain increased access for American producers and investors into the Japanese market and, at the same time, to limit Japanese access into different segments of the American domestic market. But this objective, in turn, has been based on certain perceptions, whether valid or not, about the nature of economic forces at work in both countries; and it also suggests certain perceptions about proper government responses to pressures from various domestic interest groups. The Japanese market is perceived as being "closed"; the American market, as the most open in the world. The Japanese government is perceived as a major force behind Japan's economic performance; the American government is seen as having no coherent industrial policy, relying instead on make-shift measures to promote and protect the country's industrial structure.

Actually, the American and Japanese industrial structures show both similarities and differences. Thus, in both countries capital-intensive high-technology industries enjoy relative advantage and are internationally competitive, while labor-intensive industries are at a disadvantage and face strong competition from developing and newly industrialized countries. The basic structural differences, on the other hand, consist of the facts that: 1) while the U.S. agricultural and natural-resource industries are the most productive and competitive in the world, Japanese agriculture is far less competitive and requires protection of several products; and 2) whereas traditional U.S. industries (e.g., steel, auto, machine tool, etc.) are relatively old and their equipment and machinery often dated, the same Japanese industries, being younger, are better equipped and, hence, more efficient. It can be reasonably argued, therefore, that the recurring U.S.-Japanese trade conflicts over the years, and particularly in recent years, have been largely due to such similarities and differences in their industrial structures, and to differences in policy responses of the governments concerned. While Japan, apart from its agricultural protection, has typically protected its high-growth industries which, in turn, became a major source of competition for American producers, the United States has generally protected its relatively inefficient or declining industries. With the two nations' high technology industries locked in fierce competition, in which at present the Japanese appear to have an edge, the underlying American objective has been pursued more vigorously and the conflicts have naturally intensified.

RECENT PAST AND FUTURE PROSPECTS

In the 1980s several new elements have been added to the equation. Beginning in 1980-81, the United States and most other industrialized countries (including Japan) found themselves in the midst of an economic downturn, which by the end of 1982 appeared to be deeper and longer lasting than expected. The United States and Western Europe, in particular, experienced severe growth and productivity problems; and their domestic problems were further aggrevated by increasing competition from newly industrialized countries. Moreover, some governments, notably the United States and the United Kingdom, chose to control inflation (a legacy of the 1970s) by means of tight monetary policies. Thus, although inflation in the United States and the United Kingdom was finally reduced, prohibitively high interest rates stunted investment activities and recovery efforts. The United States, in fact, experienced its most severe and longest recession, from which it did not begin to emerge until early 1984. The recovery which followed was relatively strong, but it left two problems: a huge budget deficit and a rising dollar which, in turn, rendered American exports less competitive, and facilitated increased foreign sales in the U.S. domestic market. Hence a third problem: the continuing and growing U.S. trade deficit--a deficit financed by massive inflows of foreign capital which, in turn, served to keep the value of the dollar high and further reduce U.S. international competitiveness. Under the circumstances, it is hardly surprising that domestic pressures for protection have been rising and strong demands for import relief have been pouring into Washington. And it is also understandable that much of the protectionist fire has been aimed at Japan--the country whose export performance alone accounted for almost one-third of the U.S. global trade deficit in 1985.

Faced with the growing protectionist pressures, and mindful of possible congressional action to accommodate them, the U.S. Administration took several initiatives during 1985. At the Economic Summit meeting in May, the United States urged on its major trading partners the need to undertake a new round of multilateral trade negotiations under the auspices of GATT. And in September of that year, the United States and four of its allies (France, Japan, the United Kindgom, and West Germany) agreed to concerted effort aimed at pushing down the value of the dollar. Meanwhile at home various measures were pursued so as to reduce the budget deficit and lower interest rates, the latter move designed to reduce the attractiveness of holding dollar assets.

As is well known, the dollar has indeed declined against the four currencies involved in the September 1985 agreement, and U.S. interest rates have fallen down. Since the celebrated agreement was announced, the yen has risen by 35% against the dollar, and the interest-rate spread between long-term U.S. and Japanese government bonds has narrowed from 4.5 percentile points to 2.2. In Japan, Prime Minister Nakasone has appealed to his people to increase their purchases of imported goods and pledged to further reduce Japanese trade restrictions.

Yet as these lines are written, there is no clear sign that the declining dollar has brought relief to the U.S. trade balance or that lower U.S. interest rates have acted as a brake on the inflow of foreign capital. In fact, as noted above, foreign investment in the United States continues to grow; and the global U.S. trade deficit for 1986 is now estimated at over $170 billion. Nor is there a sign that the trade imbalance with Japan is narrowing or is about to narrow in the near future. On the contrary, despite the rise of the yen, Japan's trade surplus with the United States for 1986 is expected to reach about $60 billion, and some Japanese estimates point to a higher surplus yet in 1987.

Thus, while American officals continue to impress on their Japanese counterparts the gravity of the situation and the urgent need to open the Japanese home market to increased imports, the patience of the U.S. Congress is wearing thin. Despite the threat of a presidential veto (which was carried out) Congress passed, in the summer of 1986, a bill limiting textile imports. Moreover, it has been considering an omnibus trade legislation which would, among other things, impose specific restrictions against imports from Japan. Indeed, in 1986 the United States and Japan are facing perhaps the gravest crisis in their postwar trading relations--a crisis which may well produce adverse consequences for both their economies.

Unfortunately, there are no quick and easy solutions to the current state of affairs influencing U.S.-Japanese bilateral economic relations. Nor is it really possible to predict either the short-term or long-term course of relevant developments (e.g., how far will the dollar decline, and what will be the precise effects on the U.S. trade balance). But while exact predictions are impossible, one may nevertheless conclude with one general observation. It is, that since both the United States and Japan, singly or bilaterally, constitute two of the three major elements of the international trading system, their present and future relations must be considered and treated within a _multilateral_, rather than a strict bilateral, framework. Or to put it differently: however specific their bilateral problems may be, their solutions must ultimately grow out of a multilateral perspective. In the final analysis, _this_ is what the challenge of U.S.-Japanese economic relations should mean.

NOTES

1. Edwin Spencer, "Japan: Stimulus or Scapegoat?" _Foreign Affairs_ (Fall 1983):137.

2. During 1960/70, manufacturing productivity in Japan averaged 10.8%, compared to 2.8% in the United States, 6.7% in France, 5.8% in West Germany, and 3.7% in the United Kingdom. Although during 1970/80 Japanese productivity was

lower than during 1960/70, it was still higher than in the other four countries. The same held true for 1984 and 1985.

3. See OECD, OECD Observer (March 1984):3-4.

4. For an interesting discussion of the Occupation period and early U.S.-Japanese relations, see William Borden, The Pacific Alliance (Madison, Wisconsin: The University of Wisconsin Press, 1984).

5. See, for example, Peter F. Druker, "Behind Japan's Success," Harvard Business Review (January-February, 1981).

6. On the eve of World War II Japan was the fourth largest exporting nation in the world, exceeded only by the United States, United Kingdom, and Germany.

7. See Alfred K. Ho, Japan's Trade Liberalization in the 1960s (White Plains, New York: IAS Press, 1973), p. 5.

8. See Borden, The Pacific Alliance, p. 220.

9. Ibid., p. 3.

10. As of 1981, Japan buys about $1.6 billion of technology per year, while it sells only $500 million. See U.S. Congress, Committee on Science and Technology, Japanese Technological Advances and Possible United States Responses Using Research Joint Ventures, 98th Congressional Hearings, 1st Session, Washington, D.C., 1984.

11. See Druker, "Behind Japan's Success," for cases in point.

12. For interesting details concerning conflicts between Japanese government agencies with regard to policy questions, see Chikara Higashi, Japanese Trade Policy Formulation (New York: Praeger, 1983).

13. See Ho, Japan's Trade Liberalization..., p. 16.

14. For details of Japanese tariff concessions during the Kennedy Round, see Ernest Preeg, Traders and Diplomats (Washington, D.C.: Brookings Institution, 1970), especially p. 211.

15. See Patricia H. Kuwayama, "The Evolution of Trade with Japan," in U.S. Trade in the Sixties and Seventies, ed., K. Jameson and R. Skurski (Lexington, Mass.: D.C. Heath, 1974), p. 21.

16. Mostly on agricultural products; ibid.

17. Japan's global trade surplus stood at $20 billion in 1981; $31 billion in 1983; and is estimated at $75 billion for 1986.

18. See, for example, Kuwayama, "Evolution of Trade with Japan;" also Higashi, Japanese Trade Policy....

19. See John Greenwood, "U.S.-Japan Economic Relations, 1970-73," in Proceedings of a Conference on Japan-U.S. Economic Policy Japan-U.S. Assembly (Washington, D.C.: American Enterprise Institute, 1975).

20. At first there was no perceptible change in the bilateral trade imbalance, but the revaluation may well have contributed to the reduction in the U.S. deficit between 1972 and 1973.

21. Until the late 1960s, Japanese exports consisted chiefly of textiles, apparel, toys, china, etc. In recent years, over 20% of total U.S. manufactured imports have come from Japan. Moreover, in 1983, 98% of U.S. imports from Japan consisted of manufactured products while only 45% of U.S. exports to Japan comprised such products.

22. The following discussion draws on Wilbur F. Monroe, Japanese Exports to the United States: Analysis of "Import Pull" and "Export Push" Factors (Washington, D.C.: U.S.-Japan Trade Council, 1978).

23. For specific examples, see ibid., pp. 206-214.

24. Thus, for example, Japan's share of the U.S. automobile market has increased from less than 10% in 1976, to about 23% in 1982; her share of the U.S. machine tool market rose from 10% in 1979, to 62 and 68 percent in 1982 and 1983, respectively.

25. Prior to 1973, there are only two postwar years which show Japanese foreign investment in the United States. These are 1968 and 1972, and in each case the value of the investment was about $100 million.

26. See "Japan, U.S.A.," Business Week, 14 July 1986, p. 46.

27. A good example is the Japanese steel industry which has been hard hit by the stronger yen, as well as by increased competition from such steel producing countries as Brazil, South Korea, and Taiwan. During the first quarter of 1986, Japanese steel exports were down 15.5% compared to the same period in 1985, while imports rose by 51.4%. Reacting to these developments, companies such as Nippon Steel Corporation and Nippon Kokan have, in recent years, bought manufacturing facilities in the United States and have formed several joint ventures with American firms. See, "Japanese Steel Darkest Days," New York Times, 3 August 1986

28. Nevertheless, another U.S.-Japanese textile agreement was signed in 1978; and as of this writing, the United States still maintains quotas on several textile products imported from Japan. For an illuminating discussion of the textile controversy, see I.M. Destler, H. Fukui, and H. Sato, The Textile Wrangle (Ithaca, N.Y.: Cornell University Press, 1979).

29. Ibid., pp. 332-333.

30. Actually, as early as 1969, steel producers in Japan and Europe had signed Voluntary Restraint Agreements with the United States, limiting to 5% the annual growth of their exports to that country. These agreements, effective for three years, were later revised and renewed for another three-year period. But they were not renewed upon expiration in 1974.

31. Although Japan was not regarded as the only culprit by American steel producers, most of the attention, for obvious reasons, had been focused on it.

32. It has been recently estimated that these VER's have cost American consumers $15.7 billion in higher prices on cars since mid-1981, with an average increase of $1,300 per car for Japanese cars and about $660 for American cars. See Wall Street Journal, 14 February 1985.

33. For details see Higashi, Japanese Trade Policy..., pp. 83-96.

34. Ibid., pp. 106-114.

35. Japan is, in fact, the largest destination of U.S. agricultural exports. In 1982, over 20% of total U.S. agricultural exports went to Japan, including 60% of total U.S. exports of beef.

36. See U.S. Department of Commerce, Business America, 20 August 1984, p. 38.

13

Trade Relations of Australia, New Zealand and South Africa with East Asia

P. D. F. Strydom

The trade relations between East Asia, Australia, New Zealand and South Africa can only be understood within the global context of trade. Thus trade between these countries will be analyzed within the framework of major changes in the patterns of world trade during the past decade or so. Since our major emphasis is on trade between the Far East, Australia, New Zealand and South Africa, this chapter will not elaborate on world trade patterns as such, although they will be discussed when necessary to support our exposition.

The analytical framework adopted in this paper is based on a synthesis of trade theories along the lines suggested by Hirsch (1974) as well as by Batchelor, Major and Morgan (1980). We are therefore setting ourselves the task of explaining trade in terms of types of commodities. Furthermore, we shall establish shifts of lower to higher stages of manufacturing as suggested by Michaely (1968).

We define East Asia in line with the convention of the GATT; viz. South and East Asia excluding Bangladesh, India, Pakistan and Sri Lanka.1/ In view of the importance of Japan in this region, we shall extend our analysis to include it when necessary.

ANALYTICAL FRAMEWORK

Conventional international trade theory explains trade in terms of competing hypotheses. The Ricardian model explains trade by comparative advantage, determined by production conditions within the framework of one factor of production. Within the general equilibrium assumptions of neoclassical economics, international trade is explained in terms of relative factor endowments and the availability of different techniques of production which ensure production in different factor proportions across countries. The extensive literature on the Leontief paradox as well as the mounting empirical evidence against the hypotheses of conventional trade theories clearly support the skepticism against them.2/ Alternative hypotheses were developed, such as those which highlighted intra-industry trade, and technology-based theories within the framework of the so-called dynamic trade thoeries. Hirsch (1974) proposed a synthesis which emphasized the complementarity of trade theories by dividing the global set of traded goods into a small number of categories to which existing trade models were applicable. Accordingly, he distinguished between Ricardian goods, Heckscher-Ohlin goods, and Product Cycle goods. Ricardian goods are those containing a high proportion of domestic natural resources. Comparative advantage is determined by the natural endowment of the country. Heckscher-Ohlin goods are characterized by the conditions that their production techniques are known and easily available. Comparative advantage depends on the relative endowment of the different countries. Product Cycle goods are produced by means of advanced technologies which are not readily available. The product passes through a cycle which entails the intensive use of skilled manpower during the first stage of the production cycle. As the product becomes more mature and it reaches the later stage of the cycle, other factors of production become relatively more important in production.

This analytical framework has also been applied by Batchelor, Major and Morgan (1980) in classifying countries into clusters by their main basis for trade. Countries whose exports comprise mainly agricultural and mineral products are expected to export according to the hypothesis of the Ricardian trade theory. Countries exporting mainly manufacturied products are likely to trade in terms of the hypothesis of the Heckscher-Ohlin or advanced technological based theories.

The advantage of applying this analytical framework is that it stresses the complementarity of international trade theories. Moreover, we steer clear of many of the problems associated with the empirical testing of trade theories such as those which have emerged in terms of the Leontief paradox.3/

TABLE 1
GROWTH OF WORLD PRODUCTION AND TRADE
(Average Annual Percentage change in Volume Terms)

	1963-73	1973-83	1981	1982	1983	1984
Production						
All Merchandise	6.0	2.0	1.0	-2.0	2.0	5.5
Agriculture	2.5	2.0	4.0	2.5	0.0	5.0
Mining	5.5	0.5	-2.0	-7.5	-1.5	2.0
Manufacturing	7.5	2.5	0.5	-2.0	3.5	7.5
Exports						
All Merchandise	9.0	3.0	1.0	-3.0	3.0	9.0
Agricultural Prod.	4.0	3.0	4.0	-1.0	1.0	7.0
Minerals*	7.5	-2.0	-10.0	-6.0	-1.0	3.0
Manufactures	11.5	4.5	4.0	-2.0	5.0	12.0

*Includes fuels and non-ferrous metals.
Source: GATT. International Trade 1984/85, Geneva, 1985.

CHANGING PATTERNS IN WORLD TRADE

As indicated in Table 1, the rate of world production and trade slowed down markedly during the 1970s and early 1980s. During 1982, the volume of world trade declined, the third decline during the post-war period, the other two occurred in 1975 and 1958, while the 9% growth in 1984 was the largest increase since 1963. This pattern is in sharp contrast with the period from 1960 to the mid-1970s when trade in manufactures trebled in volume terms, as demonstrated by Batchelor, Major and Morgan (1980, Chapter 2). A detailed discussion of the reasons for this performance in world production and trade falls beyond the scope of this paper. Suffice it to say that the major factors which affected production and trade adversely were the following: decline in the growth of world demand; capital shortage in the major industrial countries; the international debt problem; import substitution policies; volatile exchange rates; and protectionist measures.4/

Of particular importance to our analysis is the rising importance of certain countries in world trade during these testing times in the international economy. These countries are generally referred to as the Newly Industrializing countries, or NICs.5/ The NICs in East Asia, that is, Hong Kong, Republic of Korea, Singapore and Taiwan, are of particular importance to our analysis, and these countries will be looked at in more detail later on.

The changing patterns in world trade which occurred during the 1970s and early 1980s are clearly illustrated in Table 2. The major industrial countries still play a dominant role in world trade, but they have lost part of their share, whether measured in imports or exports. This conclusion holds despite the recovery in trade volumes during 1984. Japan is an important exception since it increased its share in world trade, particularly through exports. Similarly, the share of the non-oil developing countries in world trade declined over the period 1965 to 1984, but these counties gained a bigger share of world trade during the 1970s, primarily because of the rising share of the NICs. The redistribution in respect of world trade as measured by relative shares, largely benefited the developing oil exporting countries.

As indicated in Table 2, those NICs in East Asia have been very effective in raising their share in world trade. They were, for instance, more successful than the Latin American countries. Measured by imports and exports, the Republic of Korea and Singapore have increased their share in world trade markedly. In terms of exports, for instance, the Republic of Korea has quadrupled its share in world exports from 1970 to 1982, followed by a sustained improvement in 1984. Singapore more than doubled its share over the period 1970 to 1984.

By losing their relative share in world trade, Australia, New Zealand and South Africa followed a similar pattern as the industrial countries. New Zealand constitutes a special case in the sense that its falling share in world exports and imports has been dramatic. Several aspects of these changing patterns will be addressed in more detail below. It should nevertheless be kept in mind that, economically South Africa is dissimilar from Australia and New Zealand.

TABLE 2
PERCENTAGE SHARE IN WORLD TRADE
(Value terms, M=Imports, X=Exports)

Areas	X/M	1965	1970	1975	1980	1982	1984
Industrial Countries	M	73.2	75.5	71.4	71.0	67.7	71.1
	X	73.7	76.8	70.0	66.1	67.6	68.7
Oil Developing Exporting	M	3.4	3.2	6.2	6.8	9.5	7.0
Countries	X	5.9	5.8	13.9	15.7	12.6	9.6
Non-oil Developing	M	23.1	20.8	21.7	21.2	21.7	21.0
Countries	X	20.1	16.9	15.4	17.1	18.5	20.0
Asia	M	7.8	6.4	6.6	7.7	9.7	10.4
	X	6.4	5.0	5.1	6.5	9.0	10.2
Latin America	M	5.4	5.2	5.7	5.4	5.4	4.1
	X	5.4	4.6	4.0	4.5	5.7	5.9
Countries							
Japan	M	4.5	6.3	7.0	7.3	7.3	7.4
	X	5.0	7.0	7.0	7.0	9.9	9.6
Hong Kong	M	0.9	1.0	0.8	1.2	1.3	1.6
	X	0.7	0.9	0.7	1.1	1.2	1.6
Korea	M	0.3	0.7	0.9	1.2	1.3	1.7
	X	0.1	0.3	0.6	0.9	1.3	1.7
Singapore	M	0.7	0.8	1.0	1.2	1.6	1.6
	X	0.6	0.5	0.7	1.0	1.2	1.4
Taiwan	M				1.1	0.8	1.2
	X				1.1	1.2	1.7
Australia	M	2.1	1.7	1.3	1.2	1.5	1.4
	X	1.8	1.7	1.5	1.2	1.3	1.4
New Zealand	M	0.6	0.4	0.4	0.3	0.3	0.3
	X	0.6	0.4	0.3	0.3	0.3	0.3
South Africa	M	1.4	1.3	1.0	1.0	1.0	0.9
	X	1.5	1.2	1.1	1.4	1.0	1.0

Sources: IMF, International Financial Statistic; Council for Economic Planning and Development, Industry of Free China.

EAST ASIA IN WORLD TRADE

The rising share of East Asia in world trade has already been signaled above. The contribution of the Asian NICs is of particular importance since their dynamic economies made a substantial contribution towards the export boom in East Asia. The rise in exports of manufactures from the NICs in Asia as well as in Latin America has been analysed extensively in the literature, and it suffices to mention the major factors only briefly.6/

Firstly, the NICs adjusted more rapidly than the major industrial countries to the effects of the more expensive energy era of the 1970s. Secondly, the rise in the oil price during the 1970s and early 1980s disrupted the economies of the industrial countries relatively more than the NICs because of the NIC's dependence for the manufacturing industry on oil imports. Thirdly, the major industrial countries have experienced deep structural changes in manufacturing since the 1970s, particularly in declining smokestack industries. Fourthly, many NICs adopted outward-looking development policies which encouraged economic growth and exports as has been demonstrated by Krueger (1973) and Balassa (1971a, 1971b). Fifthly, the NICs, particularly in Asia, have encouraged trade through economic cooperation such as the Association of South East Asian Nations (ASEAN)7/ which was formed in 1967.8/

During 1981, for instance, 17% of ASEAN trade was generated within the Association. Apart from these typical structural forces there were also those which discouraged trade in the major industrial countries and therefore indirectly encouraged trade in the NICs. In this respect Brakman, Jepma and Kuipers (1982) established that the weakening export performance of the Netherlands after 1973, could be explained by a deterioration in the commodity and country composition of exports as well as a loss of competitiveness. Another factor which has been of particular importance in the NICs of Asia is the investment activities of Japanese multinationals. The importance of investments by multinationals and intra-firm trade has been discussed in detail by Batchelor, Major and Morgan (1980, pp. 76-93)9/ and needs no further emphasis. As indicated in Table 3, Japanese foreign investment in Asia over the period 1951-1982 almost matched that of its foreign investment in the United States. Japanese foreign investment became important after the liberalization of its capital movements toward the end of 1969, and Japanese investments in East Asia have, no doubt, expanded the region's foreign trade.

TABLE 3
JAPANESE DIRECT FOREIGN INVESTMENT IN MAJOR AREAS
(FY 1951 to FY 1982)

Region/Country	$ Amount	% of Total Japanese Foreign Investment
North America	5,225	28.7
Western Europe	6,146	11.6
Latin America	8,852	16.7
Asia	14,552	27.4
Indonesia	7,268	13.0
Hong Kong	1,825	3.4
Singapore	1,383	2.6
South Korea	1,312	2.5
Malaysia	764	1.4
Philippines	721	1.4

Source: Industrial Review of Japan 1984.

TABLE 4
SOUTH AND EAST ASIA MAJOR TRADING PARTNERS
(Percentage of Total Exports)

Country/Region	1963	1973	1979	1981	1982	1983	1984
North America	16.7	23.9	23.5	23.2	23.5	28.3	30.0
Devel. Countries	35.0	26.7	30.0	34.2	33.9	33.3	31.0
Japan	11.1	22.4	20.7	18.7	19.0	16.9	17.1
Western Europe	25.9	19.4	19.3	15.2	15.1	13.9	13.2
Eastern Europe	7.0	4.2	3.1	4.3	4.3	4.3	4.9
Aust., N. Zealand S. Africa	3.8	2.7	2.7	3.2	3.3	2.4	2.8
Other	0.5	0.7	0.4	1.2	0.9	0.9	1.0

Source: GATT, International Trade 1984-85, Geneva, 1985.

The major trading partners of East Asia are identified in Table 4. East Asia is very dependent on the progress of the U.S. economy. Moreover, their dependence on the U.S. market has increased markedly from 1963 to 1984. This dependence, of course, renders them very vulnerable to the new protectionist policies followed by the United States in recent years. Trade with Japan also expanded, while a fairly stable market share has been maintained with respect to the developing countries. East Asia has lost market share in Western Europe, while Australia, New Zealand and South Africa are fairly insignificant trading partners. As indicated below, from a trading point of view East Asia is far more important to Australia, New Zealand and South Africa. In view of the protectionist policies in the United States, East Asia should not overlook the possibility of expanding trade with these three countries.

East Asia, and the Asian NICs in particular, were export oriented in their development during the 1970s and early 1980s. Unfortunately the mutual trade between the NICs of Asia is relatively small. During 1981 for instance, the mutual trade between Hong Kong, Singapore and South Korea amounted to only 7.4% of their total trade. As is evident from Table 5, the export sectors of the Asian NICs show important structural changes. The Asian NICs have gradually lost competitive advantage in respect of industrial goods such as processed agricultural products. But they have definitely improved their overall comparative advantage in terms of Heckscher-Ohlin goods. During 1981, for instance, 99.1% of Hong Kong's exports were in this category. These countries lost market share in conventional Heckscher-Ohlin goods such as textiles, though Hong Kong is probably still an important apparel exporter. The rising importance of chemicals in total exports in the case of South Korea, and after 1979 in the case of Singapore, signals a shift from labor-intensive to capital-intensive Heckscher-Ohlin goods. The rising share of Hong Kong and Singapore in the category, "other manufactures," signals the growing importance of product cycle or advanced technology based products.10/ Recently Pine (1984) confirmed the growing importance to these countries of advanced technology products in the manufacturing of 64K RAM chips and other sophisticated microelectronic equipment.

The Asian NICs have therefore moved out of industrial processed agricultural products and in some cases out of Ricardian goods. They have concentrated on labor-intensive Heckscher-Ohlin goods like textiles in the past, but they are moving into the field of capital-intensive Heckscher-Ohlin goods. The evidence is that these countries are gradually concentrating on advanced technology based products. This means that we can establish a definite shift from a lower to higher stage of manufacturing in the terminology of Michaely (1968).

This conclusion is not generally applicable to other countries in East Asia. Thailand's largest export item is still agricultural in nature viz. Ricardian goods, while Indonesia is also still very dependent on Ricardian goods in the sense that liquefied natural gas and oil are its major export products.

TABLE 5
ASIAN NICs MAJOR EXPORTS BY INDUSTRIAL ORIGIN
(Percentage of Total Value)

Country	1975	1976	1977	1979	1980	1981	1982	1983
Agriculture								
Hong Kong	3.1	1.2	1.2	0.9	0.6	0.7	0.7	0.6
South Korea	8.6	5.9	9.0	6.8	5.3	5.2	---	---
Singapore	4.6	16.7	16.6	14.0	11.3	9.1	8.1	8.0
Manufacturing								
Hong Kong	92.9	98.4	98.3	98.7	99.1	99.1	99.0	99.2
South Korea	89.7	93.1	90.0	92.6	94.2	94.4	---	---
Singapore	83.9	82.3	81.7	84.8	87.5	89.7	90.6	90.3
Textiles								
Hong Kong	46.0	54.6	49.1	45.8	43.4	44.4	43.2	41.9
South Korea	40.5	42.6	37.7	37.4	35.8	36.1	---	---
Singapore	4.9	5.8	5.2	5.4	4.3	4.1	4.0	4.1
Chemicals								
Hong Kong	6.9	3.9	3.7	3.1	3.1	3.3	3.2	3.2
South Korea	8.1	7.0	6.7	7.6	9.0	7.5	---	---
Singapore	37.1	33.6	33.7	28.0	32.6	35.7	36.8	32.2
Metal Manufactures								
Hong Kong	25.1	24.9	28.3	31.3	34.4	33.6	32.4	35.8
South Korea	19.1	23.1	26.3	27.4	27.2	30.3	---	---
Singapore	27.2	29.8	28.4	30.4	30.2	30.5	29.5	35.4
Other Manufactures								
Hong Kong	10.4	12.5	14.3	15.5	14.9	14.7	17.0	14.8
South Korea	4.2	4.3	4.1	3.8	3.3	3.2	---	---
Singapore	2.5	2.2	2.4	7.8	8.3	8.6	9.4	8.9

Source: United Nations, Yearbook of International Trade Statistics.

TRADING PATTERNS OF AUSTRALIA, NEW ZEALAND AND SOUTH AFRICA WITH EAST ASIA

East Asia is Australia's major trading partner, as is illustrated in Table 6. Economically East Asia is much more important to Australia than vice-versa. Foreign trade with Asia has been encouraged at the expense of trade with Western Europe, particularly in terms of imports. North America has remained a relatively stable and important supplier to Australia, while Japan has also raised its share in Australia's imports. During 1983 there appeared to be some rebound in Australian exports to Japan.

Apart from the fact that, relative to South Africa, Australia has a geographical advantage in trading with East Asia, foreign trade has been deliberately encouraged through trade agreements between Australia and the ASEAN countries as described by Arndt and Garnaut (1979). Australia has been an important market for labor-intensive manufactures from Malaysia, the Philippines and Thailand, while Singapore has concentrated on capital-intensive exports to Australia.

TABLE 6

AUSTRALIA'S MAJOR TRADING AREAS

(Value Terms as % of Total, M=Imports, X=Exports)

	X/M	1972	1976	1979	1980	1981	1982	1983
North America	X	15.7	11.7	13.8	11.9	8.9	8.4	8.0
	M	24.7	23.4	26.0	24.5	25.4	23.8	23.6
Asia, excluding USSR	X	43.2	53.2	53.5	49.8	50.4	50.5	50.5
	M	28.6	40.3	37.0	41.4	43.9	45.3	44.2
Europe, excluding USSR	X	24.8	20.1	17.1	15.0	12.4	13.4	15.7
	M	40.3	30.2	30.4	26.9	23.6	24.7	24.9
Japan	X	29.8	34.5	28.2	25.2	25.0	24.5	26.1
	M	16.4	21.1	15.7	17.0	19.7	20.0	22.1

Source: United Nations, Yearbook of International Trade Statistics.

As indicated in Table 7, Australia's export pattern does not show similar structural changes as has been observed in the Asian NICs. Australia still enjoys a comparative advantage in Ricardian goods such as in agriculture and mining, while it has improved its comparative advantage in respect to certain Heckscher-Ohlin goods. East Asia imports mainly food, manufactured goods, machinery and equipment from Australia, while Australia imports energy, primarily petroleum from East Asia. In this respect Indonesia supplies about 60% of Australia's imports from the ASEAN countries.11/ Australia is a protected market through tariffs and quotas, and it is under pressure from the ASEAN countries to open up its markets and to cooperate more extensively with East Asia. Australia is well placed to benefit by exporting Ricardian goods to East Asia, and it could improve its trade performance by exploiting Heckscher-Ohlin possibilities. The integration of Australia with East Asia could be seen as one of the challenges facing this country. Recently Australia's Joint Committee on Foreign Affairs and Defence maintained that if Australia does not become more integrated with the ASEAN countries, it may become largely irrelevant to ASEAN economic development, while politically, Australia could equally end up without influence in the Pacific Region.12/ At this juncture it would appear as if Australia does not have the political courage and the support from its labor unions to encourage closer cooperation with East Asia. Therefore Tyler (1984) concluded that Australia is a "European social democracy, with a British trade union system, Anglo Saxon attitudes and a Californian lifestyle. To preserve all that while integrating with Asia will require more than mere diplomacy."

TABLE 7
AUSTRALIA'S EXPORTS BY INDUSTRIAL ORIGIN
(Percentage of Total Value)

Source	1975	1976	1977	1978	1979	1980	1981	1982
Agriculture	26.8	24.9	22.5	20.4	23.3	24.0	22.2	23.9
Mining/Quarry	26.1	25.3	26.5	23.1	19.1	19.2	22.9	26.2
Manufacturing	47.1	49.8	51.0	56.5	57.6	56.8	54.9	49.9
Basic Metals	10.6	8.5	9.1	9.0	9.1	10.0	9.7	8.6

Source: United Nations, Yearbook International Trade Statistics.

As illustrated in Table 8, New Zealand's comparative advantage is well established in Ricardian goods. Moreover, it has a stable comparative advantage in Heckscher-Ohlin goods. New Zealand's comparative advantage is fairly narrowly based, and it remained relatively stable over the period 1975 to 1983. The same is not true of its trading pattern, which has changed markedly during recent years, as is evident from Table 9.

TABLE 8
NEW ZEALAND'S MAJOR EXPORTS BY INDUSTRIAL ORIGIN
(Percentage of Total Value)

	1975	1976	1977	1978	1979	1980	1981	1982	1983
Agriculture	14.6	17.9	16.0	15.9	16.0	15.2	14.6	13.9	15.8
Food, Bev. Tobacco	54.7	49.5	48.8	47.8	46.1	45.7	47.8	50.2	46.9
Manufacturing	84.7	81.6	83.4	83.2	83.3	84.1	84.6	85.4	83.4
Textiles	10.8	12.4	13.7	13.4	14.2	13.6	11.6	11.1	11.4

Source: United Nations, Yearbook of International Trade Statistics.

TABLE 9
NEW ZEALAND'S MAJOR TRADING AREAS
(Imports (M) and Exports (X) as % of Total)

Country/Region		1972	1976	1978	1979	1980	1981	1982	1983
North America	X	17.3	13.5	16.4	17.3	15.0	14.2	15.9	15.9
	M	13.8	16.0	16.3	15.8	16.2	20.3	20.5	17.8
Asia excluding USSR	X	17.9	25.9	29.3	27.4	31.8	33.9	31.3	36.1
	M	23.0	32.5	29.2	32.5	38.3	38.6	36.4	36.2
Europe excluding USSR	X	44.8	34.9	32.0	29.9	25.2	22.2	24.2	21.2
	M	37.1	28.3	29.6	27.4	22.8	19.1	21.3	23.0
Japan	X	10.8	13.8	13.8	13.4	12.5	13.0	13.1	15.0
	M	12.0	15.5	13.9	14.2	14.4	17.2	17.6	18.3

Source: United Nations, Yearbook of International Trade Statistics.

During the past decade New Zealand has been transformed from a European trading based country to a Pacific trading country, in the terminology of Hickman, Kurado and Lau (1979). After 1979 East Asia claimed the major share of New Zealand's exports and imports. The United Kingdom was the main loser in this process, while Japan and the ASEAN countries gained. In terms of the 1984 IMF trade statistics, Japan was New Zealand's second largest export market after Australia, while the ASEAN countries were its fifth largest export partner. This structural change in New Zealand's foreign trade pattern, indicated in Table 2, led Hickman, Kurado and Lau (1979) to ascribe the sharp fall in New Zealand's share in world trade, primarily to the transformation of this country to a Pacific-based trading area. The loss in trade with Western Europe has therefore not yet been offset for by the rise in trade with East Asia.

Throughout the period under consideration, Western Europe has been South Africa's major trading partner, as is evident from Table 10. From 1979 the data have been adjusted for balance of payments purposes, and the data in Table 10 should therefore be seen as two sets. Measured in terms of imports, North America is its second largest trading partner,13/ while in terms of exports, Asia takes the second place. Although the relative position of the major trading blocks did not change much vis-a-vis each other, it is nevertheless evident that Asia has become a more important supplier to South Africa. A similar conclusion would apply to its relation with Japan. East Asia is therefore more important to South Africa than vice-versa.

TABLE 10

SOUTH AFRICA'S MAJOR TRADING AREAS

(Imports (M) and Exports (X) as % of Total)

Country/Region		1972	1976	1977	1978	1979	1980	1981	1982	1983
North America	X	10.0	12.9	15.8	18.7	9.9	8.1	8.4	7.6	9.1
	M	19.1	23.1	20.3	17.1	13.5	14.6	15.6	16.1	16.2
Asia excl. USSR	X	17.8	14.8	15.8	16.9	10.3	9.1	10.4	12.0	11.8
	M	14.1	12.3	14.3	15.2	9.9	11.1	13.6	13.1	15.3
Europe excl. USSR	X	54.4	55.5	50.8	47.4	29.9	22.4	22.3	27.5	27.9
	M	56.1	54.6	54.9	59.6	41.5	39.8	40.9	44.0	41.6
Japan	X	13.2	11.5	12.0	12.0	7.1	6.5	7.6	8.7	7.5
	M	10.1	10.2	12.2	13.2	8.1	9.0	10.6	10.1	11.8

Source: United Nations, Yearbook of International Trade Statistics.

South Africa's export trade with the major geographic trading blocks has, on average, deteriorated during the 1970s, while little improvement in market share became evident from 1979 to 1983. There are several reasons for this.14/ A major factor is certainly the fact that South Africa is geographically isolated from the major trading areas, mentioned in Table 10, while it has very few formal trade agreements outside GATT with its major trading partners. South Africa has a special trade agreement with one of the countries in East Asia viz. Taiwan, but this agreement puts Taiwanese trade with South Africa on equal terms with that of GATT partners. Political pressures in favor of isolation have enhanced the effects of the geographical disadvantage, particularly in view of its inward-looking industrial strategy in recent years, coupled with the international wave of newly invented protectionist measures. The new protectionism relies on trade restrictive actions other than tariffs, and has affected trade relations adversely in recent years, not only within the South African context but also in a global sense.15/ Moreover, South Africa's performance has been affected adversely through its unilateral trade liberalization policies during the early 1980s. More importantly, South Africa's international competitiveness has been affected adversely because of its relatively high inflation rate. Scheepers (1982) demonstrated that South Africa relied heavily on import substitution policies, and one may also maintain that when it started encouraging exports during the 1980s, it nevertheless continued flirting with import substitution. Recent research by Balassa (1981a, 1981b) and Krueger (1983) have unambiguously supported the conclusion that outward-looking trade policies have been more successful in stimulating trade and growth. In view of the outcome of this research, it requires little argument to discover the reasons for the relatively poor export performance of South Africa during the 1970s. South Africa's export performance has also been hampered by structural changes as shown in Table 11.

South Africa has lost competitiveness, in terms of Ricardian goods such as agricultural products, while it has gained in terms of certain Heckscher-Ohlin goods such as manufacturing. Van Zyl (1984) established the following gaining areas: footwear, clothing, furniture, miscellaneous petroleum and coal products, pulp and paperboard, basic industrial chemicals, fertilizers, basic iron and steel products, and railroad equipment. Heckscher-Ohlin goods such as basic metals have also been losing their share in total exports. A more detailed investigation into

TABLE 11
SOUTH AFRICA'S MAJOR EXPORTS BY INDUSTRIAL ORIGIN
(Percentage of Total Value)

	1975	1976	1977	1978	1979	1980	1981	1982
Agriculture	19.3	14.5	12.2	12.6	9.9	5.7	7.2	7.0
Mining Quarry	19.8	24.2	26.1	23.7	23.8	12.7	13.7	14.5
Manufacturing	60.9	61.3	61.8	63.7	66.4	81.6	79.1	78.5
Basic Metals	19.9	23.6	17.3	16.5	17.4	8.0	8.6	8.8

Source: United Nations, Yearbook of International Trade Statistics.

South Africa's foreign trade by products would suggest that its trade with East Asia is primarily characterized by Ricardian and Heckscher-Ohlin goods. This confirms the conclusion above, i.e., South Africa has lost competitiveness in terms of certain Ricardian goods such as agriculture. Export trade from South Africa in advanced technology-based product-cycle goods is virtually non-existent, and South Africa relies increasingly on East Asia for these imports, particularly from Taiwan and Hong Kong. An application of advanced technologies could nevertheless improve the competitiveness of South Africa's Heckscher-Ohlin export goods.

CONCLUSION

During the 1970s and early 1980s the patterns of world trade have changed markedly because of the oil crises and structural changes which affected the comparative advantage of the world's major trading countries dissimilarly. Although the Western industrial countries are still the world's biggest traders they have lost some of their share. Apart from the gains in world trade by oil exporting countries, the NICs have improved their relative share, primarily through outward-looking development strategies. The Asian NICs have been particularly successful in improving their share in world trade. These countries have concentrated on Heckscher-Ohlin type goods to encourage their exports while they have gradually switched to technology-based goods during recent years to concentrate more on Heckscher-Ohlin and technology-based exports.

Australia, New Zealand and South Africa are economically relatively unimportant to East Asia, while the converse is not true. Australia, New Zealand and South Africa have imported Heckscher-Ohlin goods from East Asia over a fairly long period, and recently they have increased their imports of technology-based product-cycle goods as well. Australia, New Zealand and South Africa supply Heckscher-Ohlin and Ricardian goods, but their export pattern is probably dominated by Ricardian goods, particularly in the case of South Africa. Although New Zealand has switched from a European-based trading country to a Pacific-based trading country, the integration with East Asia has not been completed yet, and it could restore its previous share in world trade by encouraging closer trading links with East Asia. Although Australia is ahead of New Zealand in terms of integrating its foreign trade with East Asia, it appears to be reluctant to encourage this process in recent years. South Africa is geographically isolated from East Asia and owing to the fact that it has lost some of its competitiveness in certain Heckscher-Ohlin goods, it will be difficult for it to expand exports to East Asia. Nevertheless, one should not underestimate South Africa's importance regarding certain Ricardian goods, particularly those which are important in the production of advanced technology-based products such as nickel, chromium, manganese, and cobalt.[16]

East Asia has become an important supplier of advanced technology-based product-cycle goods to Australia, New Zealand and South Africa, and this is likely to become an area for expanding trade, particularly in view of the competitiveness of the Asian NICs in the production of these goods. The Heckscher-Ohlin export products of the NICs have been the subject of protectionist measures in the West, and recently these measures have been extended to the advanced technology-based exports of these countries. An expansion of trade with Australia, New Zealand and South Africa could prove to be an interesting option to East Asia in order to circumvent some of the protectionist effects. These protectionist measures are nevertheless detrimental to trade and international economic growth. The only long-term answer of the West to the competition from the NICs is to improve its competitiveness in world markets in respect of those goods in which it has a comparative advantage.

NOTES

1. These countries are Afghanistan, Brunei, Burma, Democratic Kampuchea, Hong Kong, Indonesia, Lao People's Democratic Republic, Macao, Malaysia, Maldives, Philippines, Republic of Korea, Singapore and Thailand.

2. For a survey of the literature on these issues, see R.M. Stern, "Testing Trade Theories," in International Trade and Finance: Frontiers for Research, ed. P.B. Kenen (London: Cambridge U. Press, 1975); and L. Stein, Trade and Structural Change (New York: St. Martin's Press, 1984).

3. See also Fatima M. Roque, "Trade Theory and the Portuguese Pattern of Trade," Economia 7 (1983):455-469.

4. For a more detailed discussion, see P. Van veen, "Trends in World Trade," South African Journal of Economics 51 (1983):486-506; GATT, International Trade 1982/83 (Geneva, 1983); J.C. Van Zyl, "South Africa in World Trade," South African Journal of Economics 52 (1984):42-62; M.A. Akhtar and R.S. Hilton,"Effects of Exchange Rate Uncertainty on German and U.S. Trade," Federal Reserve Bank of New York Quarterly Review (Spring 1984):7-16.

5. They are Argentina, Brazil, Chile, Mexico, Uruguay, Hong Kong, Israel, Korea, Singapore, Taiwan and Yugoslavia. See B. Balassa, "The Newly-Industrializing Developing Countries After the Oil Crises," Weltwirtshaftliches Archiv 117 (1981):142-194.

6. See for instance, L.B. Krause, "Europea and the Advanced Developing Countries," in The New Economic Nationalism ed. O. Hieronymi (London: MacMillan, 1980); B. Balassa, "Trade in Manufactured Goods: Patterns of Change," World Development 9 (1981):263-275; and Balassa, "The Newly Industrializing Developing Countries...".

7. Comprising Brunei, Indonesia, Malaysia, Philippines, Singapore and Thailand. All ASEAN countries except Brunei are members of the GATT.

8. See H.W. Arndt and R. Garnaut, "ASEAN and the Industrialization of East Asia," Journal of Common Market Studies 17 (1979):191-212.

9. For an overview of the literature, see Stein, Trade and Structural Change.

10. Although Table 5 does not show data on Taiwan, similar tendencies as those for Hong Kong, Korea and Singapore are evident in the case of Taiwanese exports. For a detailed analysis of structural changes in the Taiwanese export sector which could be interpreted as a definite change away from Ricardian to Heckscher-Ohlin goods, followed by advanced technology-based exports, see K. Liang and C.H. Liang, "Trade, Technology Transfers, and the Risks of Protectionism: The Experience of the Republic of China," Industry of Free China 61 (1984):7-22.

11. M. Mohamad, "ASEAN's Trading Relationship with Japan and Australia Requires Review," Japan Economic Journal (Tokyo) (June 1984).

12. M. Thompson-Noel, "Australia Urged to Look to ASEAN," Financial Times (London), 27 November 1984.

13. Despite a sustained rising share since 1979.

14. See Van Zyl, "South Africa in World Trade."

15. P.D. Henderson, "Trade Policies: Trends, Issues and Influences," Midland Bank Review (Winter 1983):8-19.

16. See M. Murase, "Japan's Dependence on Southern Africa is Rising for Rare Metals Supply," Japan Economic Journal (Tokyo) 13 November 1984.

REFERENCES

Akhtar, M.A. and Hilton, R.S. "Effects of Exchange Rate Uncertainty on German and U.S. Trade." Federal Reserve Bank of New York Quarterly Review (Spring 1984):7-16.

Arndt, H.W. and Garnaut, R. "Asean and the Industrialization of East Asia." Journal of Common Market Studies 17 (1979):191-212.

Balassa, B. "Trade in Manufactured Goods: Patterns of Change. World Development 9 (1981):263-275.

--------. "The Newly-Industrializing Countries After the Oil Crises. Welwirtshaftliches Archiv 117 (1981):142-194.

Batchelor, R.A.; Major, R.L.; and Morgan, A.D. Industrialisation and the Basis for Trade. London: Cambridge University Press, 1980.

Brakman, S.; Jepma, C.J.; and Kuipers, S.K. "The Deterioration of the Netherlands Export Performance during the late 1970s: A Matter of Competitiveness or Export Structure?" De Economist 130 (1982):360-379.

General Agreement on Tariffs and Trade (GATT). International Trade 1982-83. Geneva, 1983.

Henderson, P.D. "Trade Policies: Trends, Issues and Influences." Midland Bank Review (Winter 1983):8-19.

Hickman, B.G.; Kurodo, Y.; and Lau, L.J. "The Pacific Basin in World Trade: An Analysis of Changing Trade Patterns, 1955-1975." Empirical Economics 4 (1979):63-65.

Hirsch, S. "Hypotheses Regarding Trade Between Developing and Industrial Countries." In The International Division of Labour Problems and Perspectives. Edited by H. Giersh. Tubingen: Mohr, 1974.

Krause, L.B. "Europe and the Advanced Developing Countries." In The New Economic Nationalism. Edited by O. Hieronymi. London: MacMillan, 1980.

Krueger, A.O. "The Effects of Trade Strategies on Growth." Finance and Development (June 1983):6-8.

Liang, K. and Liang, C.H. "Trade, Technology Transfers, and the Risks of Protectionism: The Experience of the Republic of China." Industry of Free China 61 (1984): 7-22.

Michaely, M. "International Trade IV: Patterns of Trade." International Encyclopedia of the Social Sciences, Vol. 8. Crowell Collier & Macmillan, 1968.

Mohamad, M. "ASEAN's Trading Relationship with Japan and Australia Requires Review." Japan Economic Journal (June 1984).

Murase, M. "Japan's Dependence on Southern Africa is Rising for Rare Metals Supply." Japan Economic Journal (13 November, 1984).

Pine, A. "Third World's gains in the Basic Industries Stir a Sharp Backlash." Wall Street Journal, 16 April 1984.

Roque, Fatima M. "Trade Theory and the Portugese Pattern of Trade." Economia 7 (1983):455-469.

Scheepers, C.F. "The International Trade Strategy of South Africa." South African Journal of Economics 50 (1982): 13-25.

Stein, L. Trade and Structural Change. New York: St. Martins Press, 1984.

Stern, R.M. "Testing Trade Theories." In International Trade and Finance: Frontiers for Research. Edited by P.B. Kenen. London: Cambridge University Press, 1975.

Thompson-Noel, M. "Australia Urged to Look to ASEAN." Financial Times, 27 November 1984.

Tyler, C. "Exporters with a Nervous Outlook on the World." Financial Times, 19 November 1984.

Van Veen, P. "Trends in World Trade." South African Journal of Economics 51 (1983):486-506.

Van Zyl, J.C. "South Africa in World Trade." South African Journal of Economics 52 (1984):42-62.

PART FOUR

Conclusion

14

The Pacific Rim and the Western World: Conclusions and Perspectives

Frans A.M. Alting von Geusau

Contemporary interest in the countries on the Asia Pacific Rim has been stimulated primarily by the swift and sustained economic growth in these countries. In this volume we have made a deliberate effort to look beyond the growth of their economies and the challenge they present to North America and Western Europe. Any effort to understand the extraordinary economic development in the Pacific Rim countries and the future of their relations with the West, requires at least some insight in their cultural-historical development. Chapter 1 offers such a framework for understanding and comparison with developments in the West. To paraphrase Philip West's recommendation: Westerners would do well to spend more time defining the cultural and historical problem before moving on to trade-policy answers.

Economic development and economic relations, also, occur in the broader context of political development and strategic-political relationships. The first part in this volume dealt with the Pacific Rim and world politics and more in particular with the post-Second-World-War policies of the Soviet Union, the United States, China and Japan towards the area and their mutual relations. In terms of both its actual and its potential future influence in the Pacific region, China clearly stands apart from the other powers discussed in Part I. The analysis of China's influence in Chapter 4 therefore distinguished itself from the analysis of the policies of the Soviet Union, the United States and Japan in Chapters 2, 3 and 5.

Writing about economic development in the Pacific Rim Countries--the chapters in Part II of this volume--meant dealing with great diversity in cultural-historical background and in economic performance. While Klein, in Chapter 6, outlined those features he found distinctive about the area as a whole, the authors in Chapters 7, 8 and 9 discussed economic development separately for Japan, the group of countries commonly referred to as the Newly Industrialized Countries (NICs) in East Asia and the countries belonging to ASEAN.

Economic relations between the Pacific Rim and Western Europe and South Africa have been the subject of Part III in this volume. As the authors were primarily interested in the challenges of Pacific economic development to the Western world, relations between Japan on the one side, and the EEC and the United States on the other, obviously received priority treatment. Chapters 10 and 11 are concerned with relations between Japan and the EEC; the one offering a conceptual framework for analyzing the question of protectionism or cooperation, the other dealing with Japanese and European trade policies. Chapter 12 reviewed Japan's relations with the United States as they evolved since the Second World War. In Chapter 13, Strydom offered both an analytical framework for and a detailed description of trade relations between Australia, New Zealand and South Africa, and the Pacific Rim countries.

In this concluding chapter, I have no intention to summarize or compare the conclusions reached by each of the authors in this volume. This chapter rather offers a broader reflection on three themes to which the previous chapters have led.

ON THE PACIFIC AND ATLANTIC RIMS OF THE EUR-ASIAN CONTINENT

Situated on the rims of the largest and most populous continent of our globe--whether on the Atlantic Rim for the West Europeans or on the Pacific one for the East Asians--some similarities and identifiable comparable interests are surely there to be seen. Such is all the more so in view of the political situation existing since the end of the Second World War. The Soviet Union, the most formidable military power on the Eurasian continent, has expanded its domination to the Elbe in the West and to the Pacific islands in the East. On both sides expanding Soviet power is perceived as a threat to the security of the area.

The United States as the major power from another continent considers itself to be both an Atlantic and a Pacific power; since the Second World War especially, it has become involved in the economic development and the security arrangements of both the Pacific and the Atlantic rims.

On both rims, American policies of containment reacted to Soviet policies of expansion and brought the two powers in conflict and confrontation with each other. American strategic involvement found its clearest manifestations in the formation of alliances and in the economic recovery and political re-orientation of the two former enemy-states, the German Federal Republic and Japan. Both states, with American guidance, adopted democratic constitutions, became pivotal in the American security arrangements and evolved into leading participants in the U.S. made postwar world economic order.

China, as the most populous state on the Eur-Asian continent, has re-emerged as a unified state. The awe felt for its potential influence and power is widespread and not limited to the Soviet Union and the United States, and it will bear upon the security and independence of the other states as well, whether on the Atlantic or the Pacific rims of the Eur-Asian continent.

On both sides, as a consequence, the interplay between the two principal continental powers of the Eur-Asian heartland and the smaller countries on the rim, has changed in character and concern.

The Soviet Union by the sheer size of its territory and of its built-up military power can no longer be said to be threatened by invasion from the West or by suffocation in the East. Its formidable military bases on the Pacific, in Vietnam, or in the Northern Atlantic do constitute a security threat to countries on both rims. Hence the concern expressed about the Soviet global reach, the continuing build-up of its military and naval power and the methods it employs for solving its perceived security problems. The concern is all the more widespread in view of the totalitarian nature of the Soviet regime, the closed character of Soviet society, and the expansionist doctrine of communist ideology.

At the same time and increasingly so, concern is being expressed on both sides about the willingness of the United States to remain involved in the area's security for an indefinite period to come, or about the lack of consistency in American containment policies.

At this point, however, the apparent similarities cease to exist. On the Atlantic Rim, Western Europe forms a bridge-head on the continent facing Soviet military power across a long land border, called the iron curtain, running through the heart of Germany and Europe. Western Europe perceives the Soviet Union as a clear and direct threat to its security.

On the Pacific Rim, most states are archipelagos of islands and have no common border with the Soviet Union. The perception of threats to their security is different and more diffuse for historical as well as geopolitical reasons. The security problems faced, say by Japan or by Indonesia, can hardly be perceived as common security problems.

On the Atlantic Rim, the states of Western Europe belong to a multilateral alliance with the United States. The institutions set up after the war for multilateral economic cooperation, emerged from and within the special relationship between the U.S. and West European countries.

On the Pacific Rim, bilateral relationships prevail. The normalization of relations between the United States and China and the emergence of Vietnam as an expansionist power (after the American withdrawal) have fundamentally altered the security arrangements promoted by the United States in the 1950s. None of the security treaties concluded in the 1950s have been formally abrogated. Still SEATO (Southeast Asian Treaty Organization) was disbanded in 1975 and New Zealand left the ANZUS in 1986. For the states of Southeast Asia, ASEAN has become the preferred framework for a slow growth in military cooperation and political coordination. The United States remains committed to the defense of South Korea and has so far maintained its important military bases in the Philippines. As has been explained in Chapter 3, the United States is now focusing its efforts on developing its security relationship with Japan in the framework of their bilateral Treaty for Mutual Cooperation and Security.

Despite these dissimilarities, a few other similarities between the Atlantic and Pacific Rim countries can be pointed out. On both rims, most countries are generally poor in natural resources. They distinguish themselves in this respect from the large continental powers like China, the Soviet Union and the United States. They are dependent on external trade and on the security of sea lanes and therefore need allies to protect their security. As a consequence they have an interest in cooperating with each other and with the United States and in participating in the work of international economic organizations. For all of them, economic relations with the Soviet Union are a separate matter or even no issue at all.

Here again, the apparent similarities cease to exist. On the Atlantic Rim, the states of Western Europe show a high degree of cultural homogeneity. There is strong similarity in their forms of government, and economic expansion has generally been preceded by effective and relatively stable domestic political organization. On the Pacific Rim, cultural diversity prevails. Social and religious differences are substantial, and so are differences in form of government. In most countries, economic development has preceded effective political organization and political structures in many countries are still weak. Drastic changes in government--whether by externally inspired subversion or by domestic upheaval--are still a realistic possibility for governments to reckon with. Participation in a "liberal" international economic order is not rooted in domestic political traditions or developments.

On the Atlantic Rim, patterns of mutual economic relations are largely determined by postwar developments in the Western world and (increasingly so) by the existence of the European Communities. In economic terms, the Common Market may be more uncommon than most Europeans would like it to be. Its political significance for the stability and well-being of the participating states is substantial however. On the Pacific Rim, no such common focus exists. Japan is a category of its own, the only country (besides Australia and New Zealand) that has joined the OECD. South Korea, Taiwan, Hong Kong and Singapore have little more in common than the Western label: "Newly Industrialized Countries." Even the term countries is doubtful for two of them, and challenged for another. The countries belonging to ASEAN are part of a vibrant region in dynamic economic development. They are very different, however, in terms of size, population, religion, culture and level of development. Their relations with third countries (Japan and the United States in particular) are stronger and more important than with each other.

In a broader political perspective, the diversity in the Pacific area reflects a still open ended process of adjustment to the predominant form of political organization in the late twentieth century. The long era in which China had been the center of the East and South East Asian world has been followed by an era of European colonial expansion, and the Second World War in which Japan attempted by military power to become the dominant state. Each of these historical eras has left its mark on the map of the area, together with the postwar extension to Asia of Soviet and American power and the Soviet-American adversarial relationship. Many countries still have a sizeable population of Chinese descent; all countries have adopted the Western sovereign state as their form of political organization. Japan has been militarily defeated but has built up substantial economic influence in the area. Korea remains divided and a source of concern. Soviet policy and its relations with Vietnam, and the awe felt for China are sources of uncertainty and instability throughout the region.

PACIFIC CONCERNS

The extent to which those sources of uncertainty and instability generate feelings of concern cannot be easily measured in an area as diverse as the Pacific Rim. Popular feelings of concern cannot be easily expressed through the existing political institutions. Governments tend to express their concerns with the utmost care for internal political and international political reasons. Despite the sources of uncertainty referred to, the Pacific Rim has experienced a period of fast economic growth and relative international political stability.

Still, a number of broad concerns underlay the general discussion at the Eindhoven conference, the first being the threats to national security. As we have already seen, these threats tend to be diffused and varied, both in terms of identifying the country from which the threat originates and the nature of the threat. Concern about China is apparent in the ASEAN countries and for specific reasons in Taiwan and Hong Kong. Apprehension in ASEAN countries stems from historical experience and the support China still gives to local communist parties. The threat to their national security is perceived primarily in terms of possible internal destabilization. Recent changes in China and the Chinese-British agreement on Hong Kong seem to have lessened Taiwan's fears for a military conflict with China. No country now reckons with the possibility of renewed Japanese expansion, but apprehension towards Japan is still considerable in ASEAN countries and South Korea for both historical and economic reasons. Concern about the Soviet threat is felt primarily in Japan and China. Japan is concerned about the nearby build-up of Soviet forces and the potential naval threat to the security of sea lanes. China's concern about the Soviet Union has somewhat shifted from concern over border conflicts to concern with growing Soviet influence elsewhere and its alliance with Vietnam in particular. ASEAN countries are concerned about Vietnam, but would be reluctant to associate themselves too closely with China in this respect. Several countries share the American concern about the Soviet control over the military bases at Cam Ranh Bay in Vietnam. They apparently feel more reassured by policies of the present U.S. Administration in the area, but are clearly unwilling to become involved in the global U.S.-Soviet conflict. Political rivalry between major Asian powers as a source of national insecurity, seems to be a distant concern.

Concern about destructive economic competition in the area focused mainly on two potential effects: the effect it may have on national industrial and economic development; and the effect it may have on relatively free trade. Inside ASEAN countries there is concern about Japanese economic dominance. More widespread is concern about growing protectionism in the West as a consequence of trade policy differences between Japan and the West. Few are inclined to look at China as a threat in economic terms. The principal unanswered question with respect to China appears to be whether economic reform will continue along present patterns, or whether radical changes with unforseeable consequences must be reckoned with.

CHALLENGES TO THE WEST

For a substantial number of years following the Second World War, the principal challenge perceived by the West was communist expansion and the need for a policy containing Soviet influence in Europe. In recent years Western perceptions of the principal challenge have shifted to the growing importance of East Asia in economic terms. With respect to this more recent economic challenge, attention has been focused primarily on how to cope with Japan's current industrial and trade policies.

Western views on the organization of a workable international economic order are naturally linked to Western experiences and developments in domestic, social and political organization. Western concepts on state and authority are rooted in Western concepts about man and the place of the individual in society. In such a society emphasis is given to managing a variety of relations, to maintaining pluralism and to solving problems that arise. The Asians' world view is profoundly different. In domestic social and political organization, importance is given to the group rather than to the individual. There is less fear of authority and central administration. In society, emphasis is laid more on preserving a hierarchical structure than on managing relations, more on continuing from experience than on devising new means for solving problems. In countries like Japan or China, there is no liberal philosophical tradition as understood in the West. Western concepts of an international economic order have no roots in East Asian societies. They therefore tend to look at the prevailing world trade system more in terms of opportunities offered than in terms of rules to be preserved.

In the case of Japan, the world market is an instrument for reaching industrial development and rapid expansion. As it turned out in the previous chapters, it was less easy to identify the driving forces behind Japan's development and policies, than to determine some of their effects. In Japan, labeled "a capitalist development state" in Chapter 7, one cannot easily differentiate between state and private enterprise. Japan shows a strong group spirit and a difficult-to-grasp network of intricate relations, producing the effects of a highly protected domestic economy, an undervalued yen, and a trade policy of "industrial targeting." Japan's trade policies move from one target to another, trying through development, export and investment to acquire a dominant position on the world market in specific products, thus creating major survival problems for specific industrial products in the Western markets.

Various Western efforts to cope with the Japanese challenge seem not to have worked. Despite arrangements for mutual self restraint in trade practices, pressure on Japan to open up its domestic market to imported products and bilateral talks, no solution has as yet been found to the European and American trade deficits with Japan. The EEC is hampered in its efforts by its own internal lack of unity (in particular in its relations with Japan). The American trade deficit has reached proportions of such magnitude that the U.S. Congress shows an increasingly hostile mood towards Japan. The pressure towards protectionist measures, if submitted to, might well create an explosive situation with negative effects going beyond the field of trade.

The argument that economic developments in Japan could be looked at as a "model" for other Pacific countries, did not extend to the challenge of such developments to the West. Japan's economic challenge has been approached as a specific and quite separate problem. Korea and Taiwan are unlikely to be in a position to follow the Japanese example in their trade relations with the West. The larger ASEAN countries are still to be considered as developing countries for many years to come. They will continue to be dependent on the West for trade and economic aid.

In the short run, the United States and the European Community shall have to deal primarily with Japan's trade practices in such a way that key industries are adequately protected, without resorting to harmful protectionism.

Although bilaterally negotiated arrangements may temporarily be called for, the strengthening of international legal rules and multilateral procedures for negotiation on trade and for managing monetary relations should be aimed at. Although immediate and specific trade issues must be solved, a more comprehensive approach to relations with the Pacific and other non-Western industrialized nations should also be explored.

Unlike the former British historian Arnold Toynbee, I would be surprised indeed, if the twenty-first century would prove to be an East-Asian century of human history. Human history is not made by economic growth alone, and the growing economic importance of East Asia has been too recent a phenomenon to enable us to draw such far-reaching conclusions.

The growing economic importance of the Pacific Rim does challenge the primarily Western-made organization of a workable international economic order. As such it poses a challenge to the West, in its understanding of and ability to cope with a world of cultural diversity. In the longer run, the organization of a workable international economic order shall have to be adjusted to a world of cultural and political diversity, without however abandoning the principles and practices of market-oriented multilateralism.

Contributors

James David ARMSTRONG: Lecturer in International Studies and Director of Graduate School of International Studies, University of Birmingham; Ph.D., Australian National University 1975; Chinese Foreign Policy and the United Front Doctrine (University of California Press, 1977); The Rise of International Organization, Macmillan Ltd., 1982.

Laszlo Lajos S. BARTALITS: Senior Research Fellow at the John F. Kennedy Institute at Tilburg University; Hongarije en de Anschluss 1918-1938 [Hungary and the Anschluss 1918-1933] (H. Gianotten, 1968).

Janamitra DEVAN: Senior Consultant, Ernst & Whinney Management and Consulting Services, Singapore; Research Associate, Institute for Southeast Asian Studies, Singapore, 1985-86; Ph.D. 1987, Indiana University, "An Intercountry Analysis of the ASEAN Preferential Trading Arrangement: Expost and Exante."

Reinhard DRIFTE: Assistant Director for Regional Security Studies at the International Institute for Strategic Studies in London; Ph.D. 1979, University of Bochum, East Asian Studies; chapters on Japan and the Korean peninsula in Strategic Survey, 1984-85, International institute for Strategic Studies, London, 1985.

Lawrence R. KLEIN,: Professor of Economics, University of Pennsylvania; Ph.D. Massachusetts Institute of Technology (1944); Nobel Memorial Prize in economic sciences, 1980; An Introduction to Econometrics (Prentice Hall 1962); editor, Economic Growth: The Japanese Experience Since the Meiji Era (1968); collected essays, Economic Theory and Econometrics: Lawrence Klein (University of Pennsylvania Press, 1985).

Jacques PELKMANS: Professor of Economics, European Institute of Public Administration in Maastricht; Ph.D. Tilburg University, 1975; Market Integration in the European Community (St. Martin's Press, 1984); "GATT As An Instrument in Atlantic Trade Policy," in L. Tsoukalis, ed., Europe, America and the World Economy, Oxford/Basil Blackwell, 1985; "The Institutional Economics of European Integration," in M. Cappelletti, ed., Integration Through Law (New York/Berlin, Walther de Gruyter, 1985).

F. H. SAELENS: Corporate Planner, Philips International, Eindhoven; Lecturer, European University, Antwerp 1979-1985; Ph.D. Tilburg University; "The European Investments of Japanese Financial Institutions," Columbia Journal of World Business, Winter 1986.

Johannes Wilhelmus H.C.M. SCHNEIDER: Professor of International Law, Tilburg University; Ph.D. Amsterdam, 1959; "Non-tariff Barriers in Benelux," in A. Scaperlanda ed., Non-Tariff Distortions, Leiden, 1973; editor, From Nine to Twelve: Europe's Destiny? Sythoff Leyden, 1980.

P. D. F. STRYDOM: Chief Strategic Researcher, Sanlam Investment Corporation (Sankorp), Johannesburg; Senior Economist, Senbank, Johannesburg, 1979-1985; Professor of Economics, University of South Africa, Pretoria, 1969-1979; "Exchange Rates in South Africa," South African Journal of Economics, 1979.

Pieter VAN VEEN: Profesor of International Economics, Tilburg University; Ph.D. University of Amsterdam; Assistant Professor of Economics, Erasmus University, 1963-1968; Publications on export promotion, East-West trade, structures of world trade, exchange rate policies, and industrial policy.

Frans A.M. Alting VON GEUSAU: Professor of Law of International and European Organizations at Tilburg University, The Netherlands, Director of the John F. Kennedy Institute, Tilburg University since 1967; Doctor of Law, 1962, Leyden University; Visiting Professor at MIT and Harvard University, 1971-72; Uncertain Detente, Sythoff Leyden, 1979; editor, Allies in a Turbulent World: Challenges to U.S. and Western European Cooperation, New York, D. C. Heath, 1982; The Security of Western Europe. A Handbook, London, Sherwood Press, 1985.

Karel G. VON WOLFEREN: East Asia correspondent for the Dutch daily NRC Handelsblad, with residence in Japan since 1962; "The Japan Problem," Foreign Affairs, Winter 1986-87; currently working on a book on how power is exercised in Japan, to be published by Macmillan, London.

Philip WEST: Associate Professor of History and of East Asian Languages and Cultures, Director of the East Asian Studies Center, Indiana University; Ph.D., Harvard University, 1971; Yenching University and Sino-Western Relations, 1916-1952 (Harvard University Press, 1976); Strategic Planning and the Pacific Rim: A Handbook, Indiana University, 1984.

Imanuel WEXLER: Professor of Economics, University of Connecticut; Ph.D. Harvard University, 1959; Fundamentals of International Economics (Random House, 1968, second edition, 1972); The Marshall Plan Revisited: The European Recovery (Greenwood Press, 1983).

Rong-I WU: Professor of Economics at the National Chung Hsing University and the Asia and World Institute in Taipei, Taiwan; Ph.D. 1971, Universite Catholique de Louvain; with S. C. Tsiang, "Foreign Trade and Investment as Boosters for Take-off: The Experience of the Four Asian NICs" in Walter Galenson, ed., Economic Development in Asia's Newly Industrializing Nations, University of Wisconsin Press, 1985.

Index